THE CLINICIAN'S GUIDE TO TREATING HEALTH ANXIETY

THE CLINICIAN'S GUIDE TO TREATING HEALTH ANXIETY

Diagnosis, Mechanisms, and Effective Treatment

Edited by

ERIK HEDMAN-LAGERLÖF

Karolinska Institutet, Stockholm, Sweden

ELSEVIER

ACADEMIC PRESS

An imprint of Elsevier

Academic Press is an imprint of Elsevier
125 London Wall, London EC2Y 5AS, United Kingdom
525 B Street, Suite 1650, San Diego, CA 92101, United States
50 Hampshire Street, 5th Floor, Cambridge, MA 02139, United States
The Boulevard, Langford Lane, Kidlington, Oxford OX5 1GB, United Kingdom

Library of Congress Cataloging-in-Publication Data
A catalog record for this book is available from the Library of Congress

British Library Cataloguing-in-Publication Data
A catalogue record for this book is available from the British Library

ISBN: 978-0-12-811806-1

For information on all Academic Press publications
visit our website at https://www.elsevier.com/books-and-journals

Publisher: Nikki Levy
Acquisition Editor: Nikki Levy
Editorial Project Manager: Karen R. Miller
Production Project Manager: Vijayaraj Purushothaman
Cover Designer: Mark Rogers

Typeset by SPi Global, India

CONTENTS

CONTRIBUTORS

Gordon J.G. Asmundson
Department of Psychology, University of Regina, Regina, SK, Canada

Erland Axelsson
Department of Clinical Neuroscience, Karolinska Institutet, Stockholm, Sweden

Thomas A. Fergus
Department of Psychology and Neuroscience, Baylor University, Waco, TX, United States

Per Fink
The Research Clinic for Functional Disorders and Psychosomatics, Aarhus University Hospital, Aarhus, Denmark

Lisbeth Frostholm
The Research Clinic for Functional Disorders and Psychosomatics, Aarhus University Hospital, Aarhus, Denmark

Erik Hedman-Lagerlöf
Department of Clinical Neuroscience, Karolinska Institutet, Stockholm, Sweden

Ditte Hoffmann
The Research Clinic for Functional Disorders and Psychosomatics, Aarhus University Hospital, Aarhus, Denmark

Charlotte U. Rask
Research Unit, Department of Child and Adolescent Psychiatry, Aarhus University Hospital, Skejby; Research Clinic for Functional Disorders and Psychosomatics, Aarhus University Hospital, Aarhus, Denmark

Peter Tyrer
Centre for Psychiatry, Imperial College, London, United Kingdom

Helen Tyrer
Centre for Psychiatry, Imperial College, London, United Kingdom

CHAPTER ONE

The Concept of Health Anxiety

Gordon J.G. Asmundson[*] and Thomas A. Fergus[†]
[*]Department of Psychology, University of Regina, Regina, SK, Canada
[†]Department of Psychology and Neuroscience, Baylor University, Waco, TX, United States

Health Anxiety Defined

Health anxiety occurs when perceived bodily sensations or changes are interpreted as symptoms of a serious disease. Everyone experiences health anxiety at some point in their lives, and in some cases, it can be persistent and distressing. Contemporary cognitive behavioral models conceptualize health anxiety as existing along a continuum, ranging from mild to severe, and as being a core facet of several psychiatric diagnoses. Maladaptive presentations of health anxiety, often referred to as severe health anxiety, are associated with various dysfunctional beliefs and several forms of health-related checking behavior. These maladaptive presentations are often personally debilitating and associated with considerable societal costs. The purpose of this chapter is to introduce contemporary cognitive behavioral models proposed to understand health anxiety, to provide an overview of its clinical profile, to describe the core features associated with its etiology and maintenance, and to introduce considerations for assessment and treatment.

The Case of Paul

Paul is a 40-year-old man who works in a fast-paced and often demanding information technology department of a large corporation. About 6 months ago, he began experiencing pain in his left chest and shoulder and recently noticed increased shortness of breath and coughing when active. He was concerned by the persistence of the pain and breathing issues, particularly given that his father had poor cardiac health and had died following a stroke. His cousin, Sarah, a triathlete also in her 40s, was also struggling with some cardiac issues for the past few years. Paul went to see his family physician, who performed an EKG and immediately thereafter referred him to a cardiac specialist for a stress test. Paul began to worry that his chest pain and breathing issues may be related to a problem with his heart and, although his family physician did not recommend any changes in activity, stopped

The Clinician's Guide to Treating Health Anxiety
https://doi.org/10.1016/B978-0-12-811806-1.00001-9

exercising and playing with his children. During the several months that he waited for his stress test, his chest and shoulder pain became progressively worse, and he noticed increasing difficulties with his breathing. Paul was relieved following his stress test, which the cardiologist noted as being indicative of a healthy heart, but his relief faded quickly as he began to wonder whether his pain, breathlessness, and coughing might be a consequence of cancer, COPD, or some other disease process. Against the advice of his family physician and his own best judgment, he now spends many hours every day searching online information for a potential explanation for his concerns and is constantly anxious and worried about his well-being.

Contemporary Cognitive-Behavioral Models

Available research findings generally converge on viewing health anxiety as a dimensional, rather than a categorical, construct (Ferguson, 2009; Longley et al., 2010); however, there is preliminary evidence that qualitatively distinct forms may exist (Asmundson, Taylor, Carleton, Weeks, & Hadjistavropoulos, 2012). Conceptualizing health anxiety as a dimensional construct has several important implications for theory, research, and clinical practice (Asmundson, Abramowitz, Richter, & Whedon, 2010). First, if differences in health anxiety are one of severity rather than qualitative differences in experience, then contemporary conceptualizations are in line with the available evidence. Second, research seeking to examine health anxiety should include a range of potential vulnerability and maintenance factors, such as biological and environmental correlates, dysfunctional beliefs, and maladaptive coping behaviors. Third, when examining potential vulnerability and maintenance factors for health anxiety, research would benefit from examining large unselected samples that include a full range of health anxiety rather than focusing exclusively on samples of individuals with severe levels of health anxiety. Finally, from a clinical perspective, a dimensional conceptualization highlights the possibility of identifying points along the continuum where health anxiety rapidly worsens and for developing prevention efforts for individuals at risk for developing severe presentations.

There have been several contemporary cognitive behavioral models proposed to understand and explain health anxiety (Abramowitz, Schwartz, & Whiteside, 2002; Salkovskis & Warwick, 2001; Taylor & Asmundson, 2004; also see Abramowitz & Braddock, 2011). In essence, each of these models posits that severe presentations of health anxiety develop from underlying vulnerability factors (e.g., biological factors that influence somatosensory stimulation and experiences that influence the way somatosensory changes are perceived and interpreted) that interact with dysfunctional beliefs about maladaptive coping in response to bodily sensations and changes. For example, the perception of "bodily noise"—an ache or pain, racing heart, tightness in the chest, a rash, or feeling itchy—may be viewed through the lens of underlying beliefs (e.g., overestimating likelihood and the cost of a health problem) that lead to concern, worry, and more "bodily noise." Paul likely overestimated the probability that his chest pain and breathing difficulties were indicative of a serious health problem given a familial history of related health problems. He also likely concurrently held beliefs about the costliness of a serious health problem, as his father died as a consequence of health problems. In Paul's case and like many individuals with severe health anxiety, body vigilance rendered him more likely to notice innocuous bodily sensations or changes (e.g., monitoring the propensity of shortness of breath when active) and misinterpret them as indicative of a potentially serious health issue. Cognitive behavioral models hold that for individuals with severe health anxiety, the perception of bodily sensations or symptoms is met by persistent "what if" thinking surrounding the possible catastrophic nature and consequences of those bodily states. In Paul's case, that type of thinking related to "what if my chest pain and shortness of breath relate to a problem with my heart?"

Cognitive behavioral models also posit that, in response to such health-related worries, individuals engage in maladaptive coping. Typical forms of maladaptive coping associated with health anxiety include body checking, Internet searches, seeking out advice from multiple health professionals, or reassurance seeking from friends or family. In Paul's case, he visited his family physician and a cardiac specialist and also began spending hours searching the Internet. Although these behaviors temporarily reduced his health anxiety, Paul's health-related worries reemerged and persisted given that dysfunctional beliefs and body vigilance remained unchanged. Consequently, Paul remained locked into a pattern of monitoring for the presence of feared bodily states and was prone to catastrophizing about the meaning of those bodily states when they occurred. As Paul did not get the corrective experience that his health-related worries are unfounded, he became increasingly preoccupied by those worries and engaged in additional maladaptive coping in the form of repeated Internet searches that served to maintain his health anxiety.

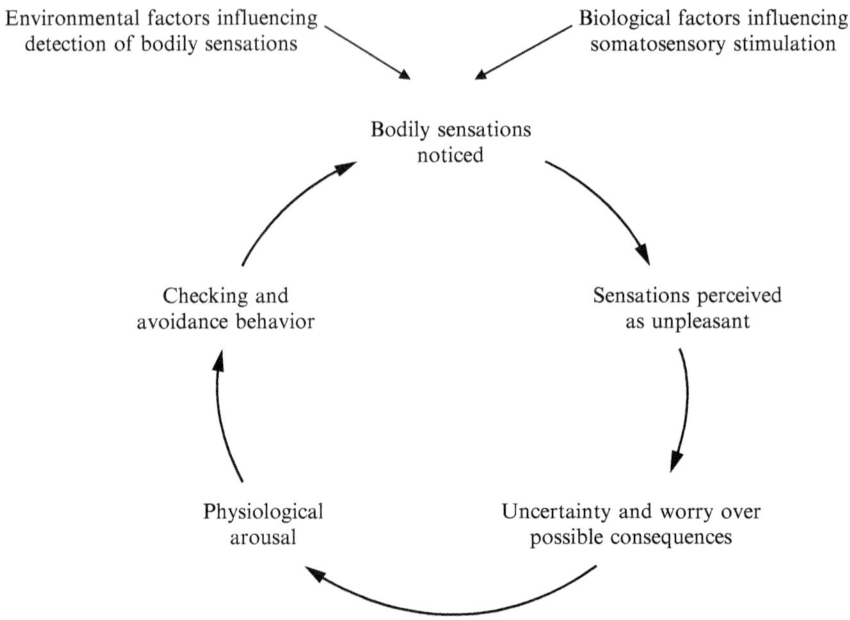

Fig 1 The cognitive behavioral model of health anxiety. *(Adapted from Asmundson, G. J. G., Taylor, S. (2005).* It's not all in your head: How worrying about your health could be making you sick and what you can do about it. *New York: Guilford.)*

For Paul and others with severe health anxiety, a repetitive cycle (see Fig. 1) develops. He notices bodily sensations and changes, perceives these changes as unpleasant, worries about the causes and potential consequences of his bodily sensations and changes, engages in coping that temporarily reduces his health anxiety, notices more bodily sensations, and so forth. The cycle is, unfortunately, self-perpetuating and chronic without intervention.

Clinical Profile

Severe health anxiety typically manifests during periods of significant stress, following serious illness or the loss of a family member, or subsequent exposure to disease-related stories in the popular media (Barsky & Klerman, 1983; Taylor & Asmundson, 2004). The bodily sensations and changes that Paul was concerned about began during a particularly demanding several months at work and were similar in nature to those experienced by his now deceased father and his cousin. In cases where health anxiety is sufficiently severe and prolonged and where conceptualization as continuous may be less than ideal (e.g., where required for insurance purposes), there are several diagnoses that may be warranted. Below, we highlight various conceptualizations of maladaptive presentations of health anxiety (also see Chapter 2), their prevalence (also see Chapter 3), and associated societal and personal costs.

Maladaptive Presentations and Related Psychiatric Disorders

In cases where diagnostic nomenclature and classification schemas are applied, contemporary cognitive behavioral models often conceptualize severe presentations of health anxiety as hypochondriasis (Abramowitz et al., 2002; Salkovskis & Warwick, 2001; Taylor & Asmundson, 2004), a psychiatric disorder marked by the misinterpretation of normal bodily states as a serious health problem. Whereas the diagnosis of hypochondriasis still exists in the ICD-10 (1992), major changes to the classification of somatoform disorders occurred in the DSM-5 (American Psychiatric Association, 2013), and the diagnosis of hypochondriasis was removed from DSM nomenclature.

Despite considerable controversy regarding issues of reclassification (Collimore, Asmundson, Taylor, & Abramowitz, 2009; Starcevic, 2013), the DSM-5 now classifies hypochondriasis and several other somatoform disorders (i.e., somatization disorder and pain disorder) within a new diagnosis of somatic symptom disorder. Another new diagnosis—illness anxiety disorder—applies to people who experience severe health anxiety without any salient bodily sensations or changes. The ramifications of these changes to the diagnostic classification of severe presentations of health anxiety remain to be determined (Rief, 2013); yet, there are already proposed modifications to DSM-5 criteria for severe presentations of health anxiety (Rief & Martin, 2014), with some researchers proposing diagnostic criteria for a distinct health anxiety disorder (Fink et al., 2004). Such modifications and alternative diagnostic criteria have yet to be formally adopted and require further examination. Importantly, diagnostic changes surrounding severe presentations of health anxiety have minimal impact on either contemporary cognitive behavioral models or associated approaches to assessment and treatment where the focus is on the health anxiety construct.

Preliminary research has examined potential differences in the presentation and associated characteristics of somatic symptom disorder and illness anxiety disorder, respectively (Bailer et al., 2016; Newby, Hobbs, Mahoney,

Wong, & Andrews, 2017). This research has produced mixed findings as to whether individuals previously diagnosed with hypochondriasis primarily meet criteria for somatic symptom disorder versus illness anxiety disorder, with Bailer et al.'s (2016) findings providing evidence of a greater prevalence split favoring somatic symptom disorder than did Newby et al.'s (2017) findings. Newby et al. (2017) found greater levels of health anxiety among individuals meeting criteria for somatic symptom disorder, whereas Bailer et al. (2016) generally did not find differences. A consistent pattern across these two studies is that individuals with somatic symptom disorder endorse greater somatic symptom severity than individuals with illness anxiety disorder. Additionally, somatic symptom disorder may be marked by greater levels of maladaptive coping, in the form of the overutilization of medical care and increased functional impairment relative to illness anxiety disorder. There is a need for additional research comparing somatic symptom disorder and illness anxiety disorder; yet, results from these two preliminary studies suggest differences between the disorders are likely best conceptualized in terms of severity rather than substantive qualitative differences (Bailer et al., 2016; Newby et al., 2017).

Paul's presentation seems best characterized as somatic symptom disorder (American Psychiatric Association, 2013), which requires the experience of one or more somatic symptoms that are distressing or disruptive and associated with excessive cognitive, emotional, or behavioral responsivity to the somatic symptom or related health concerns. Paul has substantive concern surrounding both chest pain and shortness of breath. Paul experiences disproportionate and persistent thoughts about the severity of these somatic states and persistent high levels of health anxiety. Paul finds himself constantly plagued by worries that his bodily sensations and changes are the sign of a serious health problem. Finally, Paul spends excessive time and energy in response to his health anxiety, ultimately spending hours nightly searching for the meaning of his symptoms and finding himself preoccupied by health-related worries.

How to best classify health anxiety is not isolated to considering somatic symptom disorder versus illness anxiety disorder, as health anxiety shares considerable overlap with other anxiety disorders (Olatunji, Deacon, and Abramowitz, 2009). Overlap includes the tendency to make catastrophic misinterpretations of bodily states (e.g., panic disorder; Noyes Jr., et al., 1994), the occurrence of distressing thoughts and engagement in repetitive safety behaviors to mitigate the threat surrounding the thoughts (e.g., obsessive-compulsive disorder; Asmundson et al., 2010), and the tendency to worry (e.g., generalized anxiety disorder; Taylor & Asmundson, 2004).

Despite this overlap, severe presentations of health anxiety have been posited to be conceptually and empirically distinct from anxiety disorders (e.g., Barsky, 1992; Hedman et al., 2017; Salkovskis & Clark, 1993; Starcevic, Fallon, Uhlenhuth, & Pathak, 1994; Warwick & Salkovskis, 1990). Nonetheless, the overlap does raise the possibility that severe presentations of health anxiety may be best conceptualized as a manifestation of severe anxiety as opposed to intense somatic focus (Collimore et al., 2009; Olatunji, Deacon, et al., 2009).

Prevalence

A detailed discussion of the prevalence of health anxiety appears in Chapter 3 of this volume. Briefly, extant prevalence estimates for clinically severe presentations of health anxiety are based upon the prevalence of hypochondriasis and range from 0.5% (Bleichhardt & Hiller, 2007; Looper & Kirmayer, 2001; Martin & Jacobi, 2006) in community samples to 0.4%–6% in primary care and medical clinics (Barsky, Wyshak, Klerman, & Latham, 1990; Escobar et al., 1998; Fink, Ørnbøl, & Christensen, 2010; Gureje, Ustun, & Simon, 1997; Liu et al., 2012). When considering severe forms of health anxiety that may not meet full diagnostic criteria, the extant research points to prevalence estimates in community samples from 2% to 13% (Looper & Kirmayer, 2001; Martin & Jacobi, 2006; Noyes Jr., Carney, Hillis, Jones, & Langbehn, 2005; Sunderland, Newby, & Andrews, 2013) and in medical clinics from 12% to 20% (Fink et al., 2010; Tyrer et al., 2011). Challenges in establishing accurate prevalence estimates, including differing definitions of health anxiety and recent changes to diagnostic categories in the DSM-5, are discussed elsewhere (Asmundson and Le Bouthillier, 2018).

Cost

Because medical overutilization is considered a core form of reassurance seeking among individuals experiencing severe health anxiety (Abramowitz et al., 2002; Salkovskis & Warwick, 2001; Taylor & Asmundson, 2004), the cost of severe presentations of health anxiety has typically be assessed in the form of the impact on the health-care system. The estimated medical cost of patients with somatization is around $256 billion (USD) annually (Barsky, Orav, & Bates, 2005). This estimate is relevant to severe presentations of health anxiety, as somatic symptom disorder includes individuals previously diagnosed with somatization disorder (American Psychiatric Association, 2013). Within primary care settings, patients experiencing severe health anxiety utilize between 41% and 78% more health-care services per year than individuals with a well-defined medical condition (Fink et al., 2010). The mean cost of a single primary care patient with heightened health anxiety and somatic symptoms, a symptom presentation akin to DSM-5 somatic symptom disorder, is around $1500 per year (Barsky, Ettner, Horsky, & Bates, 2001). Spontaneous recovery from severe health anxiety is rare (olde Hartman et al., 2009), suggesting that the concerns of individuals with severe health anxiety are likely to be chronic if left untreated. Individuals with severe health anxiety are more likely to initially present to a physical health provider (Taylor & Asmundson, 2004), relative to a mental health provider, and severe health anxiety typically goes unrecognized by physicians (Fink, Sorensen, Engberg, Holm, & Munk-Jorgensen, 1999). Difficulties recognizing severe health anxiety delay potential treatment and perpetuate a maintaining factor of medical service overutilization.

Core Features of Severe Health Anxiety

Severe health anxiety is characterized by one or more core features that contribute to its development, exacerbation, and maintenance (also see Chapter 4). These core features include a variety of dysfunctional beliefs and maladaptive coping behaviors, environmental factors, and biological influences. As discussed elsewhere (Asmundson, Thibodeau, Peluso, & Taylor, 2013), we find it useful to separate the vulnerability factors from exacerbation and maintenance factors. Understanding which factors (e.g., biological predispositions and traumatic event exposure) contribute to initial development of severe health anxiety can inform both theoretical conceptualizations and relapse prevention (e.g., identifying what factors could lead to severe health anxiety in the future), whereas factors that maintain health anxiety (e.g., environmental factors, cognitive distortions, and maladaptive behaviors) are often direct targets of treatment.

Vulnerability Factors

Environmental and biological factors are emphasized in contemporary cognitive behavioral models as playing an important role in the development of severe health anxiety. Environmental influences include various learning experiences, such as parental modeling of illness behaviors and early aversive experiences (e.g., childhood hospitalizations, receiving rewards for being sick, and adverse childhood experiences), that teach children to catastrophically misinterpret bodily sensations or changes and believe that they are vulnerable to disease (Taylor & Asmundson, 2004). Indeed, individuals experiencing parental illness growing up endorse significantly greater levels of health anxiety and dysfunctional beliefs related to overestimating the likelihood of experiencing a health problem than individuals who do not experience parental illness growing up (Alberts, Hadjistavropoulos, Sherry, & Stewart, 2016). Also interesting is that there is evidence to suggest that learning of the health struggles of strangers may also play a role in the development of severe health anxiety (Karademas, 2009).

Specific genes contributing to severe presentations of heath anxiety remain to be determined. Behavioral-genetic (twin) research indicates that the core maintenance factors of health anxiety (i.e., dysfunctional beliefs and maladaptive behavior) are shaped by a combination of genetic and environmental influences (Taylor, Thordarson, Jang, & Asmundson, 2006). This suggests that severe presentations of health anxiety may, at least in part, be heritable. However, environmental factors and gene by environment interactions appear important as well. When examining genetic contributions to health anxiety, the magnitude of heritability estimates differs depending on how the data are analyzed. More precisely, when examining severe health anxiety as a categorical construct, heritability estimates range from 0.54 to 0.69 (Taylor & Asmundson, 2012). Alternatively, Taylor and Asmundson (2012) found heritability estimates ranging from 0.10 to 0.37 when examining genetic contributions in relation to a dimensional assessment of health anxiety. One possibility is that genetic factors contributing to pain or autonomic arousal could contribute to the development of dysfunctional health-related beliefs that ultimately contribute to health anxiety (Taylor & Asmundson, 2012).

Maintenance Factors

Dysfunctional beliefs and maladaptive behavior are emphasized in contemporary cognitive behavioral models as playing primary roles in the maintenance of severe health anxiety. In addition to their developmental roles, certain environmental and biological influences may also play a role in the maintenance and exacerbation of health anxiety. For example, media reports regarding various health risks, understimulating environments, deconditioning as a result of physical inactivity, changes in daily routine and diet, and minor ailments may all promote bodily sensations and changes that are perceived as threatening and lead to dysfunctional beliefs and maladaptive coping (Taylor & Asmundson, 2004).

Dysfunctional Beliefs

Dysfunctional beliefs include disease conviction (i.e., the belief that bodily sensations and changes are due to disease processes) and health-related fears (e.g., fear of succumbing to disease), with disease conviction being considered a core dysfunctional belief underlying health anxiety (Asmundson et al., 2010). Existing research supports disease conviction and health-related fears as being separate dimensions of health anxiety (Fergus & Valentiner, 2010).

Cognitive behavioral models posit that dysfunctional beliefs serve as a primary maintaining (and, to some extent, causal) factor of anxiety disorders (Clark & Beck, 2010). An accumulating body of research suggests that health anxiety may share dysfunctional beliefs with anxiety disorders. For example, anxiety sensitivity, which represents the fear of arousal-related sensations (Taylor et al., 2007), is related to health anxiety (Deacon & Abramowitz, 2008) and anxiety disorders more broadly (Naragon-Gainey, 2010). Additionally, intolerance of uncertainty, which reflects the reduced capacity to endure states that coincide with the perception of missing salient, key, or sufficient information (Carleton, 2016), is related to health anxiety (Deacon & Abramowitz, 2008) and anxiety disorders more broadly (Carleton et al., 2012). Both anxiety sensitivity and intolerance of uncertainty each contribute unique information to our understanding of health anxiety (Fergus & Bardeen, 2013), suggesting both sets of beliefs are potentially important causal or maintaining factors. Unfortunately, existing experimental and longitudinal research in this area of research is generally lacking. One longitudinal study casts doubt as to whether anxiety sensitivity actually confers risk to health anxiety (Olatunji, Wolitzky-Taylor, et al., 2009), underscoring a need for future research to help clarify how anxiety sensitivity and intolerance of uncertainty contribute to health anxiety.

Based upon the cognitive specificity hypothesis (Beck & Haigh, 2014), which posits that each anxiety disorder is marked by dysfunctional beliefs that are more relevant to the respective disorder than other anxiety disorders, researchers have put forward dysfunctional beliefs that are putatively specific to health anxiety. Salkovskis and Warwick (2001) described four health-related dysfunctional beliefs of particular importance to health anxiety. These beliefs are the perceived (a) likelihood of experiencing a health problem, (b) awfulness of experiencing a health problem, (c) inability to cope with an experienced health problem, and (d) inadequacy of medical resources to treat an experienced health problem. To date, existing research has found that these four beliefs relate to health anxiety and potentially more so than to symptoms of other anxiety disorders (Fergus, 2014; Hadjistavropoulos et al., 2012). Future research examining how these four dysfunctional beliefs contribute to health anxiety is warranted.

The dysfunctional beliefs described above can broadly be conceptualized as content-based beliefs about the self and world. Although informative to our understanding of health anxiety, metacognitive conceptualizations suggest that emotional distress largely develops because of our beliefs about thinking (i.e., metacognitive beliefs; Wells, 2009). Bailey and Wells (2015) found three sets of metacognitive beliefs underlying health anxiety, including that thoughts can cause illness (e.g., "Worrying about illness is likely to make it happen"), biased thinking (e.g., "Worrying about my health will help me cope"), and that thoughts are uncontrollable (e.g., "Dwelling on thoughts of illness is uncontrollable"). Using a longitudinal design, Bailey and Wells (2016) found support for metacognitive beliefs serving as a moderator of the longitudinal relationship between catastrophic misinterpretations of bodily states and health anxiety. These findings highlight the possibility that metacognitive beliefs may play a causal role in relation to health anxiety.

Importantly, preliminary research suggests that content-based beliefs and metacognitive beliefs account for unique variance in health anxiety scores, suggesting that both sets of beliefs offer incremental explanatory power (Melli, Carraresi, Poli, & Bailey, 2016). Future research is needed to better understand the interplay among these sets of beliefs and whether one set is more important to health anxiety than the other set of beliefs.

Maladaptive Coping

Maladaptive coping takes several forms, including reassurance seeking and excessive health-related checking behaviors (e.g., repeated palpation of subcutaneous lumps) and functional impairment (Taylor & Asmundson, 2004). Reassurance seeking and checking behaviors provide transient relief but serve to maintain or exacerbate health anxiety in the long term (Abramowitz & Moore, 2007). As discussed above, the overutilization of medical services is considered a core form of maladaptive coping among severe presentations of health anxiety (Abramowitz et al., 2002; Salkovskis & Warwick, 2001; Taylor & Asmundson, 2004). Preliminary research suggests that the overutilization of medical services among individuals with severe health anxiety may depend upon the age of the individual, as health anxiety is associated with greater primary care service utilization among older, relative to younger, adults (Fergus, Griggs, Cunningham, and Kelley, 2017). Whether age influences the type of maladaptive coping engaged in by individuals with severe health anxiety remains to be more fully examined in future research.

As illustrated in Paul's case, using the Internet to look up symptoms and other health concerns is an additional form of maladaptive coping common among individuals with severe health anxiety. It is important to underscore that the use of the Internet to access health-related information is associated with potential benefits for some individuals, including leading them to experience more long-term versus transient relief from health concerns and leading to a sense of being better informed (Starcevic & Berle, 2013). However, at least one study found that around 30% of individuals who search for health-related information on the Internet report an escalation of health anxiety following their searching behavior (Fergus & Dolan, 2014). When health anxiety specifically occurs because of Internet searches for health-related information, it is commonly referred to as cyberchondria (Taylor & Asmundson, 2004). Defining features of cyberchondria include excessive or repeated Internet searches for health-related information that is associated to distress, typically in the form of health anxiety (Starcevic & Berle, 2013). There is not yet consensus on the directionality of associations between health anxiety and the repeated Internet searches that mark cyberchondria (Starcevic & Berle, 2015), with preliminary longitudinal data raising the possibility that repeated Internet searches for health-related information may emerge even among individuals without elevated health anxiety (te Poel, Baumgartner, Hartmann, & Tanis, 2016).

Summary of Core Features

There are a number of core features that promote development of health anxiety and serve to exacerbate and maintain it over time. Understanding these features and distinguishing those that play a developmental role from those that contribute to severity and persistence can facilitate case conceptualization and direct treatment choices and focus.

Primer on Assessment and Evidence-Based Treatment

Treatments based on the contemporary cognitive behavioral model of health anxiety are generally accepted as the frontline intervention for individuals presenting with severe health anxiety (Abramowitz & Braddock, 2011; Taylor & Asmundson, 2004), although other treatment options are available (e.g., pharmacotherapy and psychodynamics). Detailed descriptions of the treatment of severe presentations of health anxiety have been provided elsewhere (Taylor & Asmundson, 2004; Taylor, Asmundson, & Coons, 2005; Thibodeau, Asmundson, & Taylor, 2013). Overviews of pharmacotherapy for severe health anxiety and evidence indicating a marked patient preference for cognitive behavioral treatment are provided by Asmundson et al. (2010). Below, we provide a brief primer on assessment and treatment from a cognitive behavioral perspective.

Treatment always begins will comprehensive assessment, the details of which are described elsewhere (Taylor & Asmundson, 2004). To summarize, critical steps in assessment include ruling out medical conditions that may be responsible for presenting concerns, establishing that the presenting disease-based concerns are associated with severe health anxiety, and gathering information pertinent to understanding the presenting concerns (e.g., personal history and reasons for seeking treatment). People with severe health anxiety are often unwilling or reluctant to accept that their concerns are caused by anything other than disease. This poses a considerable challenge to the cognitive behavioral therapist—how to engage the reluctant patient in psychotherapy. A combination of validating statements (e.g., "I understand that what you are experiencing is real") and motivational interviewing ("You've tried many other things that haven't provided relief. If these other things haven't helped, isn't this at least worth a try?") is often helpful in this regard, establishing trust and initiating the treatment process.

The general goal of cognitive behavioral treatment for severe health anxiety is not to reduce bodily sensations or changes (although it often does so); instead, the goal is to help the person discover explanations for his or her concerns that are not rooted in disease. For example, Paul might discover that his shoulder pain and breathing difficulties he thought likely to be indicative of a cardiac issue are consequences of recent increases in stress at work combined with physical deconditioning as a result of spending less time working out. Psychoeducation, behavioral stress management, exposure and response prevention, and cognitive therapy are particularly effective in reducing disease conviction and checking behavior while improving overall functioning and quality of life (Taylor & Asmundson, 2004); however, metaanalytic findings indicate that the largest effect sizes are for treatments that combine cognitive and behavioral strategies (Taylor et al., 2005). Several chapters of this volume detail the specifics of cognitive and behavioral treatments (Chapter 6), acceptance and commitment therapy (Chapter 7), and technology-based innovation (Chapter 8) for severe presentations of health anxiety.

Paul Revisited

Paul continued to struggle with worries about the seriousness of his chest pain and breathing difficulties for many months following his stress test with the cardiologist. He continued searching the Internet for information on diseases that had similar symptom profiles to his own. He stopped all physical activity, including playing with his children, because it made his pain, breathlessness, and coughing worse. And after a few months, as his participation in social activities also dwindled, he started staying home from work more days than not. With increasing fatigue and weakness and emerging fears that he may have ALS, he traveled thousands of miles for a comprehensive medical workup, which ultimately revealed no disease-based explanations for his presentation. At the urging of his family, supported by the doctors who conducted the comprehensive medical workup, he visited a psychologist who specialized in health anxiety. The psychologist discussed with Paul the nature of his bodily sensations and presentations, assured him that his experiences were real and asked him to consider other possible explanations that were not rooted in disease, and upon gaining Paul's trust, worked with him on exploring those possibilities using a cognitive behavioral framework.

Summary and Conclusion

Health anxiety occurs when perceived bodily sensations or changes are interpreted as symptoms of a serious disease. Health anxiety can be conceptualized as existing along a continuum, ranging from mild to severe, and as being a core facet of several psychiatric diagnoses. Key characteristics of maladaptive presentations of health anxiety, that is, severe health anxiety, are dysfunctional beliefs and several forms of health-related checking behavior. It is not long ago that severe presentations of health anxiety, particularly hypochondriasis, were viewed as the bane of physicians and believed to be largely untreatable. This belief changed with the introduction of the contemporary cognitive behavioral conceptualization of health anxiety. The cognitive behavioral model and the treatment strategies that stem from it, although still undergoing refinement and requiring additional empirical evaluation, have proved beneficial in reducing distress and improving the quality of life for people who experience severe health anxiety. Other related issues, such as refining the DSM-5 reclassification of conditions characterized by severe health anxiety and innovative applications of cognitive behavioral strategies, may prove to further impact the present state of the science.

References

Abramowitz, J. S., & Braddock, A. E. (2011). *Hypochondriasis and health anxiety*. Germany: Hogrefe.

Abramowitz, J. S., & Moore, E. L. (2007). An experimental analysis of hypochondriasis. *Behaviour Research and Therapy*, *45*, 413–424.

Abramowitz, J. S., Schwartz, S. A., & Whiteside, S. P. (2002). A contemporary conceptual model of hypochondriasis. *Mayo Clinic Proceedings*, *77*, 1323–1330.

Alberts, N. M., Hadjistavropoulos, H. D., Sherry, S. B., & Stewart, S. H. (2016). Linking illness in parents to health anxiety in offspring: Do beliefs about health play a role? *Behavioural and Cognitive Psychotherapy*, *44*, 18–29.

American Psychiatric Association (2013). *Diagnostic and statistical manual of mental disorders* (5th ed.). Washington DC: Author.

Asmundson, G. J. G., Abramowitz, J. S., Richter, A. A., & Whedon, M. (2010). Health anxiety: Current perspectives and future directions. *Current Psychiatry Reports*, *12*, 306–312.

Asmundson, G. J. G., & Le Bouthillier, D. (2018). Somatic symptom and related disorders. In D. C. Beidel & B. C. Frueh (Eds.), *Adult psychopathology and diagnosis* (pp. 429–449). (8th ed.). New York: Wiley.

Asmundson, G. J. G., Taylor, S., Carleton, R. N., Weeks, J. W., & Hadjistavropoulos, H. D. (2012). Should health anxiety be carved at the joint? A look at the health anxiety construct using factor mixture modelling in a non-clinical sample. *Journal of Anxiety Disorders*, *26*, 246–251.

Asmundson, G. J. G., Thibodeau, M. A., Peluso, D. L., & Taylor, S. (2013). Hypochondriasis. S. Hofmann & W. Rief (Eds.), *Cognitive behavioral therapy: A complete reference guide* (pp. 489–504). Vol. II(pp. 489–504). Chichester: Wiley.

Bailer, J., Kerstner, T., Witthöft, M., Diener, C., Mier, D., & Rist, F. (2016). Health anxiety and hypochondriasis in the light of the DSM-5. *Anxiety, Stress, & Coping*, *29*, 219–239.

Bailey, R., & Wells, A. (2015). Development and initial validation of a measure of metacognitive beliefs in health anxiety: the MCQ-HA. *Psychiatry Research*, *230*, 871–877.

Bailey, R., & Wells, A. (2016). Is metacognition a causal moderator of the relationship between catastrophic misinterpretation and health anxiety? A prospective study. *Behaviour Research and Therapy*, *78*, 43–50.

Barsky, A. J. (1992). Hypochondriasis and obsessive compulsive disorder. *Psychiatric Clinics of North America*, *15*, 791–801.

Barsky, A. J., Ettner, S. L., Horsky, J., & Bates, D. W. (2001). Resource utilization of patients with hypochondriacal health anxiety and somatization. *Medical Care*, *39*, 705–715.

Barsky, A. J., & Klerman, G. L. (1983). Overview: hypochondriasis, bodily complaints, and somatic styles. *American Journal of Psychiatry*, *140*, 273–283.

Barsky, A. J., Orav, E. J., & Bates, D. W. (2005). Somatization increases medical utilization and costs independent of psychiatric and medical comorbidity. *Archives of General Psychiatry*, *62*, 903–910.

Barsky, A. J., Wyshak, G., Klerman, G. L., & Latham, K. S. (1990). The prevalence of hypochondriasis in medical outpatients. *Social Psychiatry and Psychiatric Epidemiology*, *25*, 89–94.

Beck, A. T., & Haigh, E. A. P. (2014). Advances in cognitive theory and therapy: the generic cognitive model. *Annual Review of Clinical Psychology*, *10*, 1–24.

Bleichhardt, G., & Hiller, W. (2007). Hypochondriasis and health anxiety in the German population. *British Journal of Health Psychology, 12*, 511–523.

Carleton, R. N. (2016). Into the unknown: a review and synthesis of contemporary models involving uncertainty. *Journal of Anxiety Disorders, 39*, 30–43.

Carleton, R. N., Mulvogue, M. K., Thibodeau, M. A., McCabe, R. E., Antony, M. M., & Asmundson, G. J. G. (2012). Increasingly certain about uncertainty: intolerance of uncertainty across anxiety and depression. *Journal of Anxiety Disorders, 26*, 468–479.

Clark, D. A., & Beck, A. T. (2010). *Cognitive therapy of anxiety disorders: Science and practice.* New York, NY: Guilford.

Collimore, K. C., Asmundson, G. J. G., Taylor, S., & Abramowitz, J. S. (2009). Classification of hypochondriasis and other somatoform disorders. In D. McKay, J. S. Abramowitz, & S. Taylor (Eds.), *Current perspectives on the anxiety disorders: Implications for DSM-V and beyond* (pp. 431–447). New York, NY: Springer.

Deacon, B., & Abramowitz, J. S. (2008). Is hypochondriasis related to obsessive-compulsive disorder, panic disorder, or both? An empirical evaluation. *Journal of Cognitive Psychotherapy, 22*, 115–127.

Escobar, J. I., Gara, M., Waitzkin, H., Silver, R. C., Holman, A., & Comptom, W. (1998). DSM-IV hypochondriasis in primary care. *General Hospital Psychiatry, 20*, 155–159.

Fergus, T. A. (2014). Health-related dysfunctional beliefs and health anxiety: Further evidence of cognitive specificity. *Journal of Clinical Psychology, 70*, 248–259.

Fergus, T. A., & Bardeen, J. R. (2013). Anxiety sensitivity and intolerance of uncertainty: Evidence of incremental specificity in relation to health anxiety. *Personality and Individual Differences, 55*, 640–644.

Fergus, T. A., & Dolan, S. L. (2014). Problematic internet use and internet searches for medical information: the role of health anxiety. *Cyberpsychology, Behavior, and Social Networking, 17*, 761–765.

Fergus, T. A., Griggs, J. O., Cunningham, S. C., & Kelley, L. P. (2017). Health anxiety and medical utilization: the moderating effect of age among patients in primary care. *Journal of Anxiety Disorders, 51*, 79–85.

Fergus, T. A., & Valentiner, D. P. (2010). Disease phobia and disease conviction are separate dimensions underlying hypochondriasis. *Journal of Behavior Therapy and Experimental Psychiatry, 41*, 438–444.

Ferguson, E. (2009). A taxometric analysis of health anxiety. *Psychological Medicine, 39*, 277–285.

Fink, P., Ørnbøl, E., & Christensen, K. S. (2010). The outcome of health anxiety in primary care. A two-year follow-up study on health care costs and self-rated health. *PLoS ONE, 5*, e9873.

Fink, P., Ørnbøl, E., Toft, T., Sparle, K. C., Frostholm, L., & Olesen, F. (2004). A new, empirically established hypochondriasis diagnosis. *American Journal of Psychiatry, 161*, 1680–1691.

Fink, P., Sorensen, L., Engberg, M., Holm, M., & Munk-Jorgensen, P. (1999). Somatization in primary care: prevalence, health care utilization, and general practitioner recognition. *Psychosomatics, 40*, 330–338.

Gureje, O., Ustun, T. B., & Simon, G. E. (1997). The syndrome of hypochondriasis: a cross-national study in primary care. *Psychological Medicine, 27*, 1001–1010.

Hadjistavropoulos, H. D., Janzen, J. A., Kehler, M. D., Leclerc, J., Sharpe, D., & Bourgault-Fagnou, M. D. (2012). Core cognitions related to health anxiety in self-reported medical and non-medical samples. *Journal of Behavior Medicine, 35*, 167–178.

Hedman, E., Ljótsson, B., Axelsson, E., Andersson, G., Rück, C., & Andersson, E. (2017). Health anxiety in obsessive compulsive disorder and obsessive compulsive symptoms in severe health anxiety: an investigation of symptom profiles. *Journal of Anxiety Disorders, 45*, 80–86.

Karademas, E. C. (2009). Effects of exposure to the suffering of unknown persons on health-related cognitions, and the role of mood. *Health, 13*, 491–504.
Liu, L., Bi, B., Qin, X., Wei, S., Wang, W., Li, Y., ... Dong, G. (2012). The prevalence of somatoform disorders in internal medicine outpatient departments of 23 general hospitals in Shenyang, China. *General Hospital Psychiatry, 34*, 339–344.
Longley, S. L., Broman-Fulks, J. J., Calamari, J. E., Noyes, R., Wade, M., & Orlando, C. M. (2010). A taxometric study of hypochondriasis symptoms. *Behavior Therapy, 41*, 505–514.
Looper, K. J., & Kirmayer, L. J. (2001). Hypochondriacal concerns in a community population. *Psychological Medicine, 31*, 577–584.
Martin, A., & Jacobi, F. (2006). Features of hypochondriasis and illness worry in the general population in Germany. *Psychosomatic Medicine, 68*, 770–777.
Melli, G., Carraresi, C., Poli, A., & Bailey, R. (2016). The role of metacognitive beliefs in health anxiety. *Personality and Individual Differences, 89*, 80–85.
Naragon-Gainey, K. (2010). Meta-analysis of the relations of anxiety sensitivity to the depressive and anxiety disorders. *Psychological Bulletin, 136*, 128–150.
Newby, J. M., Hobbs, M. J., Mahoney, A. E. J., Wong, S., & Andrews, G. (2017). DSM-5 illness anxiety disorder and somatic symptom disorder: comorbidity, correlates, and overlap with DSM-IV hypochondriasis. *Journal of Psychosomatic Research, 101*, 31–37.
Noyes, R., Jr., Carney, C. P., Hillis, S. L., Jones, L. E., & Langbehn, D. R. (2005). Prevalence and correlates of illness worry in the general population. *Psychosomatics, 46*, 529–539.
Noyes, R., Jr., Kathol, R. G., Fisher, M. M., Phillips, B. M., Suelzer, M. T., & Woodman, C. L. (1994). Psychiatric comorbidity among patients with hypochondriasis. *General Hospital Psychiatry, 16*, 78–87.
Olatunji, B. O., Deacon, B. J., & Abramowitz, J. S. (2009). Is hypochondriasis an anxiety disorder? *The British Journal of Psychiatry, 194*, 481–482.
Olatunji, B. O., Wolitzky-Taylor, K. B., Elwood, L., Connolly, K., Gonzales, B., & Armstrong, T. (2009). Anxiety sensitivity and health anxiety in a nonclinical sample: specificity and prospective relations with clinical stress. *Cognitive Therapy and Research, 33*, 416–424.
olde Hartman, T. C., Borghuis, M. S., Lucassen, P. L. B. J., van de Laar, F. A., Speckens, A. E., & van Weel, C. (2009). Medically unexplained symptoms, somatisation disorder and hypochondriasis: course and prognosis. A systematic review. *Journal of Psychosomatic Research, 66*, 363–377.
Rief, W. (2013). A commentary on: Somatic symptom disorder: an important change in DSM. *Journal of Psychosomatic Research, 75*, 584.
Rief, W., & Martin, A. (2014). How to use the new DSM-5 somatic symptom disorder diagnosis in research and practice: a critical evaluation and a proposal for modifications. *Annual Review of Clinical Psychology, 10*, 339–367.
Salkovskis, P. M., & Clark, D. M. (1993). Panic disorder and hypochondriasis. *Advances in Behaviour Research and Therapy, 15*, 23–48.
Salkovskis, P. M., & Warwick, H. C. (2001). Making sense of hypochondriasis: a cognitive model of health anxiety. In G. J. G. Asmundson, S. Taylor, & B. J. Cox (Eds.), *Health anxiety: Clinical and research perspectives on hypochondriasis and related disorders* (pp. 46–64). London: John Wiley and Sons Ltd.
Starcevic, V. (2013). Hypochondriasis and health anxiety: conceptual challenges. *British Journal of Psychiatry, 202*, 718.
Starcevic, V., & Berle, D. (2013). Cyberchondria: towards a better understanding of excessive health-related Internet use. *Expert Reviews of Neurotherapeutics, 13*, 205–213.
Starcevic, V., & Berle, D. (2015). Cyberchondria: an old phenomenon in a new guise? In E. Aboujaoude & V. Starcevic (Eds.), *Mental health in the digital age: grave dangers, great promise* (pp. 106–117). New York, NY: Oxford University Press.

Starcevic, V., Fallon, S., Uhlenhuth, E. H., & Pathak, D. (1994). Generalized anxiety disorder, worries about illness, and hypochondriacal fears and beliefs. *Psychotherapy and Psychosomatics*, *61*, 93–99.

Sunderland, M., Newby, J. M., & Andrews, G. (2013). Health anxiety in Australia: Prevalence, comorbidity, disability and service use. *British Journal of Psychiatry*, *202*, 56–61.

Taylor, S., & Asmundson, G. J. G. (2004). *Treating health anxiety: a cognitive-behavioral approach*. New York, NY: Guilford Press.

Taylor, S., & Asmundson, G. J. G. (2012). Etiology of hypochondriasis: a preliminary behavioral-genetic investigation. *International Journal of Genetics and Gene Therapy*, *2*, 1–5.

Taylor, S., Asmundson, G. J. G., & Coons, M. J. (2005). Current directions in the treatment of hypochondriasis. *Journal of Cognitive Psychotherapy*, *19*, 291–310.

Taylor, S., Thordarson, D. S., Jang, K. L., & Asmundson, G. J. G. (2006). Genetic and environmental origins of health anxiety: a twin study. *World Psychiatry*, *5*, 47–50.

Taylor, S., Zvolensky, M., Cox, B., Deacon, B., Heimberg, R., Ledley, D. R., … Cardenes, S. J. (2007). Robust dimensions of anxiety sensitivity: development and initial validation of the anxiety sensitivity index-3 (ASI-3). *Psychological Assessment*, *19*, 176–188.

te Poel, F., Baumgartner, S. E., Hartmann, T., & Tanis, M. (2016). The curious case of cyberchondria: A longitudinal study on the reciprocal relationship between health anxiety and online health information seeking. *Journal of Anxiety Disorders*, *43*, 32–40.

Thibodeau, M. A., Asmundson, G. J. G., & Taylor, S. (2013). Health anxiety. In S. Hofmann & G. Simos (Eds.), *CBT of anxiety disorders: A practitioner book* (pp. 135–160). New York: Wiley.

Tyrer, P., Cooper, S., Crawford, M., Dupont, S., Green, J., Murphy, D., … Tyrer, H. (2011). Prevalence of health anxiety problems in medical clinics. *Journal of Psychosomatic Research*, *71*, 392–394.

Warwick, H. M. C., & Salkovskis, P. M. (1990). Hypochondriasis. *Behaviour Research and Therapy*, *28*, 105–117.

Wells, A. (2009). *Metacognitive therapy for anxiety and depression*. New York, NY: Guilford.

Further Reading

Faravelli, C., Salvatori, S., Galassi, F., Aiazzi, L., Drei, C., & Cabras, P. (1997). Epidemiology of somatoform disorders: A community survey in Florence. *Social Psychiatry and Psychiatric Epidemiology*, *32*, 24–29.

Taylor, S., Jang, K. L., Stein, M. B., & Asmundson, G. J. G. (2008). A behavioral-genetic analysis of health anxiety: implications for the cognitive-behavioral model of hypochondriasis. *Journal of Cognitive Psychotherapy*, *22*, 143–153.

CHAPTER TWO

A Diagnostic Perspective on Health Anxiety

Per Fink
The Research Clinic for Functional Disorders and Psychosomatics, Aarhus University Hospital, Aarhus, Denmark

Classification—A Historical Perspective

The term health anxiety has at least partly replaced the older eponym hypochondriasis, which is a diagnosis that has been used since antiquity. However, the meaning of the diagnosis has changed over time. Hippocrates used the term *hypochondria* about the anatomical region that is located under the left curvature, a region that still bears this name today. The Roman doctor, Galen, described hypochondria as a condition with indigestion problems with flatulence, abdominal pain, nervousness, and melancholy. The condition was believed to be caused by disturbances in the pelvic organs, the gastrointestinal tract, the liver, and the spleen. The mental symptoms were attributed to an effect of a body fluid on the brain (Hansen, 1976). Early in history, hysteria was perceived as a uterine variant of hypochondriasis, and Sydenham thus described hypochondriasis as the male counterpart to hysteria in women (Kenyon, 1965), a view that prevailed until about 1900 (Veith, 1965). In the 18th century, hypochondriasis was perceived as a fashionable disorder in Britain associated with the modern way of life and the environmental threats due to the industrialization. Hypochondriasis was viewed as a disorder of the abdominal organs, and many of the cases of hypochondriasis from the 19th century can today be classified as well-defined physical diseases, which were unknown at the time. Therefore, there is only a partial overlap between the early described disorder and our current understanding of this disorder. The term achieved its modern sense, namely, an exaggerated fear of physical disease, with Feuchtersleben in the first part of the 19th century (Veith, 1965) and in the Anglo-Saxon world with Gillespie in 1928.

The Clinician's Guide to Treating Health Anxiety
https://doi.org/10.1016/B978-0-12-811806-1.00002-0

Hypochondriac worries are frequent in a variety of mental disorders of both psychotic and nonpsychotic nature. In the last century, hypochondriasis was believed to be the precursor to melancholia (depression) and dementia praecox (schizophrenia). Melancholy was believed to be caused by a disturbance in the black bile meaning that the cause of the disturbance was to be found in the same anatomical region as hypochondriasis. This may be one of the reasons why the link between depression and hypochondriasis has attracted so much interest.

When Beard introduced the neurasthenia diagnosis, it almost completely engulfed the hypochondriasis diagnosis. From around the 19th century and until a renewed interest arose in the 1960s, hypochondriasis was only sparsely described in the literature because it was considered a manifestation of neurasthenia (Hansen, 1976). Right up to now, the existence of hypochondriasis as a distinct diagnostic entity has been challenged, and whether it is always secondary to another mental disorder has been debated. Kenyon (Kenyon, 1964, 1965) proposed in the 1960s to divide hypochondriasis into a primary and a secondary type. The primary type was included in the official classification system of International Classification of Diseases (ICD)-8 in 1965 and Diagnostic and Statistical Manual of Mental Disorders (DSM)-II in 1968 under the designation hypochondriacal neurosis. The main symptoms were preoccupation with the body and fear of having a disease. In the DSM-III from 1980 (American Psychiatric Association, 1980), it was added that the patient misinterpreted physical signs and sensations as evidence of physical illness and that these symptoms were not better explained by another condition. Furthermore, the patient did not respond to repeated medical reassurance. Hypochondriasis was moved to the new diagnostic group of somatoform disorders that includes a group of mental disorders predominantly manifesting themselves with somatic symptoms. In the ICD-10 from 1992 (WHO, 1992), the concept of neurosis was omitted, and somatoform disorders were included in the ICD-10 under which heading the hypochondriasis diagnosis was placed. The duration was set to a minimum of 6 months, a criterion that was also included in the revision of the DSM-III. The definition of hypochondriasis was further revised in the DSM-IV in 1994 (American Psychiatric Association, 1994) in which specific exclusion criteria were added to delineate hypochondriasis from other disorders, and it was specified that the symptoms should be distressing or with functional impairment.

The Current DSM-5 and ICD-10 (−11) Classifications of Health Anxiety

In Table 1, the diagnostic criteria for ICD-10 hypochondriasis are displayed, and Tables 2 and 3 display the criteria for illness anxiety (IAS) and

Table 1 ICD-10 Hypochondriacal Disorder[a]

(A)	Persistent belief in the presence of at least one serious physical illness underlying the presenting symptom(s), even though repeated investigations and examinations have identified no adequate physical explanation or a persistent preoccupation with a presumed deformity or disfigurement
(B)	Persistent refusal to accept the advice and reassurance of several different doctors that there is no physical illness or abnormality underlying the symptoms

[a]WHO (1993). The ICD-10 Classification of Mental and Behavioral Disorders. Diagnostic Criteria for Research. Geneva: WHO.

Table 2 Illness Anxiety Disorder—DSM-5[a]

A	Preoccupation with having or acquiring a serious illness
B	Somatic symptoms are not present or, if present, are only mild in intensity. If another medical condition is present or there is a high risk for developing a medical condition (e.g., strong family history is present), the preoccupation is clearly excessive or disproportionate
C	There is a high level of anxiety about health, and the individual is easily alarmed about personal health status
D	The individual performs excessive health-related behavior (e.g., repeatedly checks his or her body for signs of illness) or exhibits maladaptive avoidance (e.g., avoids doctor appointments and hospitals)
E	Illness preoccupation has been present for at least 6 months, but the specific illness that is feared may change over that period of time
F	The illness-related preoccupation is not better explained by another mental disorder, such as somatic symptoms disorder, panic disorder, generalized anxiety disorder, body dysmorphic disorder, obsessive-compulsive disorder or delusional disorder, and somatic type

Specify whether:

Care-seeking type: Medical care, including physician visits or undergoing tests and procedures, is frequently used

Care-avoidant type: Medical care is rarely used

[a]American Psychiatric Association (2013). *Diagnostic and statistical manual of mental disorders (DSM-5).* Arlington, VA: American Psychiatric Association.

Table 3 Somatic Symptom and Related Disorders—DSM-5[a]

A One or many somatic symptoms that are distressing or result in significant disruption of daily life
B Excessive thoughts, feelings, or behaviors related to the somatic symptoms or associated health concerns as manifested by at least one of the following:
1. Disproportionate and persistent thoughts about the seriousness of one's symptoms
2. Persistently high level of anxiety about health or symptoms
3. Excessive time and energy devoted to these symptoms or health concerns (typically more than 6 months)

C Although any somatic symptom may not be continuously present, the state of being symptomatic is persistent (typically more than 6 months)

Specify if:

With predominant pain (previously pain disorder): This specifier is for individuals whose somatic symptoms predominantly involve pain

Specify if:

Persistent: A persistent course is characterized by severe symptoms, marked impairment, and long duration (more than 6 months)

Specify current severity:

Mild: Only one of the symptoms specified in criterion B is fulfilled
Moderate: Two or more of the symptoms specified in criterion B are fulfilled

[a]American Psychiatric Association (2013). *Diagnostic and statistical manual of mental disorders (DSM-V)*. Arlington, VA: American Psychiatric Association.

somatic symptom disorder (SSD) in DSM-5 (American Psychiatric Association, 2013). A main change in the DSM-5 was that the somatoform diagnosis group was obliterated and replaced by SSD. Some of the previous somatoform disorders were merged into the three diagnoses of SSD, IAS, and conversion disorder. In fact, somatization and the undifferentiated somatization disorder and somatoform pain disorder were erased as only patients who also have health anxiety symptoms besides their somatic symptoms now qualify for the SSD diagnosis. The DSM-IV hypochondriasis diagnosis was thus split into the two new diagnoses, the IAS and SSD (see also below).

The hypochondriasis diagnosis in ICD-11 has been moved from the somatoform chapter to the anxiety chapter, and the bodily distress disorder diagnosis has been introduced to at least partly include the other somatoform disorders of the ICD-10. The strongly stigmatizing name hypochondriasis is kept in the ICD-11 despite the fact that most publications and researchers today use the eponym health anxiety.

Neither the ICD-10 nor the DSM-IV and DSM-5 diagnoses build on scientific principles for establishing diagnostic categories like those introduced by Robins and Guze in connection with the development of DSM-III in which they took a phenotype approach (Robins & Guze, 1970; Kendell, 1989; Fink & Rosendal, 2008). Instead, the former diagnoses are almost entirely consensus-driven based on a clinical utility approach and by consensus in small expert groups (First et al., 2004). The empirical foundation of the diagnoses is poor as they are mainly based on clinical observations by members of the expert groups and/or are derived from severely skewed patient samples in psychiatric settings even though health anxiety is predominantly seen in medical settings.

Diagnostic categories based on clinical consensus have shown to fail to align with findings from clinical and epidemiological studies as well as studies on neuroscience and genetics. Diagnoses based on phenotype, that is, the identification of characteristic symptom pattern or symptom clustering, illness course, prognosis, etc. by the use of scientific principles like those introduced by Robins and Guze, are very much needed for research and clinical purposes (Insel et al., 2010).

For this chapter, a phenotype approach complying with the Robins and Guze approach with later modifications for construction and validation of diagnoses will also be used. In 2004, Fink et al. introduced the empirically based criteria for health anxiety displayed in Table 4 (Fink et al., 2004). The study builds on an exhaustive diagnostic examination of consecutive patients in primary care and statistical analyses using factor and latent class analyses. The symptom rumination with thoughts of harboring an illness stood out as a very specific symptom of health anxiety (Table 4). The diagnosis has been shown to be well accepted by patients and helpful in providing patients with a positive explanation of their symptoms, to predict a poor outcome when untreated (Eilenberg, Frostholm, Schroder, Jensen, & Fink, 2015; Fink, Ørnbøl, & Christensen, 2010) and to identify a group of patients with a good chance of responding to psychotherapy (Eilenberg, Fink, Jensen, Rief, & Frostholm, 2015; Tyrer, Eilenberg, Fink, Hedman, & Tyrer, 2016). The diagnostic concept is used in some specialized clinics, but it has not been tested more widely and in less specialized settings. The criteria have been adopted by the ICD-11 PC draft for primary care.

These positive diagnostic criteria for health anxiety make the diagnosis easy to establish and to demarcate from other somatoform disorders or functional somatic disorders or bodily distress syndrome, and it speaks strongly

Table 4 Empirically Derived Diagnostic Criteria for Severe Health Anxiety (Fink et al., 2004)[a]

A	Obsessive rumination with thoughts or ideas and fears of suffering from a disease; thoughts that the person cannot stop or can only stop with great difficulty
B	One or more of the following five symptoms
	1 a and/or b
	(a) Worry or concern accompanied by fear of having a serious physical disease or thoughts about getting a disease in the future or concern with other health-related issues
	(b) Exaggerated attention to and awareness of bodily functions, physical sensations, physiological reactions, or minor bodily issues that are misinterpreted as signs of serious illness
	2 Suggestivity and autosuggestivity. If the patient hears or reads about disease, he/she is prone to think that he/she has that disease
	3 Exaggerated fascination with medical information
	4 Unrealistic fear of being infected/contaminated by something eaten or touched (e.g., a person you have touched)
	5 Fear of taking prescription drugs
C	The patient's reaction is far excessive to what would be reasonably expected in response to an illness
D	The symptoms cannot be better explained by another disorder
E	The symptoms should be present most of the time and persist for at least 2 weeks
F	Specification:
	Severe: At least one of the symptoms A–B strongly disturbs or affects the patient's activities of daily living
	Mild: All others

[a]Fink, P., Ørnbøl, E., Toft, T., Sparle, K. C., Frostholm, L., Olesen, F. (2004). A new, empirically established hypochondriasis diagnosis. *The American Journal of Psychiatry* 09;161 (0002-953, 9): 1680–1691.

against the DSM-5 approach in which more or less all the old somatoform disorders are merged into a single construct. Health anxiety/hypochondriasis stands out as distinct dimension/diagnosis that is different from and independent of diagnoses including patients whose primary problem is their somatic symptoms despite the fact that there is a high comorbidity (Fink et al., 2010; van den Heuvel, Veale, & Stein, 2014; Scarella, Laferton, Ahern, Fallon, & Barsky, 2016). In Table 5, differences in characteristics between the two diagnoses are summarized.

Table 5 Differences Between Health Anxiety and Conditions Presenting With Physical Symptoms (BDS, FSS, or SD)

	Health/Illness Anxiety	Bodily Distress Disorder/ Functional Somatic Syndrome/Somatization Disorder
Gender	No difference	75% female
Social status	As general population	Low social status/income
Illness identity	A mental disorder (well accepted by patients)	Does not fit into mental/ nonmental dichotomy
Disability	Mildly to moderately increased	Moderately to severely increased
Working capacity	Somewhat reduced	Very reduced
Disability pension	As general population	Very high risk
Treatment response (psychological therapy and pharmacological)	Very good	Modest
Central characteristics	Disturbed by worriers for symptoms/bodily signals and thoughts about illness	Disabled by physical symptoms
Course	Fluctuating	Persistent
Physical function (SF-36 PCS)	Unaffected	Severely reduced
Mental health (SF-36 MCS)	Affected	Unaffected in mild cases/ affected in severe cases
Avoidance behavior	May avoid information on illness etc. or are very active in information seeking	Avoid physical activities
Somatic symptom score	Modest	High
Use of health care	Slightly increased	Very high

Abbreviations: BDS: Bodily distress syndrome, FSS: Functional somatic syndromes, MCS: Mental component summary, PCS: Physical component summary, SD: Somatization disorder.

Duration

The 6-month duration criterion included in both the DSM and the ICD-10 criteria seems to be arbitrary. No studies have supported this time criterion (Fink et al., 2004; Barsky, Ettner, Horsky, & Bates, 2001; Barsky, Wyshak, & Klerman, 1990). Furthermore, it means that early intervention and prevention are not possible as the patients cannot be diagnosed before they become chronically ill.

Symptoms and Clinical Presentation

Most definitions agree that an essential feature of health anxiety is pathological *worries, concerns, or fears of having or acquiring a serious physical disease* or concern with other health-related issues (a video clip of patients with health anxiety talking about their symptoms and suffering can be viewed here, http://www.en.auh.dk/departments/the-research-clinic-for-functional-disorders-and-psychosomatics/clinical-treatment/) (The Research Clinic for Functional Disorders and Psychosomatics, 2016). The patient has *obsessive rumination* about these thoughts or ideas about suffering from a disease meaning that the patient cannot, or only with great difficulty, stop thinking about this. All thoughts are centered on a suspected disease, and the patient finds more and more "evidence" that he/she suffers from an often severe disease.[1] The growing anxiety spiral ultimately makes the patient seek medical attention. Rumination is specific for health anxiety in the sense that other functional or somatoform disorders, in which illness worries may be prominent, for example, OCD, do not display this symptom, and it is hence of high differential diagnostic importance (Fink et al., 2004). However, despite these facts, the symptom of rumination is not specifically included, neither in the DSM-5 illness anxiety nor in the ICD-10 hypochondriasis or the ICD-11 draft.

The patient is *excessively preoccupied by bodily sensations and body functions* and with anything that may appear to be a sign of a pathological condition. The patient may have *autonomic hypersensitivity* hearing his/her own pulse or being aware of other natural physical phenomena of which others are rarely conscious. The patient may *misinterpret these natural bodily sensations* and develop ideas that it is something unnatural or abnormal. For example, if getting bruises or irritated skin, he/she will be worried that it is a sign of a serious undetected disease. The patient is inclined to *catastrophize* and to always choose the worst possible explanation and misinterpret trivial illness or symptoms as serious ailment. The patient may also *display health-related behavior* repeatedly checking his/her bodily functions and inspect the body's waste products and secretions and may, for example, frequently measure body temperature and blood pressure.

[1] To inquire into rumination, you may ask the following: "If you think about having a disease or being seriously ill, do you find it difficult to get it off your mind again?" "Are you thinking about it constantly or are you winding yourself up?"

Patients with health anxiety also have a significant *suggestive* or *autosuggestive* potential. Hearing or reading about a disease, he/she is easily alarmed and inclined to fear having that disease. Likewise, if someone in the family or among friends, acquaintances, or work colleagues falls ill, the patient may fear having this disease. The patient may also *fear becoming contaminated or infected* with a disease if he/she has been with an ill person or if the patient touches dirty things or things that could be contaminated such as a toilet seat.

A patient with health anxiety may have an *exaggerated fascination with medical and health information*, frequently looking up symptoms and diseases on the Internet and scrutinizing newspaper articles, magazines, popular medical books, and television programs. However, because of a raised level of suggestivity, this may in some cases be such a significant burden for the patient that he/she instead may avoid reading or hearing about health matters and stop seeing doctors. Patients may thus be divided into a *care- or help-seeking type* and a *care-avoidant type*. The latter may also, for instance, avoid visiting family members or friends who are hospitalized or ill, because it is too anxiety-provoking and may trigger the rumination.

The patient is often *afraid to take any medication* based on a fear of getting contaminated.

In some cases, the patient is worried about his/her child's health and is afraid that the child has a disease. This is called *health anxiety by proxy* (Thorgaard et al., 2017; Lockhart, 2016). This may lead to multiple doctor visits with the child.

The patient may seek *reassurance* by consulting a doctor but have *difficulties in believing the doctor* when told that there is nothing to worry about, and when reassured, the worrying returns rapidly.

Differences Between Different Diagnostic Constructs of Health Anxiety

In the DSM-5, health anxiety is split into two diagnostic labels: somatic symptom disorder (SSD) and illness anxiety disorder (IAD). The main difference between the two diagnoses is that in IAD, the patient is not required to have somatic symptoms or, if present, only mild in intensity, whereas in SSD, the patient must have at least one distressing somatic symptom. As studies have shown that somatic symptoms are very prevalent in health anxiety and in the general population, illness anxiety will be a diagnosis nearly impossible to use (Fink et al., 2004). However, a small study in a highly specialized clinic showed that the IAD diagnosis could be established and that the new SSD and IAD diagnoses were more reliable than the DSM-IV hypochondriasis diagnosis (Newby, Hobbs, Mahoney, Wong, & Andrews, 2017).

The ICD-10 hypochondriasis diagnosis also requires that the patient has persistent beliefs in suffering of at least one and not more than two serious physical disease or a persistent preoccupation with a presumed bodily deformity. Why this maximum of two diagnoses is included is a mystery as there seems to be no publications supporting this and no studies seem to have tested it. Preoccupation with a presumed bodily deformity is a separate diagnosis of body dysmorphic disorder in the DSM diagnostic system, which also is the case in the ICD-11 draft. Furthermore, in the ICD-10 diagnosis (like in the DSM-IV), the patient must *refuse to accept reassurance* from doctors that there is no physical illness or abnormality underlying the symptoms. However, it has been shown that it is only about half of the patients with health anxiety that are difficult to reassure, and therefore, it cannot be used diagnostically although it may be of importance for the treatment (Fink et al., 2004). Furthermore, this characteristic may not necessarily be a problem on the patient's part but may be attributable to doctors' communication skills, which is probably very important in this aspect. In the ICD-11 draft, hypochondriasis also seems to include delusional hypochondriacal beliefs.

Delineation from Normality, Differential Diagnoses, and Comorbidity

Delineation from Normality and Normal Reactions to a Health Threat

Being attentive about one's health and bodily functions is important for the survival of human beings as it is a precondition for taking care of ourselves and seeking help if necessary. Illness worrying or health anxiety is thus on a dimension from being too little aware of their body signals and functioning to patients severely disabled by unfounded health worries. The demarcation between normal reactions and pathological health anxiety cannot be established rigorously as it is the case in many other disorders. Clinically, the difference between normality and the pathological behavior may be based on a clinical judgment on how impaired and distressed the patient is by the health anxiety.

Severe health worrying is a normal reaction when a severe disease such as cancer is suspected. The reaction has similar characteristics as other stress reactions to life events and is transient disappearing when the suspected disease is excluded or treated. The preoccupation is not excessive or disproportionate in the light of the condition that is suspected, and usually, patients do not panic but cope with their fear. However, such a real threat to health may trigger the onset of health anxiety. In health anxiety, the patient is usually aware that the worries and preoccupations are unfounded or disproportionate if asked in a considerate way, despite the fact that it may be difficult for the patient to realize this during an attack of overwhelming health anxiety.

Pain, Functional and Somatoform Disorders Primarily with Somatic Symptoms

Between 20% and 30% of patients with health anxiety also fulfill criteria for another comorbid somatoform or functional disorder. Also, except for rumination, many of the symptoms of health anxiety described above may also be present in other somatoform or functional disorders, even if health anxiety is not in play (Fink et al., 2004; Hiller, Leibbrand, Rief, & Fichter, 2005). This may be the reason for confusion among some clinicians and in parts of the medical literature about whether health anxiety is an independent condition distinct from other somatoform or functional disorders. The confusion has been worsened by the introduction of the DSM-5, splitting the old hypochondriasis diagnosis into two. As displayed in Table 5, there are however marked differences between health anxiety and functional disorder/bodily distress syndrome, and both scientific evidence and clinical experience unambiguously point toward them being indeed different conditions. Many patients also find that they are different conditions as they do not identify themselves with the descriptions of the other condition. At the Research Clinic for Functional Disorders in Aarhus, Denmark, group therapy is the applied treatment for both groups, and if a patient with health anxiety by mistake is included in a bodily distress syndrome group or vice versa, it is very clear that the two patient groups do not identify with each other. The patients with health anxiety are fully aware that the problem is not the somatic symptoms but rather the worrying about symptoms or health, and they easily accept that they have a mental disorder. In contrast, patients with a functional disorder presenting with physical symptoms are troubled by the somatic symptoms more than worries about their symptoms.

This is expressed by this patient statement during a diagnostic interview: "Doctor, you have to understand that it's not the somatic symptoms that bother me, but that they make me worry so much."

To establish a differential diagnosis or to judge whether the patient has two independent conditions, it should be explored if both types of symptoms occurred at the same time or if the health anxiety symptoms occurred first. Furthermore, it should be explored what the patient finds most bothersome: the worrying or the somatic symptoms. This, combined with a compiling of all clinical information on illness picture and illness course, may determine whether the patient suffers from health anxiety alone or from another somatoform or functional disorder or both conditions simultaneously.

Depression

A comorbid depression disorder may be present in 15%–30% of patients with health anxiety (Fink et al., 2004; Scarella et al., 2016). As somatic health worrying is also very common in depression, it may be a diagnostic challenge to decide whether the health worrying is caused by the depression or whether both disorders are present independently. The worries in depression are typically mood-congruent influenced by the patient's depressive mood and very pessimistic beliefs. For instance, the patient may think the body is decaying, cancer is eating him/her up, or he/she smells badly. In severe cases, it may be delusional beliefs. If the illness worries begin at the same time or after the onset of the depression or the symptoms disappear when the depression is treated, it speaks for the illness worrying being a manifestation of the depression.

Anxiety and OCD

Anxiety disorder is a very frequent comorbid conditions in health anxiety presenting in as high as 1/3 of the patients (Fink et al., 2004; Scarella et al., 2016).

Health worries and concerns about ones health may also be prominent in various anxiety disorders. Autonomic somatic symptoms in anxiety disorders may be misinterpreted as caused by a medical condition by the patients (and doctors for that matter). However, in generalized anxiety disorders, the patients' focus is not primarily on the body but on worries and concerns centered around a wide range of situations and events. The anxiety is triggered by multiple factors. When the diagnosis of anxiety disorder is established, the patients readily accept this and will, contrary to patients with health anxiety, not continue being preoccupied by the physical health status but accept the somatic distress as being part of their anxiety disorder albeit they may need occasional reassurance. However, it may be a problem if the correct diagnosis is not established as the doctor and the patient may continue seeking medical explanations.

In panic disorder, during a panic attack, the patients have prominent, alarming somatic symptoms such as palpitations, difficulty breathing when hyperventilating, and other autonomic symptoms, and they feel an impending catastrophe like having a heart attack or a stroke with the fear of dying. But like in generalized anxiety disorder, the patients accept that their somatic symptoms are caused by the panic disorder when the diagnosis is established, and their fear of suffering from a severe medical condition is centered around the autonomic symptoms caused by the panic attack. They do not misinterpret other bodily symptoms they may experience or do not fear diseases not associated with anxiety-related autonomic symptoms.

Despite the fact that there may seem to be some clinical similarities between OCD and health anxiety, there is little evidence for this. In OCD, the compulsions and obsessions are not limited to worries about health but consist of a variety of obsessions and compulsions such as repeated hand washing or counting, and the compulsions are intended to neutralize the obsessions. A patient with health anxiety feels compelled to see a doctor to get reassurance, but this is caused by fear of a health problem, not because it is a compulsion to see a doctor. Patients with health anxiety do not usually have other compulsions or obsessions. In OCD, the patients fear getting a disease in the future, whereas patients with health anxiety rather fear being ill here and now. In health anxiety, the rumination is usually triggered by an external or internal stimulus like hearing about illness, and the worrying usually relates to the trigger, while obsessive thoughts in OCD are usually solely intrusive with no specific trigger, although they may be a reaction to a stressor.

Psychosis

Psychotic hypochondriacal delusions are common in schizophrenia spectrum disorders, and in more rare cases, the delusion may be focused on the body and the health only (*paranoia hypochondriaca*) (Hansen, 1976).

In psychosis, the delusions are usually bizarre, for instance, that a steel wire is moving around in the stomach, and therefore, the differential diagnosis is easy to establish. The paranoid delusions are often settled in a comprehensive network of explanations and understandings that are difficult to correct. The psychotic patient is very persistent and little flexible in modifying his/her beliefs when challenged.

In very rare cases, paranoid hypochondriacal delusions may be attributed to a physical disease like a brain tumor or dementia.

Summary and Conclusion

Health anxiety or hypochondriasis is characterized by pathological *worries of harboring a severe disease* and *preoccupation by bodily sensations and function*. Hypochondriasis has been known since antiquity but in different meanings. Research has now shown that it is a distinct phenotype that can be demarked from other conditions, but this approach is not fully adopted in the illness anxiety disorder and somatic symptom disorder of the DSM-5 or hypochondriasis in the ICD-10/11. Health worries are prominent in various mental disorders (depression, anxiety, psychosis, or functional disorders), and therefore, a meticulous diagnostic assessment is important in establishing the diagnosis. A symptom of high differential diagnostic importance is *obsessive rumination* about one's health that has been shown to be specific for health anxiety. Other symptoms are increased *suggestivity*, *fear of becoming contaminated or infected*, *fear of taking prescribed medication*, and *fascination with health information*, and some patients may be *difficult to reassure* that there is nothing wrong physically.

References

American Psychiatric Association. (1980). *Diagnostic and statistical manual of mental disorders (DSM-III)*. Washington DC: American Psychiatric Association.

American Psychiatric Association. (1994). *Diagnostic and statistical manual of mental disorders (DSM-5)*. Washington DC: American Psychiatric Association.

American Psychiatric Association. (2013). *Diagnostic and statistical manual of mental disorders (DSM-V)*. Arlington, VA: American Psychiatric Association.

Barsky, A. J., Ettner, S. L., Horsky, J., & Bates, D. W. (2001). Resource utilization of patients with hypochondriacal health anxiety and somatization. *Medical Care, 39*, 705–715. 0025-7079; 7.

Barsky, A. J., Wyshak, G., & Klerman, L. G. (1990). Transient hypochondriasis. *Archive of General Psychiatry*, *47*(8), 746–752.

Eilenberg, T., Fink, P., Jensen, J. S., Rief, W., & Frostholm, L. (2015). Acceptance and commitment group therapy (ACT-G) for health anxiety: a randomized controlled trial. *Psychological Medicine*, *46*(01), 103–115.

Eilenberg, T., Frostholm, L., Schroder, A., Jensen, J. S., & Fink, P. (2015). Long-term consequences of severe health anxiety on sick leave in treated and untreated patients: analysis alongside a randomised controlled trial. *Journal of Anxiety Disorders, 32*, 95–102. 1873-7897; 0887-6185.

Fink, P., Ørnbøl, E., & Christensen, K. S. (2010). The outcome of health anxiety in primary care. A two-year follow-up study on health care costs and self-rated health. *Plos One, 5*(3), e9873.

Fink, P., Ørnbøl, E., Toft, T., Sparle, K. C., Frostholm, L., & Olesen, F. (2004). A new, empirically established hypochondriasis diagnosis. *The American Journal of Psychiatry, 161*, 1680–1691. 0002-953; 9.

Fink, P., & Rosendal, M. (2008). Recent developments in the understanding and management of functional somatic symptoms in primary care. *Current Opinion in Psychiatry, 21*, 182–188. 0951-7367; 2.

First, M. B., Pincus, H. A., Levine, J. B., Williams, J. B., Ustun, B., & Peele, R. (2004). Clinical utility as a criterion for revising psychiatric diagnoses. *The American Journal of Psychiatry, 161*, 946–954. 0002-953; 0002-953; 6.

Hansen, E. B. (1976). *Paranoia Hypochondriaca.* København: Rigshospitalet, Psykiatrisk afd. O.

Hiller, W., Leibbrand, R., Rief, W., & Fichter, M. M. (2005). Differentiating hypochondriasis from panic disorder. *Journal of Anxiety Disorders, 19*(1), 29–49.

Insel, T., Cuthbert, B., Garvey, M., Heinssen, R., Pine, D. S., Quinn, K., & Wang, P. (2010). Research domain criteria (RDoC): Toward a new classification framework for research on mental disorders. *The American Journal of Psychiatry, 167*(7), 748–751.

Kendell, R. E. (1989). Clinical validity. *Psychological Medicine, 19*(1), 45–55.

Kenyon, F. E. (1964). Hypochondriasis: a clinical study. *British Journal of Psychiatry, 110*, 478–488.

Kenyon, F. E. (1965). Hypochondriasis: a survey of some historical, clinical and social aspects. *The British Journal of Medical Psychology, 38*, 117–133.

Lockhart, E. (2016). Health anxiety in children and parents. *BMJ (Clinical Research Ed.), 353*, i2891.

Newby, J. M., Hobbs, M. J., Mahoney, A. E. J., Wong, S. K., & Andrews, G. (2017). DSM-5 illness anxiety disorder and somatic symptom disorder: Comorbidity, correlates, and overlap with DSM-IV hypochondriasis. *Journal of Psychosomatic Research, 101*, 31–37 (doi:S0022-3999(17)30720-1 [pii).

Robins, E., & Guze, S. B. (1970). Establishment of diagnostic validity in psychiatric illness: its application to schizophrenia. *American Journal of Psychiatry, 126*, 983–987.

Scarella, T. M., Laferton, J. A., Ahern, D. K., Fallon, B. A., & Barsky, A. (2016). The relationship of hypochondriasis to anxiety, depressive, and somatoform disorders. *Psychosomatics, 57*(2), 200–207.

The Research Clinic for Functional Disorders and Psychosomatics. (2016). Statements from patients with health anxiety, http://www.en.auh.dk/departments/the-research-clinic-for-functional-disorders-and-psychosomatics/clinical-treatment/.

Thorgaard, M. V., Frostholm, L., Walker, L., Jensen, J. S., Morina, B., Lindegaard, H., & Rask, C. U. (2017). Health anxiety by proxy in women with severe health anxiety: a case control study. *Journal of Anxiety Disorders, 52*, 8–14.

Tyrer, P., Eilenberg, T., Fink, P., Hedman, E., & Tyrer, H. (2016). Health anxiety: the silent, disabling epidemic. *BMJ, 353*, i2250. 1756-1833; 0959-535.

van den Heuvel, O. A., Veale, D., & Stein, D. J. (2014). Hypochondriasis: considerations for ICD-11. *Revista Brasileira De Psiquiatria (Sao Paulo, Brazil: 1999), 1*, 21–27.

Veith, I. (1965). *Hysteria. The History of a Disease.* Chicago & London: Phoneix Books. The University of Chicago Press.

WHO. (1992). The ICD-10 classification of mental and Behavioural disorders. In *Clinical descriptions and diagnostic guidelines*. Geneva: World Health Organization.

Further Reading

Ferguson, E. (2000). Hypochondriacal concerns and the five factor model of personality. *Journal of Personality*, *68*, 705–724. 0022-3506; 4.

Sanatinia, R., Wang, D., Tyrer, P., Tyrer, H., Crawford, M., Cooper, S., & Barrett, B. (2016). Impact of personality status on the outcomes and cost of cognitive-behavioural therapy for health anxiety. *The British Journal of Psychiatry: The Journal of Mental Science*, *209*(3), 244–250.

CHAPTER THREE

Etiology and Epidemiology of Health Anxiety

Peter Tyrer and Helen Tyrer
Centre for Psychiatry, Imperial College, London, United Kingdom

In this chapter, we will be providing data and comment on studies that have been carried out on both health anxiety and hypochondriasis. These are not synonymous diagnoses, but because they overlap, it would be wrong to ignore information that could be of value to understanding the subject. We also have to acknowledge that studies and reviews on the specific subject of health anxiety are all relatively recent, with the book by Gordon Asmundson, Taylor, and Cox (2001) being a trendsetter in this process.

In reviewing past information, we have been consciously aware of the central component of health anxiety, perhaps best summarized by Forbes Winslow, the first editor of the journal, *Psychological Medicine*, in a book published in 1863, who defined hypochondriasis with rather more emphasis on the anxious component of the condition, as "a morbid anxiety as to health," with "slight bodily ailments, which eventually assume to the distempered and deluded imagination a grave significant character" (Winslow, 1874). This, admittedly somewhat antiquated, language emphasizes the anxious component of health anxiety, its incorrect interpretation, and its subsequent morbidity. It therefore predates later definitions of hypochondriasis that included the conviction of actual physical disease.

Etiology

There is little systematic study of the process by which health anxiety is generated. Worries about health are often perfectly natural, particularly when they are to some extent justified by the possibility of having a disease, awaiting medical investigation, or having been at risk of developing a disease. At any one time, 10%–20% of the population worry about illness (Kellner, 1987a, 1987b), and it is only when these worries persist unnecessarily that pathological health anxiety develops. This characteristic of persistence was also described by Forbes Winslow over 150 years ago; "many

The Clinician's Guide to Treating Health Anxiety
https://doi.org/10.1016/B978-0-12-811806-1.00003-2

Table 1 Factors Involved in the Generation of Health Anxiety

Negative life events	Single or more commonly a cluster of life events that are threatening
Family antecedents	Modeling
Triggers	Single personal events that create health concerns
Personality predisposition	Premorbid personality function in the domain of negative affectivity

(hypochondriacs) will be haunted by a set of thoughts and fancies that they can by no means get rid of, though they desire it ever so earnestly" (Winslow, 1868). Determining the reasons for persistence is a very important task, and to date, they have proved elusive or been summarized in generalities (Table 1).

Negative Life Events

Health anxiety is similar to generalized anxiety disorder (and depression) in its manifestations being associated with negative life events such as deaths in the family, financial problems, and breakup of relationships, but a large proportion are associated with conflict in different forms (Noyes Jr et al., 2002).

Family Antecedents

It is suspected, but not carefully researched, that health anxiety runs in families and, in addition to possible genetic loading, there is an element of modeling from parent to child. Children copy their parents' behavior and may easily pick up abnormal checking and body examination and repeat it accordingly until it becomes pathological. This is something that has been noted in clinical practice and is important in understanding and management. In one Danish community study (Rask, Elberling, Skovgaard, Thomsen, & Fink, 2012), nearly one in five children aged between 5 and 7 had health anxiety symptoms (according to parental report) although this reduced to 1 in 40 when the symptoms were regarded as frequent and troubling (see also Chapter 10 for a detailed description of health anxiety in children).

Triggers

Previous studies have suggested that hypochondriasis (not specifically health anxiety) is precipitated by traumatic events (Seivewright, Tyrer,

Ferguson, Murphy, & Johnson, 2000) and, in our own clinical experience, these are often related to sudden death. There is a great element of superstition here (e.g., "both my father and uncle died of heart attacks at the age of 50, and I am sure the same is going to happen to me"). The responsibility of becoming the main monitor of health is reinforced by these thoughts, and this consequently reinforces health anxiety.

A large proportion of patients with health anxiety also have high levels of generalized anxiety, and study of these associations has led Scarella, Laferton, Ahern, Fallon, and Barsky (2016) to the conclusion that health anxiety belongs firmly with the anxiety disorders.

Personality Predisposition and Health Anxiety

It has long been clear that personality factors are important in the generation and persistence of common mental illness and may possibly be the prime mover in recurrence (Tyrer, 2015). Hypochondriasis has an even stronger anecdotal association with personality than other mood disorders, possibly because of its tendency to persist. One only has to read the verbatim accounts of well-known hypochondriacs to identify personality factors lying behind the symptoms. Boswell's biography of the polymath, Samuel Johnson, is an account by one hypochondriac of another, and throughout their descriptions, the relapsing nature of the condition, together with its association with depression, is illustrated. "When I survey my past life, I discover nothing but a barren waste of time, with some disorders of body, and disturbances of the mind very near to madness" (Boswell, 1791, p. 296). Not long before Johnson's death, "he suffered a very severe return of the hypochondriac disorder, which was ever lurking about him. He was so ill, as, notwithstanding his remarkable love of company, to be entirely averse to society, the most fatal symptom of that malady" (p. 114). "He was afflicted by a bodily disease, which made him often restless and fretful, and with a constitutional melancholy, the clouds of which darkened the brightness of his fancy" (p. 500).

Although it would be wrong to assume that persistent symptoms of any mental condition entitle it to be considered as a personality disorder, it is a viable hypothesis needing enquiry (Tyrer, Ferguson, Fowler-Dixon, & Kelemen, 1990). Although hypochondriasis has been usually characterized by convention as a mental state disorder, physicians and surgeons concerned with psychological aspects of physical disorders have long considered hypochondriasis to be a personality concept. It has also been considered as a personality variable by psychologists, most notably in the Minnesota Multiphasic Personality Inventory (MMPI) (Hathaway & Meehl, 1951). When the association of hypochondriasis with personality disorder has been studied, there is a range of 35%–75% personality disorder co-occurrence, higher than most conditions (Polatin, Kinney, Gatchel, Lillo, & Mayer, 1993; Gatchel, Mayer, & Eddington, 2006; Sakai, Nestoriuc, Nolido, & Barksy, 2010). Personality disorder has also been noted to have a negative impact on outcome in some studies (Tyrer, Seivewright, & Seivewright, 1999), but opposite findings have been noted more recently (Sanatinia et al., 2016; Tyrer, Wang, Tyrer, Crawford, & Cooper, 2016), suggesting that some degree of personality disturbance is not a bar to successful treatment with psychological approaches.

Prevalence of Health Anxiety

This is not a straightforward subject. Health anxiety as a diagnosis has only recently been formalized in DSM-5 as "illness anxiety" (American Psychiatric Association, 2013) (fundamentally the same concept with reverse connotation) and not yet fully formed in the forthcoming ICD-11 classification, although there have been moves to formalize description. But until these descriptions are approved and become accepted, we have to accept a range of diagnostic criteria ranging from the older diagnosis of hypochondriasis (which overlaps with health anxiety but is much more restrictive) to threshold scores on the common scales used to record health anxious symptoms. Many of those formally diagnosed with hypochondriasis will now be reclassified as somatic symptom disorder. The three main ones are the Whiteley Index (Pilowsky, 1967), the Illness Attitude Scales (Kellner, 1987a, 1987b), and the Health Anxiety Inventory (Salkovskis, Rimes, Warwick, et al., 2002), and the thresholds for each of these for the diagnosis of severe health anxiety have been determined (Hedman et al., 2015).

The data that exist are far from satisfactory and are summarized in Table 2. This includes a mixture of estimates of current and period prevalence, and the latter is always higher. The reliability of these can be judged by the degree of variation, with 10-fold variation in the prevalence of hypochondriasis in similar settings and twofold differences in the equivalent health anxiety figures. The hypochondriasis figures are also complicated by the subcategories, abridged and transient hypochondriasis, and in the context of health anxiety, they can probably be concluded to be of relatively little value.

Table 2 Prevalence of Health Anxiety in Different Settings

		Prevalence (%) (current = Point Prevalence, 6 m, 1 year, and Lifetime Indicates forms of Period Prevalence)		
Setting	**Author(s)**	**Health Anxiety**	**Hypochondriasis**	**Comments**
Community	Faravelli et al. (1997), Bleichhardt and Hiller (2007), Sunderland, Newby, and Andrews (2013)	6 (current) 3.4 (current)	4.5 (1 year) 0.4 (current)	Sunderland et al. (5.7% lifetime prevalence found also)
General practice	Gureje, Üstün, and Simon (1997), Escobar et al. (1998), Tyrer, Cooper, Tyrer, and Bassett (2018)	12	0.8 (current) 3 (current)	
Medical clinics	Barsky, Wyshak, Klerman, and Latham (1990), Tyrer et al. (2018), Tyrer et al. (2011)	15 (current) 19 (current)	4.2–6.3 (6 m)	
Liaison psychiatry clinics	Altamura, Carta, Tacchini, Musazzi, and Pioli (1998),		1.6 (current)	
Cardiology clinics	Aydemir et al. (1997)		7.4 (current)	Low mental health literacy in this population
Range (all studies)		3.4–19	0.4–7.4	

The health anxiety figures also cover a range from severe to mild health anxiety. It remains to be seen if the divisions between them are supported by further research, but they probably account for some of the disparity in prevalence figures.

However, these figures are interpreted; they illustrate that excessive health anxiety is common. There is also the suspicion, and it cannot be said to be more than a suspicion that the group of health anxious patients who avoid medical contact because of their health fears may be underrepresented in this figures, as these people are likely to hide their beliefs in epidemiological surveys.

An important question is whether health anxiety is getting more common because of increased use of the Internet to increase knowledge of illness (cyberchondria). In two of our own studies and our personal work, we have seen an increase in its prevalence in medical patients over a 4-year period (Tyrer et al., 2018), and this could be related to greater use of the Internet and exhortations by all providers for patients to be responsible for monitoring their own health. Health anxiety is also associated with considerable comorbidity. The overlap includes generalized anxiety disorder, obsessive–compulsive disorder, and acute and chronic depressive disorders, and this partly explains the difficulties in classification and why health anxiety might be placed with the obsessional disorders in ICD-11 (Stein et al., 2016).

One of the most common comorbidities is concurrent medical illness. One of the problems with some previous definitions of hypochondriasis is that they required pathological belief in illness despite the absence of actual disease, but in practice, it is very common to get health anxiety in the context of other conditions, and this is especially relevant in older people (El-Gabalawy, Mackenzie, Thibodeau, Asmundson, & Sareen, 2013; Cooper, Gregory, Walker, Lambe, & Salkovskis, 2017).

Summary and Conclusion

This chapter illustrates more ignorance than knowledge about the etiology and epidemiology of health anxiety. We are beginning to get an impression of an increasingly common condition that has been largely underrecognized and that is increasing in frequency. Now that it is beginning to be recognized in formal diagnostic systems and will be better identified in the future, the extent of its impact and effect should become better known. It would help greatly to have a standard instrument for recording its presence unequivocally.

References

Altamura, A. C., Carta, M. G., Tacchini, G., Musazzi, A., & Pioli, M. R. (1998). Prevalence of somatoform disorders in a psychiatric population: an Italian nationwide survey. Italian collaborative group on somatoform disorders. *European Archives of Psychiatry and Clinical Neuroscience, 248*, 267–271.

American Psychiatric Association. (2013) Illness Anxiety: In 5th Revision of the Diagnostic and Statistical Manual for Mental Disorders. Washington, DC, p. 215.

Asmundson, G. J. G., Taylor, S., & Cox, B. J. (2001). *Health anxiety: Clinical and research perspectives on hypochondriasis and related conditions*. Chichester: John Wiley.

Aydemir, O., Ozmen, E., Küey, L., Kültür, S., Yeşil, M., Postaci, N., & Bayata, S. (1997). Psychiatric morbidity and depressive symptomatology in patients with permanent pacemakers. *Pacing and Clinical Electrophysiology, 20*, 1628–1632.

Barsky, A. L., Wyshak, G., Klerman, G. L., & Latham, K. S. (1990). The prevalence of hypochondriasis in medical out-patients. *Social Psychiatry and Psychiatric Epidemiology, 25*, 89–94.

Bleichhardt, G., & Hiller, W. (2007). Hypochondriasis and health anxiety in the German population. *British Journal of Health Psychology, 12*, 511–523.

Boswell, J. (1791). The Life of Dr Johnson. Abridged as Everybody's Boswell, edited by Frank Morley. London: G Bell & Son, 1930.

Cooper, K., Gregory, J. D., Walker, I., Lambe, S., & Salkovskis, P. M. (2017). Cognitive behaviour therapy for health anxiety: a systematic review and meta-analysis. *Behavioral and Cognitive Psychotherapy, 45*, 110–123.

El-Gabalawy, R., Mackenzie, C. S., Thibodeau, M. A., Asmundson, G. J., & Sareen, J. (2013). Health anxiety disorders in older adults: conceptualizing complex conditions in late life. *Clinical Psychology Review, 33*, 1096–1105.

Escobar, J. I., Gara, M., Waitzkin, H., Silver, R. C., Holman, A., & Compton, W. (1998). DSM-IV hypochondriasis in primary care. *General Hospital Psychiatry, 20*, 155–159.

Faravelli, C., Salvatori, S., Galassi, F., Alazzi, L., Drei, C., & Cabras, P. (1997). Epidemiology of somatoform disorders: a community study in Florence. *Social Psychiatry and Psychiatric Epidemiology, 32*, 24–29.

Gatchel, R. J., Mayer, T. G., & Eddington, A. (2006). MMPI disability profile: the least known, most useful screen for psychopathology in chronic occupational spinal disorders. *Spine, 31*, 2973–2978.

Gureje, O., Üstün, T. B., & Simon, G. (1997). The syndrome of hypochondriasis: a cross-national study in primary care. *Psychological Medicine, 27*, 1001–1010.

Hathaway, S. R., & Meehl, P. E. (1951). *An atlas for the clinical use of the Minnesota multiphasic personality inventory*. Minneapolis: University of Minneapolis.

Hedman, E., Lekander, M., Ljótsson, B., Lindefors, N., Rück, C., Andersson, G., & Andersson, E. (2015). Optimal cut-off points on the Health Anxiety Inventory, Illness Attitude Scales and Whiteley Index to identify severe health anxiety. *PLoS One, 10*(4) e0123412.

Kellner, R. (1987a). Hypochondriasis and somatization. *Journal of the American Medical Association, 258*, 2718–2722.

Kellner, R. (1987b). Abridged manual of the Illness Attitude Scale. Department of Psychiatry, School of Medicine, University of New Mexico.

Noyes, R., Jr., Stuart, S., Langbehn, D. R., Happel, R. L., Longley, S. L., & Yagla, S. J. (2002). Childhood antecedents of hypochondriasis. *Psychosomatics, 43*, 282–289.

Pilowsky, I. (1967). Dimensions of hypochondriasis. *British Journal of Psychiatry, 113*, 83–93.

Polatin, P. B., Kinney, R. K., Gatchel, R. J., Lillo, E., & Mayer, T. G. (1993). Psychiatric illness and chronic low-back pain. The mind and the spine—which goes first? *Spine, 18*, 66–71.

Rask, C. U., Elberling, H., Skovgaard, A. M., Thomsen, P. H., & Fink, P. (2012). Parental-reported health anxiety symptoms in 5- to 7-year-old children: the Copenhagen Child Cohort CCC 2000. *Psychosomatics, 53*, 58–67.

Sakai, R. I., Nestoriuc, Y., Nolido, N. V., & Barksy, A. (2010). The prevalence of personality disorders in hypochondriasis. *Journal of Clinical Psychiatry, 71*, 41–47.

Salkovskis, P. M., Rimes, K. A., Warwick, H. M. C., et al. (2002). The Health Anxiety Inventory: development and validation of scales for the measurement of health anxiety and hypochondriasis. *Psychological Medicine, 32*, 843–853.

Sanatinia, R., Wang, D., Tyrer, P., Tyrer, H., Cooper, S., et al. (2016). The impact of personality status on the cost and outcomes of cognitive behaviour therapy for health anxiety. *British Journal of Psychiatry, 209*, 244–250.

Scarella, T. M., Laferton, J. A., Ahern, D. K., Fallon, B. A., & Barsky, A. (2016). The relationship of hypochondriasis to anxiety, depressive, and somatoform disorders. *Psychosomatics, 57*, 200–207.

Seivewright, N., Tyrer, P., Ferguson, B., Murphy, S., & Johnson, T. (2000). Longitudinal study of the influence of life events and personality status on diagnostic change in three neurotic disorders. *Depression and Anxiety, 11*, 105–113.

Stein, D. J., Kogan, C. S., Atmaca, M., Fineberg, N. A., Fontenelle, L. E., Grant, J. E., et al. (2016). The classification of obsessive-compulsive and related disorders in the ICD-11. *Journal of Affective Disorders, 190*, 663–674.

Sunderland, M., Newby, J. M., & Andrews, G. (2013). Health anxiety in Australia: prevalence, comorbidity, disability and service use. *British Journal of Psychiatry, 202*, 56–61.

Tyrer, P. (2015). Personality dysfunction is the cause of recurrent non-cognitive mental disorder: a testable hypothesis. *Personality and Mental Health, 9*, 1–7.

Tyrer, P., Cooper, S., Crawford, M., Dupont, S., Green, J., Murphy, D., et al. (2011). Prevalence of health anxiety problems in medical clinics. *Journal of Psychosomatic Research, 71*, 392–394.

Tyrer, P., Cooper, S., Tyrer, H., & Bassett, P. (2018). Increase in the prevalence of health anxiety in medical clinics: cause for concern. *International Journal of Social Psychiatry*, under review.

Tyrer, P., Ferguson, B., Fowler-Dixon, R., & Kelemen, A. (1990). A plea for the diagnosis of hypochondriacal personality disorder. *Journal of Psychosomatic Research, 34*, 637–642.

Tyrer, P., Seivewright, N., & Seivewright, H. (1999). Long term outcome of hypochondriacal personality disorder. *Journal of Psychosomatic Research, 46*, 177–185.

Tyrer, P., Wang, D., Tyrer, H., Crawford, M., & Cooper, S. (2016). Dependent personality and its influence on the short and long-term outcomes of cognitive behaviour therapy for health anxiety: randomised controlled trial. *Personality and Mental Health, 10*, 96–105.

Winslow, F. B. (1868). *Obscure diseases of the brain and mind*: (p. 436) (third edition). Philadelphia: Lea.

Winslow, F. B. (1874). *Obscure diseases of the brain and mind*: (p. 216) (third edition). Philadelphia: Lea.

Further Reading

Axelsson, E., Andersson, E., Ljótsson, B., Wallhed Finn, D., & Hedman, E. (2016). The Health Preoccupation Diagnostic Interview: inter-rater reliability of a structured interview for diagnostic assessment of DSM-5 somatic symptom disorder and illness anxiety disorder. *Cognitive Behaviour Therapy, 45*, 259–269.

CHAPTER FOUR

Cognitive and Behavioral Mechanisms of Health Anxiety

Thomas A. Fergus* and Gordon J.G. Asmundson†
*Department of Psychology and Neuroscience, Baylor University, Waco, TX, United States
†Department of Psychology, University of Regina, Regina, SK, Canada

Overview

Conceptual models of health anxiety stem from a diverse array of theoretical positions; however, to date, cognitive behavioral models have garnered the greatest empirical support (e.g., see Abramowitz & Braddock, 2008; Marcus, Gurley, Marchi, & Bauer, 2007; Norris & Marcus, 2014; Rachman, 2012; Taylor & Asmundson, 2004; Williams, 2004) and are the focus of this chapter. One of the earliest cognitive behavioral models of health anxiety came from Warwick and Salkovskis (1990), who based their model upon Clark's (1986) cognitive behavioral model of panic. In brief, Warwick and Salkovskis's (1990) model of health anxiety posits that learning experiences lead to the development of health-related dysfunctional beliefs. Those beliefs, in turn, lead to the misappraisals of, likely, innocuous bodily states (e.g., headache is perceived as a sign of a possible brain tumor) that, in turn, evoke health anxiety. The use of safety behaviors (e.g., avoidance and self-inspection) temporarily reduces health anxiety, but those behaviors ultimately serve to maintain health anxiety because the behaviors do not allow for the disconfirmation of underlying dysfunctional beliefs (Warwick & Salkovskis, 1990).

Warwick and Salkovskis's (1990) model has since been elaborated and extended upon by several research groups (e.g., Abramowitz & Braddock, 2008; Rachman, 2012; Salkovskis & Warwick, 2001; Taylor & Asmundson, 2004; Williams, 2004). At present, there is not enough research on a single cognitive behavioral model of health anxiety to suggest that one model is a preferred over other models. There is existing research supporting central tenets of many aspects of existing cognitive behavioral models of health anxiety (Marcus et al., 2007; Norris & Marcus, 2014). For these reasons, a variety of potential causal and maintaining factors of

The Clinician's Guide to Treating Health Anxiety
https://doi.org/10.1016/B978-0-12-811806-1.00004-4

health anxiety will be reviewed in this chapter. The factors are not meant to be an exhaustive list; rather, they are ones commonly implicated in extant cognitive behavioral models and are factors that have received, at least some, empirical support. Because health anxiety parallels anxiety disorders (e.g., Olatunji, Deacon, & Abramowitz, 2009), an influential model of anxiety disorders (i.e., Barlow's, 2000, triple vulnerability model) will, at times, be used as an organizing perspective throughout this chapter.

Biological Vulnerability

Barlow (2000) posits that each anxiety disorder is marked by a generalized biological vulnerability in the form of genetic contributions expressed as negative affect. Negative affect (often referred to as neuroticism) is a risk factor for health anxiety (e.g., Williams, 2004), with health anxiety sharing substantive associations with negative affect/neuroticism (see Longley, Calamari, Noyes, Meyers, & McDowell, 2014, for a review). Negative affect/neuroticism is highly heritable (see Tackett & Lahey, 2017, for a review), and it thus seems plausible that health anxiety could be attributable to genetic contributions as well, given that health anxiety may be a manifestation of negative affect/neuroticism (Longley et al., 2014). Relatively, little behavioral genetic (twin) research of health anxiety has been completed and heritability estimates differ depending on the conceptualization of health anxiety. When examining a categorization of health anxiety (severe vs not severe), heritability estimates range from 54% to 69% (Taylor & Asmundson, 2012). Alternatively, Taylor and Asmundson (2012) found heritability estimates between 10% and 37% in relation to a continuous indicator of health anxiety. The former set of heritability estimates are on par with estimates seen in relation to negative affect/neuroticism (Tackett & Lahey, 2017). Whether individuals inherit relatively nonspecific genes to negative affect/neuroticism and/or genes more specific to health anxiety remains an important area of future investigation.

Possible structural components of the brain contributing to health anxiety remain largely understudied; however, preliminary research suggests that functional connectivity between brain regions implicated in interoception relate to health anxiety (Grossi et al., 2017). Interoception is important to health anxiety because, as reviewed more fully below, health anxiety is linked to the tendency to be vigilant to bodily states and to catastrophize about the meaning of those states. Grossi et al. (2017) found reduced connectivity between the extrastriate body area (EBA) and somatosensory areas in the brain among individuals with severe health anxiety. The EBA is thought, in part, to relate to bodily self-consciousness (Serino et al., 2013), with Grossi et al. (2017) interpreting this finding to suggest that health anxiety may be marked by a decreased ability to integrate across sensory modalities (e.g., integrating somatosensory information with other perceptual information). The possibility that health anxiety is related to reduced multisensory integration may help account for findings that health anxiety is associated with *lowered* interoceptive accuracy (Krautwurst, Gerlach, Gomille, Hiller, & Witthöft, 2014). Grossi et al. (2017) further found that health anxiety is associated with stronger connectivity between the EBA and both the amygdala and hippocampus, interpreting this finding to suggest that individuals with severe health anxiety may experience greater distress-based signals related to self-body signals in the brain. Although preliminary, such findings indicate that impaired functional connectivity may contribute to health anxiety.

Learning Experiences

Learning experiences are critical to the development of anxiety disorders, as those experiences lead individuals to focus their anxiety on specific life circumstances (Barlow, 2000). Rachman (2012) notes that there are at least three life experiences contributing to health anxiety, and anxiety disorders more broadly, including experiencing disturbing or damaging events, vicarious acquisition, or absorbing threatening information. Pursuant to these life experiences, extant research suggests that adults with severe health anxiety report greater childhood psychosocial and physical difficulties than individuals without severe health anxiety (Barsky, Wool, Barnett, & Cleary, 1994). However, such direct difficulties may not be specific to health anxiety and are likely seen across anxiety disorders more broadly (Gropalis, Bleichhardt, Witthöft, & Hiller, 2012). An extremely ill or injured close friend or family member is a correlate of health anxiety (Noyes Jr., Carney, Hillis, Jones, and Langbehn, 2005), with death of a parent correlating with health anxiety as well (Alberts & Hadjistavropoulos, 2014). Individuals may vicariously acquire a focus on health-related threats through witnessing health problems in close others (Rachman, 2012). Indeed, preliminary research suggests that witnessing parental illness as a child may predispose one to overestimate personal susceptibility to illness as an adult, which contributes to health anxiety (Alberts, Hadjistavropoulos, Sherry, & Stewart, 2016). Children may develop health-related concerns through absorbing information about the threatening nature of health concerns at home as well, as parent and child levels of health anxiety positively correlate (Wright, Reiser, & Delparte, 2017). Additionally, there is some evidence that greater knowledge of health threats relates to greater fearful responding (Blakey & Abramowitz, 2017); however, this pattern of findings has not always been consistent (Blakey, Reuman, Jacoby, & Abramowitz, 2015). Although additional research is needed to more fully connect learning experiences to the development of health anxiety, preliminary research is broadly consistent with Rachman's (2012) posited pathways.

Dysfunctional Beliefs

Dysfunctional beliefs have arguably received the most empirical attention of any factor in relation to the pathogenesis of health anxiety. Cognitive behavioral models posit that beliefs contribute to the misinterpretation of bodily states as a potential health problem and, thus, are putative vulnerability and/or maintaining factors of health anxiety (e.g., Abramowitz & Braddock, 2008; Rachman, 2012; Salkovskis & Warwick, 2001; Taylor & Asmundson, 2004; Williams, 2004). As has been reviewed elsewhere (Marcus et al., 2007; Norris & Marcus, 2014), studies examining associations between health-related beliefs and health anxiety have nearly uniformly identified effects moderate to large in magnitude. One caveat surrounding this line of research is an issue of description versus explanation, as the assessed beliefs substantively overlap with the content of the health anxiety measures (Marcus et al., 2007). Another caveat is that the health anxiety literature has largely lagged behind other literatures examining the causal role of dysfunctional beliefs in relation to manifestations of anxiety (e.g., see Hezel & McNally, 2016) in that few existing studies have used either an experimental or longitudinal design to examine if dysfunctional beliefs causally exacerbate or temporally precede health anxiety (Rachman, 2012). Nonetheless, conclusions from at least two review papers are supportive of the relevance given to beliefs within existing conceptual models (Marcus et al., 2007; Norris & Marcus, 2014). Following from Barlow (2000), we initially consider psychological vulnerability—in this case, in the form of beliefs—that is generalized in nature and then turn our attention to beliefs that are possibly relatively specific to health anxiety.

Anxiety sensitivity (AS) and intolerance of uncertainty (IU) are two generalized psychological vulnerability factors for anxiety disorders (e.g., Carleton et al., 2012; Naragon-Gainey, 2010; Sexton, Norton, Walker, & Norton, 2003) that receive considerable attention within some cognitive behavioral models of health anxiety (e.g., Abramowitz & Braddock, 2008). AS refers to individual differences in the fear of anxiety (Reiss, 1987), and an individual prone to fearing anxiety (i.e., reflecting heightened AS) may be more likely to perceive health problems from innocuous bodily states. AS may, therefore, contribute to the development and maintenance of health anxiety (Abramowitz & Braddock, 2008). Peterson and Reiss (1992) developed the Anxiety Sensitivity Index (ASI) to assess a unidimensional conceptualization of AS. Studies using the original ASI found positive associations between AS and health anxiety (e.g., Boelen & Carleton, 2012; Olatunji, Wolitzky-Taylor, et al., 2009; Otto, Pollack, Sachs, & Rosenbaum, 1992). Subsequent research, though, suggests that AS is multidimensional (Taylor, 1999).

The most recent version of the ASI is Taylor et al.'s (2007) ASI-3. The ASI-3 assesses beliefs about consequences of anxiety, with the assessed consequences including immediate medical complications (physical), mental incapacitation (cognitive), and social rejection (social). Studies using the ASI-3 have found that AS and health anxiety are distinct, yet, strongly related constructs (Stewart, Sherry, Watt, Grant, & Hadjistavropoulos, 2008). Extant research generally converges on the consequences of immediate medical complications being the AS concern most relevant to health anxiety (e.g., Abramowitz, Olatunji, & Deacon, 2007; Deacon & Abramowitz, 2008; Fergus & Bardeen, 2013; Fergus & Valentiner, 2010; Fetzner et al., 2014; Reuman et al., 2017; Wheaton, Berman, Franklin, & Abramowitz, 2010; Wheaton, Deacon, McGrath, Berman, & Abramowitz, 2012). The consequences of mental incapacitation and social rejection have, at times, emerged as relevant to health anxiety as well (e.g., Fetzner et al., 2014; Wheaton et al., 2010). It is possible that those concerns are most relevant to the perceived consequences of a potential health problem rather than overestimating the likelihood of the occurrence of a health problem (Wheaton et al., 2010). Despite these promising pattern of results linking AS and health anxiety, the lone longitudinal study examining these constructs casts doubt on whether AS actually confers risk for health anxiety (Olatunji, Wolitzky-Taylor, et al., 2009).

IU is strongly related to AS, although research findings suggest the two constructs are distinct (Carleton, Sharpe, & Asmundson, 2007). The most recent definition of IU is that the construct reflects the reduced capacity to endure states that coincide with the perception of missing salient, key, or sufficient information (Carleton, 2016). In the context of health anxiety, individuals often desire *certainty* about their health status (Abramowitz & Braddock, 2008). The remote possibility that one has, or could develop, a health problem can be distressing, particularly for someone who has difficulties tolerating uncertainty. Indeed, IU may moderate the association between catastrophic health appraisals and health anxiety. More precisely, preliminary research indicates that the tendency to form catastrophic health appraisals of innocuous bodily states only relates to health anxiety when coupled with heightened IU (Fergus & Valentiner, 2011). In addition, extant research nearly uniformly converges on there being positive associations between IU and health anxiety (e.g., Abramowitz, Deacon, & Valentiner, 2007; Boelen & Carleton, 2012; Deacon & Abramowitz, 2008; Fergus & Bardeen, 2013; Fergus & Valentiner, 2009; Fetzner et al., 2014). Whereas these studies focus on a unidimensional conceptualization of IU, research findings indicate that IU is best conceptualized as a multidimensional construct (Carleton, Norton, & Asmundson, 2007) consisting of the tendency to look to the future to address uncertainty (prospective) and becoming immobilized when faced with uncertainty (inhibitory). Preliminary studies have provided mixed findings as to whether those facets of IU differentially relate to health anxiety, with some findings indicating that inhibitory relates more strongly with health anxiety (Fergus & Bardeen, 2013) and other findings indicating that prospective relates more strongly with health anxiety (Fetzner et al., 2014). No known published study has yet examined IU as a potential risk factor of health anxiety using a longitudinal or experimental design.

In addition to generalized psychological vulnerability, like AS and IU, Barlow's (2000) triple vulnerability model posits that anxiety disorders can be differentiated based upon specific psychological vulnerability that lead individuals to focus their anxiety on specific life circumstances. In the context of cognitive behavioral models of health anxiety, health-related dysfunctional beliefs represent specific psychological vulnerability (e.g., Abramowitz & Braddock, 2008; Rachman, 2012; Salkovskis & Warwick, 2001; Taylor & Asmundson, 2004; Williams, 2004). In regard to health-related beliefs, existing research converges on beliefs about the meaning of good health being consequential to health anxiety. For example, individuals with severe health anxiety report a greater number of ambiguous bodily states (e.g., headache and stomachache) as indicative of poor physical health relative to individuals with lower levels of health anxiety (e.g., Barsky, Coeytaux, Sarnie, & Cleary, 1993; MacLeod, Haynes, & Sensky, 1998; Weck, Neng, Richtberg, & Stangier, 2012b). Moreover, health anxiety is marked by the tendency to view ambiguous bodily states as increasingly likely to be the sign of catastrophic health problems (e.g., Hitchcock & Mathews, 1992; Marcus, 1999; Marcus & Church, 2003; Neng & Weck, 2015; Weck, Neng, Richtberg, & Stangier, 2012a). The pattern of findings from these studies is suggestive of health anxiety being marked by a tendency to consider catastrophic explanations for ambiguous bodily states rather than relatively minor explanations. As such, health anxiety does not appear to broadly relate to the tendency to overestimate the likelihood of experiencing *any* health problem but, rather, seems most related to catastrophic explanations. Using a longitudinal study design, research findings suggest that daily catastrophizing about bodily sensations may account for changes in health anxiety (Gautreau et al., 2015).

Salkovskis and Warwick (2001) described four health-related beliefs putatively specific to health anxiety. These beliefs are the perceived (a) likelihood of experiencing a health problem, (b) awfulness of experiencing a health problem, (c) inability to cope with an experienced health problem, and (d) inadequacy of medical resources to treat an experienced health problem. Existing research findings support the relevance of each of these four beliefs to health anxiety via positive interrelations (e.g., Alberts & Hadjistavropoulos, 2014; Alberts et al., 2016; Fergus, 2014a; Hadjistavropoulos et al., 2012). In support of potential specificity to health anxiety, Fergus (2014a) found that Salkovskis and Warwick's (2001) beliefs correlated more strongly with health anxiety than they did with a related symptom type (i.e., obsessive-compulsive symptoms). As discussed, preliminary research suggests some of Salkovskis and Warwick's (2001) beliefs may connect learning experiences with the development of health anxiety. More precisely, parental illness may lead individuals to experience greater beliefs surrounding the likelihood of experiencing a health problem, and those beliefs may evoke health anxiety (Alberts et al., 2016). No known published study has yet examined these four beliefs as a potential risk factor of health anxiety using a longitudinal or experimental design.

The beliefs described above can broadly be conceptualized as content-based beliefs about the self and world. Alternative conceptualizations suggest that health anxiety, and anxiety more broadly, develops because of our beliefs about thinking (i.e., metacognitive beliefs; Wells, 2009). Existing research findings suggest that metacognitive beliefs generally relevant to anxiety correlate with health anxiety as well (e.g., Bailey & Wells, 2013; Bailey & Wells, 2015b; Solem et al., 2015). Some investigators have sought to examine the relevancy of metacognitive beliefs putatively specific to health anxiety (e.g., Bailey & Wells, 2015a; Bailey & Wells, 2016; Bouman & Meijer, 1999; Melli, Carraresi, Poli, & Bailey, 2016). For example, Bailey and Wells (2015a) found three sets of metacognitive beliefs underlying health anxiety. These beliefs include that thoughts can cause illness (e.g., "worrying about illness is likely to make it happen"), thoughts can cause biased thinking (e.g., "worrying about my health will help me cope"), and thoughts are uncontrollable (e.g., "dwelling on thoughts of illness is uncontrollable"). Using a longitudinal design, Bailey and Wells (2016) found support for these metacognitive beliefs serving as a moderator of the longitudinal relationship between catastrophic misappraisals of bodily states and health anxiety. It thus appears that if a person makes catastrophic misappraisals about symptoms and concurrently holds metacognitive beliefs about health-related thoughts, then the risk of experiencing health anxiety is elevated. Such findings underscore metacognitive beliefs possibly playing a causal role in relation to health anxiety. In addition, it is important to note that preliminary research suggests that content-based beliefs, such as AS and Salkovskis and Warwick's (2001) beliefs, and metacognitive beliefs each account for unique variance in health anxiety scores (Melli et al., 2016). These findings suggest that neither content-based beliefs nor metacognitive beliefs may fully account for the experience of health anxiety alone.

Whereas the above-described studies examined explicit health-related beliefs, there is growing interest in examining implicit indexes of health-related beliefs. Assessment of implicit indexes of constructs is advantageous, particularly when the construct may reside outside of conscious control given that the accessibility of constructs, chronic or temporary, impacts information processing (e.g., Higgins & Scholer, 2008). Preliminary research indicates that individuals with severe health anxiety exhibit a tendency to implicitly associate health words with the self, suggestive that individuals with severe health anxiety may have greater automatic accessibility to health-related information (Weck & Höfling, 2015). Additionally, health anxiety may relate to an implicit tendency to view symptoms as more dangerous (Schmidt, Witthöft, Kornadt, Rist, & Bailer, 2013). A replicated finding in this line of research is an association between health anxiety and the tendency to rate ambiguous stimuli as less often pleasant following health-threatening images than neutral images (Jasper & Witthöft, 2013; Schreiber, Neng, Heimlich, Witthöft, & Weck, 2014). Such findings suggest that health anxiety is associated with an automatic negative evaluation of health-related information, which may relate to selective attention to health-related information and greater misappraisals of that information. However, other research has found less evidence for altered implicit associations among individuals with severe health anxiety than other noted studies (Witthöft et al., 2016).

Attention

Attention is prominently featured in extant conceptual models of anxiety disorders, with the primary focus among existing conceptual models being an attentional bias for threat (see Mogg & Bradley, 2016, for a review). More precisely, cognitive models posit that the tendency to allocate attention toward threatening versus nonthreatening information is a causal and maintaining factor for anxiety disorders. Subsequent research has fleshed out the link between an attentional bias for threat and anxiety (see Cisler & Koster, 2010, for a review), suggesting that this bias may be reflective of both facilitated engagement with threatening information and difficulties disengaging from such information. Facilitated attention reflects the speed in which attention is oriented toward threat, and disengagement difficulties reflect the impaired switching of attention from threat. Researchers have additionally suggested that attentional avoidance of threat may characterize anxiety disorders, such that attention, at times, is preferentially allocated away from threat as a possible distraction method to regulate negative affect. The type of bias exhibited may depend on the stage of processing, with facilitated engagement occurring during earlier stages of processing and attentional avoidance occurring during later stages of processing. In addition, each type of bias may have unique mechanisms that help account for individual differences in the exhibited attentional bias (Cisler & Koster, 2010). For example, individuals with diminished attentional control may show difficulties disengaging attention from threat. Under what condition(s) specific types of attentional bias relate to anxiety has yet to be clarified, with there likely be task-related, individual difference, and situational variables affecting the association between attentional bias and anxiety (Mogg & Bradley, 2016).

To date, evidence for an attentional bias for threat in relation to health anxiety has been mixed. Using modified Stroop tasks, researchers have assessed attentional bias by presenting health-threat-related and control words in different colors. Individuals are asked to name the color of each word as quickly as possible while ignoring the word content. Using variations of such tasks, researchers have often found that health anxiety is associated with an attentional bias (e.g., Gropalis, Bleichhadt, Hiller, & Witthöft, 2013; Karademas, Christopoulou, Dimosteheni, & Pavlu, 2008; Owens, Asmundson, Hadjistavropoulos, & Owens, 2004; Witthöft et al., 2016). However, not all studies using a modified Stroop task support such a link (Kaur, Butow, & Sharpe, 2013). A limitation of the modified Stroop task is that researchers are unable to disentangle the source of interference on the task, such as through facilitated engagement or delayed disengagement (Mogg & Bradley, 2016). Using alternative tasks that can help localize the source of interference, such as the visual-probe task or visual-search task, extant research points to conflicting findings. Using a visual-probe task and health-threat-related pictures, Lees, Mogg, and Bradley (2005) found no association between health anxiety and an attentional bias. Alternatively, Jasper and Witthöft (2011) found that health anxiety is associated with facilitated engagement with health-threat-related pictures at short presentation times (175 ms) and difficulties disengaging from such stimuli during longer presentations (500 ms) using a visual-probe task. Shields and Murphy (2011) found that all individuals, irrespective of their levels of health anxiety, evidenced attentional bias toward health-threat-related words on a visual-search task. Jacoby, Wheaton, and Abramowitz (2016) also found no evidence for an association between health anxiety and an attentional bias for health-threat-related words using a visual-probe task. Findings from Lee et al. (2013) suggest that an attentional bias between health anxiety and health-threat-related words may depend on whether the words are idiographic. Using a dot-probe task that contained idiographically chosen health-threat words, Lee et al. (2013) found that health anxiety was associated with an attentional bias. Supplemental analyses suggested that the source of the bias was disengagement difficulty from threat. Potential reasons for divergent patterns of findings include the employed attentional bias task, the stimuli used, the type of sample, and the measure used to assess health anxiety. Nonetheless, at present, no firm conclusions can be drawn regarding health anxiety and an attentional bias.

Memory

Cognitive behavioral models implicate the role of a memory bias in relation to health anxiety (e.g., Taylor & Asmundson, 2004). Extending findings indicating that health anxiety is associated with a better recognition of health-related words (e.g., Brown, Kosslyn, Delamater, Fama, & Barsky, 1999; Pauli & Alpers, 2000), Ferguson, Moghaddam, and Bibby (2007) found better recognition of health-threat-related words among individuals with heightened health anxiety that was accounted for by the extent to which the words were viewed as emotionally unpleasant. Moreover, Witthöft et al. (2016) found that individuals with severe health anxiety recognized health-threat-related words significantly more accurately than neutral words and evidenced a response bias by more consistently endorsing that health-threat-related words were presented during an earlier word presentation task than comparison groups. Stronger associations of health-related information and emotional evaluations may lead to a greater availability of health-related information in working memory, which could bias information processing. Indeed, Witthöft et al. (2016) found that greater negative evaluations of health-threat-related words were associated with a response bias for certain health-threat-related words. Ferguson et al. (2007) speculated that the strength of association with health-related words may interfere with the allocation of attentional resources. Although a relatively understudied area compared with other factors putatively contributing to health anxiety, existing research findings point to the potential relevance of memory bias to health anxiety and that such a bias could contribute to additional information processing biases (e.g., attention; Ferguson et al., 2007).

Processing Somatosensory Information

As discussed, cognitive behavioral models emphasize the misappraisal of bodily states in the pathogenesis of health anxiety (e.g., Abramowitz & Braddock, 2008; Rachman, 2012; Salkovskis & Warwick, 2001; Taylor & Asmundson, 2004; Williams, 2004). It is thus not surprising that researchers have examined how health anxiety relates to indicators of somatosensory information processing. One such indicator is body vigilance, which pertains to consciously attending to internal cues (Schmidt, Lerew, & Trakowski, 1997). Like many anxiety disorders, the attention one pays to bodily sensations is putatively central to the development and maintenance of health anxiety (e.g., Abramowitz & Braddock, 2008). Extant research supports health anxiety relating to the close monitoring of bodily sensations (e.g., Hadjistavropoulos, Hadjistavropoulos, & Quine, 2000), as well as positive associations between body vigilance and health anxiety (e.g., Abramowitz, Olatunji, et al., 2007; Olatunji, Deacon, Abramowitz, & Valentiner, 2007). Excessive bodily vigilance within health anxiety may be a product of health-related dysfunctional beliefs, in which individuals feel they need to pay close attention to their bodily states to prevent the development of a health problem. However, vigilance to bodily states is likely to increase perception of such states (Schmidt et al., 1997). Increased perception of bodily states can become problematic in the escalation of health anxiety, as individuals with heightened health anxiety report greater intensity of bodily discomfort, more distress associated with that discomfort, and less control over the discomfort than do individuals with lower health anxiety (e.g., Gramling, Clawson, & McDonald, 1996; Hadjistavropoulos, Craig, & Hadjistavropoulos, 1998). As such, body vigilance may exacerbate health anxiety, as the person is more likely to perceive bodily states as threatening.

Researchers consider body vigilance as part of a broader construct known as somatosensory amplification (Köteles & Witthöft, 2017), with somatosensory amplification labeled, by some researchers, as being at the core of health anxiety (e.g., Barsky & Wyshak, 1990). Somatosensory amplification originally was conceptualized as the amplification of internal sensations (Barsky, Goodson, Lane, & Cleary, 1988) and has been most commonly assessed using the somatosensory amplification scale (Barsky, Wyshak, & Klerman, 1990). A reconceptualization of the construct suggests somatosensory amplification likely more accurately reflects an amplification of a threat response related to body integrity (Köteles & Witthöft, 2017). More precisely, Köteles and Witthöft (2017) noted that somatosensory amplification may arise because of external cues (e.g., hearing about a health threat) rather than internal cues (e.g., heartbeat) alone. Moreover, feared stimuli do not need to be physically present to initiate the amplification process, which may align with illness anxiety disorder where individuals experience an amplified threat response in the absence of any salient bodily sensations or changes. To date, research supports positive associations between somatosensory amplification and health anxiety (see Köteles & Witthöft, 2017, for a review). Somatosensory amplification purportedly increases the intensity of bodily states, thereby leading to greater catastrophizing about those states and health anxiety (e.g., Barsky & Wyshak, 1990). Some researchers suggest that somatosensory amplification, at least as assessed using the somatosensory amplification scale, may simply represent a manifestation of negative affect/neuroticism rather than an indicator of somatosensory processing (e.g., Aronson, Barrett, & Quigley, 2001).

Because health anxiety appears to be marked by heightened attention to bodily cues and the tendency to amplify possible threats to body integrity, one may expect that health anxiety would relate to improved interoceptive accuracy as well. However, existing studies examining this possibility suggest health anxiety as being either unrelated to interoceptive accuracy (e.g., Barsky, Brener, Coeytaux, & Cleary, 1995) or related to *lowered* interoceptive accuracy (e.g., Krautwurst et al., 2014). In fact, consistent with cognitive behavioral formulations, health anxiety may relate to the misinterpretation of naturally occurring fluctuations of bodily sensations (Krautwurst et al., 2014; Krautwurst, Gerlach, & Witthöft, 2016). Consequently, health anxiety does not appear to be marked by the ability to reliably detect minor changes in bodily states but, rather, to a tendency to overestimate the occurrence of bodily changes.

Safety Behaviors

Cognitive behavioral models posit that health anxiety is related to many condition-specific safety behaviors (e.g., Abramowitz & Braddock, 2008; Rachman, 2012; Salkovskis & Warwick, 2001; Taylor & Asmundson, 2004; Williams, 2004). Safety behaviors usually develop to relieve the anxiety of having or developing a health problem. These behaviors take a variety of forms, with one of the most frequent being reassurance seeking from doctors. More precisely, medical utilization may temporarily reduce health anxiety, and yet, utilization of medical services typically serves to sustain health anxiety because individuals do not get corrective experiences that dysfunctional beliefs contributing to health anxiety are unfounded. A repetitive cycle can develop in which individuals experience health anxiety and seek out reassurance from health professionals to mitigate health anxiety and health anxiety returns and individuals engage in repeated medical utilization. Existing studies support positive associations between health anxiety and medical utilization (e.g., Fergus, Bardeen, Gratz, Fulton, & Tull, 2015; Fergus & Valentiner, 2009; Fergus & Valentiner, 2010; Longley, Watson, and Noyes Jr., 2005). Moreover, preliminary research findings suggest that health anxiety may help account for the association between bodily complaints and health care use (Weiss, Rief, & Kleinstäuber, 2017).

Medical professionals are not the only sources of reassurance; as such, there are additional safety behaviors associated with medical utilization, such as bodily checking for signs of possible health problem (e.g., Abramowitz & Braddock, 2008; Taylor & Asmundson, 2004). For example, a woman with concerns of having breast cancer may repeatedly palpate her breast to reassure herself that she does not have breast cancer and, with the repeated palpation, may experience soreness and inflammation for which she then seeks out medical advice. She may seek reassurance from friends and family and also read Internet articles about breast cancer to find evidence that her symptoms are not actually indicative of breast cancer. Similar to medical service utilization, seeking reassurance from friends and family or via Internet searches is rarely beneficial; indeed, bodily checking often leads to the identification of previously unnoticed and harmless bodily states (e.g., temporary skin reddening), and the shear amount of health-related information (and misinformation) on the Internet often leads to alarming health-related information.

Excessively accessing health-related information on the Internet is a safety behavior that has been gaining increasing empirical attention. Taylor and Asmundson (2004) described this safety behavior as "cyberchondria," with existing research supporting positive associations between health anxiety and the frequency of Internet searches for health-related information (e.g., Fergus, 2013; Muse, McManus, Leung, Meghreblian, & Williams, 2012; Singh & Brown, 2014). Additional research suggests that health anxiety positively associates with distress following Internet searches for health-related information, as well as excessive completion of such searches and belief that the searches interfere with daily living (e.g., Fergus, 2014b; Fergus & Russell, 2016; Norr, Allan, Boffa, Raines, & Schmidt, 2015). There is not yet consensus on the directionality of the relationship between health anxiety and Internet searches for health-related information (Starcevic & Berle, 2015). For example, health anxiety could be a precursor to those searches, and the Internet searches could, in turn, exacerbate and/or maintain existing health anxiety. A longitudinal study completed by te Poel, Baumgartner, Hartmann, and Tanis (2016) found no longitudinal (i.e., across 2 months) relation between health anxiety and Internet searches for health-related searches among individuals with elevated health anxiety at baseline. Interestingly, for individuals without elevated health anxiety at baseline, there was a reciprocal longitudinal relation between health anxiety and Internet searches for health-related information. The researchers interpreted their data to suggest that Internet searches for health-related information could be a maintaining, versus exacerbating, factor of health anxiety among individuals with existing heightened health anxiety. Moreover, among individuals without existing heightened health anxiety, Internet searches for health-related information may be a precursor to changes in health anxiety that in turn initiate a reciprocally exacerbating process. These findings raise the possibility that excessive searches for health-related information may emerge in the absence of existing elevated health anxiety (te Poel et al., 2016).

At least two experimental studies illustrate short-term and long-term effects of safety behaviors in relation to health anxiety. Abramowitz and Moore (2007) examined the nature of safety behaviors among individuals with severe health anxiety by exposing them to health-related triggers (e.g., conjuring up images of one's own funeral) and either allowing them or preventing them from performing safety behaviors (e.g., getting reassurance). The researchers found that after exposure to the health-related triggers, both groups reported higher anxiety ratings, but the group allowed to perform safety-related behaviors reported a lower subjective anxiety rating compared with those who were prevented from performing the safety behaviors. Interestingly, the subjective anxiety ratings for the individuals in the safety behavior prevention group naturally decreased with time, but their anxiety ratings were still significantly higher than those who were allowed to perform the safety-related behaviors after 60 min.

In another experimental examination of the role of safety behaviors in relation to health anxiety, Olatunji, Etzel, Tomarken, Ciesielski, and Deacon (2011) randomized individuals to a safety behavior or control condition after an initial week of instruction to monitor their normal engagement in safety behaviors. In the safety behavior condition, individuals were asked to actively engage in safety behaviors (e.g., body checking, checking the Internet for health-related information, and seeking reassurance from family or friends) during the upcoming week. Individuals in the control condition were asked to continue to monitor their normal use of safety behaviors during the upcoming week. Olatunji et al. (2011) found that the experimental manipulation of safety behaviors caused greater increases in health anxiety and health-related beliefs. They further found that changes in health-related beliefs accounted for changes in health anxiety in the safety behavior condition. These researchers interpreted their findings to suggest that safety behaviors increase catastrophic thoughts about the likelihood and severity of health problems, thereby worsening health anxiety.

Along with examining the impact of safety behaviors within health anxiety, researchers have sought to examine motivational factors for the engagement in such behaviors. For example, Halldorsson and Salkovskis (2017) interviewed 10 individuals with severe health anxiety about why they engaged in safety behaviors. Consistently, expressed motivational factors included the perception of threat and need for safety; mood repair; and, to a lesser extent, dispersion of responsibility. The need for certainty was not expressed as a motivational factor associated with health anxiety, which diverges from some cognitive behavioral models and previously reviewed data suggesting that difficulties tolerating uncertainty are important to health anxiety.

Summary and Conclusion

This chapter reviewed putative cognitive and behavioral mechanisms commonly implicated within cognitive behavioral models of health anxiety. As discussed, it is likely that—explicit and implicit—health-related beliefs, attentional processes, and memory processes contribute to the processing of somatosensory information, including being vigilant for bodily states and amplifying perceived threats to body integrity. Underlying this sequence likely includes a genetic diathesis to experience negative emotional states, possible impaired functional connectivity in areas relevant to the self-related processing of the body, and learning experiences that lead one to focus anxiety on health threats. Safety behaviors within health anxiety are likely motivated to address perceived threats and gain a perception of safety; however, potentially through health-related beliefs, these behaviors ultimately serve to maintain health anxiety. A repetitive cycle develops—individuals experience health anxiety and repetitively engage in safety behaviors to temporarily alleviate health anxiety, health anxiety subsequently returns, and the process repeats. Whereas cognitive behavioral models have been influential in improving our understanding of health anxiety, there remains a need for future research to examine the interrelation of the processes described in this chapter to better specify the mechanisms by which each process contributes to the pathogenesis of health anxiety. Such future research efforts will likely ultimately broaden and strengthen both our understanding and treatment of health anxiety.

References

Abramowitz, J. S., & Braddock, A. E. (2008). *Psychological treatment of health anxiety & hypochondriasis: A biopsychosocial approach*. Cambridge, MA: Hogrefe & Huber.

Abramowitz, J. S., Deacon, B. J., & Valentiner, D. P. (2007a). The Short Health Anxiety Inventory: Psychometric properties and construct validity in a non-clinical sample. *Cognitive Therapy and Research*, *31*, 871–883.

Abramowitz, J. S., & Moore, E. L. (2007). An experimental analysis of hypochondriasis. *Behaviour Research and Therapy, 45*, 413–424.
Abramowitz, J. S., Olatunji, B. O., & Deacon, B. J. (2007b). Health anxiety, hypochondriasis, and the anxiety disorders. *Behavior Therapy, 38*, 86–94.
Alberts, N. M., & Hadjistavropoulos, H. D. (2014). Parental illness, attachment dimensions, and health beliefs: Testing the cognitive-behavioural and interpersonal models of health anxiety. *Anxiety, Stress, & Coping, 27*, 216–228.
Alberts, N. M., Hadjistavropoulos, H. D., Sherry, S. B., & Stewart, S. H. (2016). Linking illness in parents to health anxiety in offspring: Do beliefs about health play a role? *Behavioural and Cognitive Psychotherapy, 44*, 18–29.
Aronson, K. R., Barrett, L. F., & Quigley, K. S. (2001). Feeling your body or feeling badly: Evidence for the limited validity of the Somatosensory Amplification Scale as an index of somatic sensitivity. *Journal of Psychosomatic Research, 51*, 387–394.
Bailey, R., & Wells, A. (2013). Does metacognition make a unique contribution to health anxiety when controlling for neuroticism, illness cognition, and somatosensory amplification? *Journal of Cognitive Psychotherapy, 27*, 327–337.
Bailey, R., & Wells, A. (2015a). Development and initial validation of a measure of metacognitive beliefs in health anxiety: The MCQ-HA. *Psychiatry Research, 230*, 871–877.
Bailey, R., & Wells, A. (2015b). Metacognitive beliefs moderate the relationship between catastrophic misinterpretation and health anxiety. *Journal of Anxiety Disorders, 34*, 8–14.
Bailey, R., & Wells, A. (2016). Is metacognition a causal moderator of the relationship between catastrophic misinterpretation and health anxiety? A prospective study. *Behaviour Research and Therapy, 78*, 43–50.
Barlow, D. H. (2000). Unraveling the mysteries of anxiety and its disorders from the perspective of emotion theory. *American Psychologist, 55*, 1247–1263.
Barsky, A. J., Brener, J., Coeytaux, R. R., & Cleary, P. D. (1995). Accurate awareness of heartbeat in hypochondriacal and non-hypochondriacal patients. *Journal of Psychosomatic Research, 39*, 489–497.
Barsky, A. J., Coeytaux, R. R., Sarnie, M. K., & Cleary, P. D. (1993). Hypochondriacal patients' beliefs about good health. *American Journal of Psychiatry, 150*, 1085–1089.
Barsky, A. J., Goodson, J. D., Lane, R. S., & Cleary, P. D. (1988). The amplification of somatic symptoms. *Psychosomatic Medicine, 50*, 510–519.
Barsky, A. J., Wool, C., Barnett, M. C., & Cleary, P. D. (1994). Histories of childhood trauma in adult hypochondriacal patients. *The American Journal of Psychiatry, 151*, 397–401.
Barsky, A. J., & Wyshak, G. (1990). Hypochondriasis and somatosensory amplification. *British Journal of Psychiatry, 157*, 404–409.
Barsky, A. J., Wyshak, G., & Klerman, G. L. (1990). The Somatosensory Amplification Scale and its relationship to hypochondriasis. *Journal of Psychiatric Research, 24*, 323–334.
Blakey, S. M., & Abramowitz, J. S. (2017). Psychological predictors of health anxiety in response to the Zika virus. *Journal of Clinical Psychology in Medical Settings, 24*, 270–278.
Blakey, S. M., Reuman, L., Jacoby, R. J., & Abramowitz, J. S. (2015). Tracing "fearbola": Psychological predictors of anxious responding to the threat of Ebola. *Cognitive Therapy and Research, 39*, 816–825.
Boelen, P. A., & Carleton, R. N. (2012). Intolerance of uncertainty, hypochondriacal concerns, obsessive-compulsive symptoms, and worry. *Journal of Nervous and Mental Disease, 200*, 208–213.
Bouman, T. K., & Meijer, K. J. (1999). A preliminary study of worry and metacognition in hypochondriasis. *Clinical Psychology and Psychotherapy, 6*, 96–101.
Brown, H. D., Kosslyn, S. M., Delamater, B., Fama, J., & Barsky, A. J. (1999). Perceptual and memory biases for health related information in hypochondriacal individuals. *Journal of Psychosomatic Research, 47*, 67–78.

Carleton, R. N. (2016). Into the unknown: A review and synthesis of contemporary models involving uncertainty. *Journal of Anxiety Disorders, 39*, 30–43.

Carleton, R. N., Mulvogue, M. K., Thibodeau, M. A., McCabe, R. E., Antony, M. M., & Asmundson, G. J. G. (2012). Increasingly certain about uncertainty: Intolerance of uncertainty across anxiety and depression. *Journal of Anxiety Disorders, 26*, 468–479.

Carleton, R. N., Norton, P. J., & Asmundson, G. J. G. (2007a). Fearing the unknown: A short version of the Intolerance of Uncertainty Scale. *Journal of Anxiety Disorders, 21*, 105–117.

Carleton, R. N., Sharpe, D., & Asmundson, G. J. G. (2007b). Anxiety sensitivity and intolerance of uncertainty: Requisites of the fundamental fears? *Behaviour Research and Therapy, 45*, 2307–2316.

Cisler, J. M., & Koster, E. H. W. (2010). Mechanisms of attentional biases towards threat in anxiety disorders: An integrative review. *Clinical Psychology Review, 30*, 203–216.

Clark, D. M. (1986). A cognitive approach to panic. *Behaviour Research and Therapy, 24*, 461–470.

Deacon, B., & Abramowitz, J. S. (2008). Is hypochondriasis related to obsessive-compulsive disorder, panic disorder, or both? An empirical evaluation. *Journal of Cognitive Psychotherapy, 22*, 115–127.

Fergus, T. A. (2013). Cyberchondria and intolerance of uncertainty: Examining when individuals experience health anxiety in response to Internet searches for medical information. *Cyberpsychology, Behavior, and Social Networking, 16*, 735–739.

Fergus, T. A. (2014a). Health-related dysfunctional beliefs and health anxiety: Further evidence of cognitive specificity. *Journal of Clinical Psychology, 70*, 248–259.

Fergus, T. A. (2014b). The Cyberchondria Severity Scale (CSS): An examination of structure and relations with health anxiety in a community sample. *Journal of Anxiety Disorders, 28*, 504–510.

Fergus, T. A., & Bardeen, J. R. (2013). Anxiety sensitivity and intolerance of uncertainty: Evidence of incremental specificity in relation to health anxiety. *Personality and Individual Differences, 55*, 640–644.

Fergus, T. A., Bardeen, J. R., Gratz, K. L., Fulton, J. J., & Tull, M. T. (2015). The contribution of health anxiety to retrospectively-recalled emergency department visits within a sample of patients in residential substance abuse treatment. *Cognitive Behaviour Therapy, 44*, 1–8.

Fergus, T. A., & Russell, L. H. (2016). Does cyberchondria overlap with health anxiety and obsessive-compulsive symptoms? An examination of latent structure and scale interrelations. *Journal of Anxiety Disorders, 38*, 88–94.

Fergus, T. A., & Valentiner, D. P. (2009). Reexamining the domain of hypochondriasis: Comparing the Illness Attitudes Scale to other approaches. *Journal of Anxiety Disorders, 23*, 760–766.

Fergus, T. A., & Valentiner, D. P. (2010). Disease phobia and disease conviction are separate dimensions underlying hypochondriasis. *Journal of Behavior Therapy and Experimental Psychiatry, 41*, 438–444.

Fergus, T. A., & Valentiner, D. P. (2011). Intolerance of uncertainty moderates the relationship between catastrophic health appraisals and health anxiety. *Cognitive Therapy and Research, 35*, 560–565.

Ferguson, E., Moghaddam, N. G., & Bibby, P. A. (2007). Memory bias in health anxiety is related to the emotional valence of health-related words. *Journal of Psychosomatic Research, 62*, 263–274.

Fetzner, M. G., Asmundson, G. J. G., Carey, C., Thibodeau, M. A., Brandt, C., Zvolensky, M. J., & Carleton, R. N. (2014). How do elements of a reduced capacity to withstand uncertainty relate to the severity of health anxiety? *Cognitive Behaviour Therapy, 43*, 262–274.

Gautreau, C. M., Sherry, S. B., Sherry, D. L., Birnie, K. A., Mackinnon, S. P., & Stewart, S. H. (2015). Does catastrophizing of bodily sensations maintain health-related anxiety? A 14-day daily diary study with longitudinal follow-up. *Behavioural and Cognitive Psychotherapy, 43*, 502–512.

Gramling, S. E., Clawson, E. P., & McDonald, M. K. (1996). Perceptual and cognitive abnormality model of hypochondriasis: Amplification and physiological reactivity in women. *Psychosomatic Medicine, 58*, 423–431.

Gropalis, M., Bleichhadt, G., Hiller, W., & Witthöft, M. (2013). Specificity and modifiability of cognitive bias in hypochondriasis. *Journal of Consulting and Clinical Psychology, 81*, 558–565.

Gropalis, M., Bleichhardt, G., Witthöft, M., & Hiller, W. (2012). Hypochondriasis, somatoform disorders, and anxiety disorders. *Journal of Nervous and Mental Disease, 200*, 406–412.

Grossi, D., Longarzo, M., Quarantelli, M., Salvatore, E., Cavaliere, C., De Luca, P., ... Aiello, M. (2017). Altered functional connectivity of interoception in illness anxiety disorders. *Cortex, 86*, 22–32.

Hadjistavropoulos, H. D., Craig, K. D., & Hadjistavropoulos, T. (1998). Cognitive and behavioral responses to illness information: The role of health anxiety. *Behaviour Research and Therapy, 36*, 149–164.

Hadjistavropoulos, H. D., Hadjistavropoulos, T., & Quine, A. (2000). Health anxiety moderates the effects of distraction versus attention to pain. *Behaviour Research and Therapy, 38*, 425–438.

Hadjistavropoulos, H. D., Janzen, J. A., Kehler, M. D., Leclerc, J., Sharpe, D., & Bourgault-Fagnou, M. D. (2012). Core cognitions related to health anxiety in self-reported medical and non-medical samples. *Journal of Behavior Medicine, 35*, 167–178.

Halldorsson, B., & Salkovskis, P. M. (2017). Why do people with OCD and health anxiety seek reassurance excessively? An investigation of differences and similarities in function. *Cognitive Therapy and Research, 41*, 619–631.

Hezel, D. M., & McNally, R. J. (2016). A theoretical review of cognitive biases and deficits in obsessive-compulsive disorder. *Biological Psychology, 121*, 221–232.

Higgins, E. T., & Scholer, A. A. (2008). When is personality revealed? A motivated cognition approach. In O. P. John, R. W. Robins, & L. A. Pervin (Eds.), *Handbook of personality: Theory and research* (3rd., pp.182–207). Guilford: New York, NY.

Hitchcock, P. B., & Mathews, A. (1992). Interpretation of bodily symptoms in hypochondriasis. *Behaviour Research and Therapy, 30*, 223–234.

Jacoby, R. J., Wheaton, M. G., & Abramowitz, J. S. (2016). Attentional biases in illness anxiety: Null findings from the dot probe paradigm. *Journal of Obsessive-Compulsive and Related Disorders, 10*, 19–25.

Jasper, F., & Witthöft, M. (2013). Automatic evaluative processes in health anxiety and their relations to emotion regulation. *Cognitive Therapy and Research, 37*, 521–533.

Jasper, F., & Witthöft, M. (2011). Health anxiety and attentional bias: The time course of vigilance and avoidance in light of pictorial illness information. *Journal of Anxiety Disorders, 25*, 1131–1138.

Karademas, E. C., Christopoulou, S., Dimosteheni, A., & Pavlu, F. (2008). Health anxiety and cognitive interference: Evidence from the application of a modified Stroop task in two studies. *Personality and Individual Differences, 44*, 1138–1150.

Kaur, A., Butow, P. N., & Sharpe, L. (2013). Health threat increases attentional bias for negative stimuli. *Journal of Behavior Therapy and Experimental Psychiatry, 44*, 469–476.

Köteles, F., & Witthöft, M. (2017). Somatosensory amplification—an old construct from a new perspective. *Journal of Psychosomatic Research, 101*, 1–9.

Krautwurst, S., Gerlach, A. L., Gomille, L., Hiller, W., & Witthöft, M. (2014). Health anxiety—an indicator of higher interoceptive sensitivity? *Journal of Behavior Therapy and Experimental Psychiatry, 45*, 303–309.

Krautwurst, S., Gerlach, A. L., & Witthöft, M. (2016). Interoception in pathological health anxiety. *Journal of Abnormal Psychology, 125*, 1179–1184.

Lee, H., Turkel, J. E., Cotter, S. P., Milliken, J. M., Cougle, J., Goetz, A. R., & Lesnick, A. M. (2013). Attentional bias toward personally relevant health-threat words. *Anxiety, Stress, & Coping, 26*, 493–507.

Lees, A., Mogg, K., & Bradley, B. P. (2005). Health anxiety, anxiety sensitivity, and attentional bias for pictorial and linguistic health-threat cues. *Cognition and Emotion, 19*, 453–462.

Longley, S., Calamari, J. E., Noyes, R., Meyers, K., & McDowell, E. (2014). Health anxiety (hypochondriasis): an emotional disorder in an alternative taxonomy. *Current Psychiatry Reviews, 10*, 3–13.

Longley, S. L., Watson, D., & Noyes, R., Jr. (2005). Assessment of the hypochondriasis domain: The Multidimensional Inventory of Hypochondriacal Traits (MIHT). *Psychological Assessment, 17*, 3–14.

MacLeod, A. K., Haynes, C., & Sensky, T. (1998). Attributions about common bodily sensations: Their associations with hypochondriasis and anxiety. *Psychological Medicine, 28*, 225–228.

Marcus, D. K. (1999). The cognitive-behavioral model of hypochondriasis: Misinformation and triggers. *Journal of Psychosomatic Research, 47*, 79–91.

Marcus, D. K., & Church, S. E. (2003). Are dysfunctional beliefs about illness unique to hypochondriasis? *Journal of Psychosomatic Research, 54*, 543–547.

Marcus, D. K., Gurley, J. R., Marchi, M. M., & Bauer, C. (2007). Cognitive and perceptual variables in hypochondriasis and health anxiety: A systematic review. *Clinical Psychology Review, 27*, 127–139.

Melli, G., Carraresi, C., Poli, A., & Bailey, R. (2016). The role of metacognitive beliefs in health anxiety. *Personality and Individual Differences, 89*, 80–85.

Mogg, K., & Bradley, B. P. (2016). Anxiety and attention to threat: Cognitive mechanisms and treatment with attention bias modification. *Behaviour Research and Therapy, 87*, 76–108.

Muse, K., McManus, F., Leung, C., Meghreblian, B., & Williams, J. M. G. (2012). Cyberchondriasis: Fact or fiction? A preliminary examination of the relationship between health anxiety and searching for health information on the internet. *Journal of Anxiety Disorders, 26*, 189–196.

Naragon-Gainey, K. (2010). Meta-analysis of the relations of anxiety sensitivity to the depressive and anxiety disorders. *Psychological Bulletin, 136*, 128–150.

Neng, J. M. B., & Weck, F. (2015). Attribution of somatic symptoms in hypochondriasis. *Clinical Psychology & Psychotherapy, 22*, 116–124.

Norr, A. M., Allan, N. P., Boffa, J. W., Raines, A. M., & Schmidt, N. B. (2015). Validation of the Cyberchondria Severity Scale (CSS): Replication and extension with bifactor modeling. *Journal of Anxiety Disorders, 31*, 58–64.

Norris, A. L., & Marcus, D. K. (2014). Cognition in health anxiety and hypochondriasis: Recent advances. *Current Psychiatry Reviews, 10*, 44–49.

Noyes, R., Jr., Carney, C. P., Hillis, S. L., Jones, L. E., & Langbehn, D. R. (2005). Prevalence and correlates of illness worry in the general population. *Psychosomatics, 46*, 529–539.

Olatunji, B. O., Deacon, B. J., & Abramowitz, J. S. (2009a). Is hypochondriasis an anxiety disorder? *The British Journal of Psychiatry, 194*, 481–482.

Olatunji, B. O., Deacon, B. J., Abramowitz, J. S., & Valentiner, D. P. (2007). Body vigilance in nonclinical and anxiety disorder samples: Structure, correlates, and prediction of health concerns. *Behavior Therapy, 38*, 392–401.

Olatunji, B. O., Etzel, E. N., Tomarken, A. J., Ciesielski, B. G., & Deacon, B. (2011). The effects of safety behaviors on health anxiety: An experimental investigation. *Behaviour Research and Therapy, 49*, 719–728.

Olatunji, B. O., Wolitzky-Taylor, K. B., Elwood, L., Connolly, K., Gonzales, B., & Armstrong, T. (2009b). Anxiety sensitivity and health anxiety in a nonclinical sample: Specificity and prospective relations with clinical stress. *Cognitive Therapy and Research, 33*, 416–424.

Otto, M. W., Pollack, M. H., Sachs, G. S., & Rosenbaum, J. F. (1992). Hypochondriacal concerns, anxiety sensitivity, and panic disorder. *Journal of Anxiety Disorders, 6*, 93–104.

Owens, K. M. B., Asmundson, G. J. G., Hadjistavropoulos, T., & Owens, T. J. (2004). Attentional bias toward illness threat in individuals with elevated health anxiety. *Cognitive Therapy and Research, 28*, 57–66.

Pauli, P., & Alpers, G. W. (2000). Memory bias in patients with hypochondriacal and somatoform pain disorder. *Journal of Psychosomatic Research, 52*, 45–53.

Peterson, R. A., & Reiss, S. (1992). *Anxiety Sensitivity Index revised manual.* Worthington, OH: IDS Publishing.

Rachman, S. (2012). Health anxiety disorders: A cognitive construal. *Behaviour Research and Therapy, 50*, 502–512.

Reiss, S. (1987). Theoretical perspectives on the fear of anxiety. *Clinical Psychology Review, 7*, 585–596.

Reuman, L., Jacoby, R. J., Blakey, S. M., Riemann, B. C., Leonard, R. C., & Abramowitz, J. S. (2017). Predictors of illness anxiety symptoms in patients with obsessive compulsive disorder. *Psychiatry Research, 256*, 417–422.

Salkovskis, P. M., & Warwick, H. M. C. (2001). Making sense of hypochondriasis: a cognitive theory of health anxiety. In G. J. G. Asmundson, S. Taylor, & B. J. Cox (Eds.), *Health anxiety: Clinical and research perspectives on hypochondriasis and related conditions*. Chichester, NY: Wiley.

Schmidt, N. B., Lerew, D. R., & Trakowski, J. H. (1997). Body vigilance in panic disorder: Evaluating attention to bodily perturbations. *Journal of Consulting and Clinical Psychology, 65*, 214–220.

Schmidt, E., Witthöft, M., Kornadt, A., Rist, F., & Bailer, J. (2013). Negative automatic evaluation and better recognition of bodily symptom words in college students with elevated health anxiety. *Cognitive Therapy and Research, 37*, 1027–1040.

Schreiber, F., Neng, J. M. B., Heimlich, C., Witthöft, M., & Weck, F. (2014). Implicit affective evaluation bias in hypochondriasis: Findings from the affect misattribution procedure. *Journal of Anxiety Disorders, 28*, 671–678.

Serino, A., Alsmith, A., Costantini, M., Mandrigin, A., Tajadura-Jimenes, A., & Lopez, C. (2013). Bodily ownership and self-location: Components of bodily self-consciousness. *Consciousness and Cognition, 22*, 1239–1252.

Sexton, K. A., Norton, P. J., Walker, J. R., & Norton, G. R. (2003). Hierarchical model of generalized and specific vulnerabilities in anxiety. *Cognitive Behaviour Therapy, 32*, 82–94.

Shields, C., & Murphy, K. (2011). Selective attention and health anxiety: Ill-health stimuli are distracting for everyone. *Cognitive Therapy and Research, 35*, 241–252.

Singh, K., & Brown, R. J. (2014). Health-related internet habits and health anxiety in university students. *Anxiety, Stress, & Coping, 27*, 542–554.

Solem, S., Borgejordet, S., Haseth, S., Hansen, B., Haland, A., & Bailey, R. (2015). Symptoms of health anxiety in obsessive-compulsive disorder: Relationship with treatment outcome and metacognition. *Journal of Obsessive-Compulsive and Related Disorders, 5*, 76–81.

Starcevic, V., & Berle, D. (2015). Cyberchondria: An old phenomenon in a new guise? In E. Aboujaoude & V. Starcevic (Eds.), *Mental health in the digital age: Grave dangers, great promise* (pp. 106–117). New York, NY: Oxford University Press.

Stewart, S. H., Sherry, S. B., Watt, M. C., Grant, V. V., & Hadjistavropoulos, H. D. (2008). Psychometric evaluation of the Multidimensional Inventory of Hypochondriacal Traits: Factor structure and relationship to anxiety sensitivity. *Journal of Cognitive Psychotherapy, 22*, 97–114.

Tackett, J. L., & Lahey, B. B. (2017). Neuroticism. In T. A. Widiger (Ed.), *The Oxford handbook of the five factor model* (pp. 39–56). New York, NY: Oxford University Press.

Taylor, S. (1999). *Anxiety sensitivity: Theory, research, and treatment of the fear of anxiety.* Mahwah, NJ: Erlbaum.

Taylor, S., & Asmundson, G. J. G. (2004). *Treating health anxiety: A cognitive-behavioral approach.* New York, NY: Guilford.

Taylor, S., & Asmundson, G. J. G. (2012). Etiology of hypochondriasis: A preliminary behavioral-genetic investigation. *International Journal of Genetics and Gene Therapy, 2*, 1–5.

Taylor, S., Zvolensky, M., Cox, B., Deacon, B., Heimberg, R., Ledley, D. R., … Cardenes, S. J. (2007). Robust dimensions of anxiety sensitivity: development and initial validation of the anxiety sensitivity index-3 (ASI-3). *Psychological Assessment, 19*, 176–188.

te Poel, F., Baumgartner, S. E., Hartmann, T., & Tanis, M. (2016). The curious case of cyberchondria: A longitudinal study on the reciprocal relationship between health anxiety and online health information seeking. *Journal of Anxiety Disorders, 43*, 32–40.

Warwick, H. M. C., & Salkovskis, P. M. (1990). Hypochondriasis. *Behaviour Research and Therapy, 28*, 105–117.

Weck, F., & Höfling, V. (2015). Assessment of implicit health attitudes: A multitrait-multimethod approach and a comparison between patients with hypochondriasis and patients with anxiety disorders. *Journal of Personality Assessment, 97*, 55–65.

Weck, F., Neng, J. M. B., Richtberg, S., & Stangier, U. (2012a). Dysfunctional beliefs about symptoms and illness in patients with hypochondriasis. *Psychosomatics, 53*, 148–154.

Weck, F., Neng, J. M. B., Richtberg, S., & Stangier, U. (2012b). The restrictive concept of good health in patients with hypochondriasis. *Journal of Anxiety Disorders, 26*, 792–798.

Weiss, F. D., Rief, W., & Kleinstäuber, M. (2017). Health care utilization in outpatients with somatoform disorders: Descriptives, interdiagnostic differences, and potential mediating factors. *General Hospital Psychiatry, 44*, 22–29.

Wells, A. (2009). *Metacognitive therapy for anxiety and depression.* New York, NY: Guilford.

Wheaton, M. G., Berman, N. C., Franklin, J. C., & Abramowitz, J. S. (2010). Health anxiety: Latent structure and associations with anxiety-related psychological processes in a student sample. *Journal of Psychopathology and Behavioral Assessment, 32*, 565–574.

Wheaton, M. G., Deacon, B. J., McGrath, P. B., Berman, N. C., & Abramowitz, J. S. (2012). Dimensions of anxiety sensitivity in the anxiety disorders: Evaluation of the ASI-3. *Journal of Anxiety Disorders, 26*, 401–408.

Williams, P. G. (2004). The psychopathology of self-assessed health: A cognitive approach to health anxiety and hypochondriasis. *Cognitive Therapy and Research, 28*, 629–644.

Witthöft, M., Kerstner, T., Ofer, J., Mier, D., Rist, F., Diener, C., & Bailer, J. (2016). Cognitive biases in pathological health anxiety: The contribution of attention, memory, and evaluation processes. *Clinical Psychological Science, 4*, 464–479.

Wright, K. D., Reiser, S. J., & Delparte, C. A. (2017). The relationship between childhood health anxiety, parent health anxiety, and associated constructs. *Journal of Health Psychology, 22*, 617–626.

CHAPTER FIVE

Assessment of Health Anxiety

Erik Hedman-Lagerlöf and Erland Axelsson
Department of Clinical Neuroscience, Karolinska Institutet, Stockholm, Sweden

Psychometrically sound measures of health anxiety are a prerequisite for the clinician when conducting diagnostic assessment and evaluating the effects of interventions for health anxiety. This chapter describes commonly used dimensional measures of health anxiety and also instruments developed specifically to aid in diagnostic assessment. Here, the focus is on continuous symptom measures, whereas other parts of this book provide comprehensive reviews of differential diagnostics (Chapter 2) and functional analysis (Chapter 6).

Dimensional Measures of Health Anxiety

As outlined in Chapter 1, health anxiety is a dimensional phenomenon, which means that symptoms can vary by degrees both between individuals and within individuals over time. Dimensional measures therefore have the potential advantage of being more precise measures of health anxiety than any dichotomous (yes/no) indicators, including diagnoses. In the following, three well-established self-rated dimensional measures of health anxiety are presented: the Health Anxiety Inventory, the Illness Attitude Scales, and the Whiteley Index. We also briefly touch on the possibility of dimensional measurement by the clinician.

The Health Anxiety Inventory

Salkovskis, Rimes, Warwick, and Clark (2002) developed the Health Anxiety Inventory (HAI), which is a self-report measure designed to cover a broad spectrum of cognitive, affective, and behavioral symptoms of health anxiety. The items of the HAI are constructed to enable reliable assessment of health anxiety also in samples with somatic diseases. The full version of the HAI has 64 items, and each item is rated 0–3, which gives a total scale range of 0–192. The main section (47 items) is complemented with a negative consequence subscale (17 items), which measures the individual's perception of what it would be like to become seriously ill. The HAI also comes in a short version (SHAI), which is composed of 18 items (14 items in the

The Clinician's Guide to Treating Health Anxiety
https://doi.org/10.1016/B978-0-12-811806-1.00005-6

main section and 4 in the negative consequence subscale) and has a total scale range of 0–54. The SHAI is highly correlated with the full HAI (Salkovskis et al., 2002) and has the important advantage of requiring just a few minutes to complete. Some research has suggested that the negative consequence subscale has limited value (Alberts, Hadjistavropoulos, Jones, & Sharpe, 2013), which means that it ought to be possible to use only the 14 items of the main section, that is, an even shorter version of the scale, without compromising its psychometric properties. It should however be noted that most studies on the HAI and the SHAI have used the 64- and 18-item versions of the respective scales.

Reliability

The HAI and SHAI have been found to be highly reliable, though less is known about the 14-item scale, as compared with the 64- and 18-item scales. The HAI has been shown to have high internal consistency ($\alpha = 0.95$) and high test-retest reliability ($r = 0.90$) over a mean of 22 days in a mixed sample of individuals with anxiety disorders and healthy controls (Salkovskis et al., 2002). In a systematic review, Alberts et al. (2013) found that the internal consistency (α) of the 18-item SHAI ranged from 0.75 to 0.96 across 16 studies and that two studies on the 14-item SHAI reported αs of 0.84 and 0.81. The 18-item SHAI test-retest reliability over one week has also been found to be high ($r = 0.87$) in a sample of undergraduate students (Olatunji, Etzel, Tomarken, Ciesielski, & Deacon, 2011).

Validity

Studies have shown that the HAI has good convergent and discriminant validity, that is, the scale is significantly correlated with other measures of health anxiety and this association is stronger than the correlation to other psychiatric symptoms such as general anxiety or depression (e.g., Hedman, Ljótsson, et al., 2015). The HAI also discriminates well between patients with health anxiety, similar patient groups, and healthy controls (Hedman, Lekander, et al., 2015). The same pattern of strong associations has been shown for the SHAI. In a meta-analysis, Alberts et al. (2013) found that the SHAI was highly correlated with other measures of health anxiety ($r = 0.67$), while correlations with more remote constructs such as social anxiety and medical status were lower. The SHAI has also been found to be associated with health-care utilization and safety behaviors, which further indicates validity of the scale (Boston & Merrick, 2010; Olatunji, Deacon, Abramowitz, & Valentiner, 2007).

Clinical Cut-offs

In a study investigating the ability of the HAI to identify persons with health anxiety (DSM-IV hypochondriasis), Hedman, Lekander, et al. (2015) found that a score of ≥67 was the best cutoff for identifying clinically significant health anxiety. When using this cutoff score in a combined sample of individuals with health anxiety, individuals with obsessive-compulsive disorder, and healthy controls, both sensitivity (96%) and specificity (93%) were high. That is, the proportion of individuals with health anxiety that were correctly classified as having health anxiety was 96%, and the proportion of individuals without health anxiety that were correctly classified as not having health anxiety was 93%.

For the short-version SHAI, several different cutoff scores have been suggested for both the 14- and 18-item versions of the scale. The Improving Access to Psychological Treatment initiative (Clark, 2011), which is one of the largest projects aiming to implement evidence-based psychological treatments, uses a cutoff score of 18 or higher on the 14-item SHAI (IAPT, 2011) to identify those likely to have health anxiety (DSM-IV hypochondriasis), but no data to support this suggestion are presented in the IAPT handbook. In one study, a cutoff of ≥27 on the 18-item SHAI was the best for discriminating between persons with health anxiety and persons with other anxiety disorders (Abramowitz, Olatunji, & Deacon, 2007). As reported by Alberts et al. (2013), cutoff scores in the range of 15–20 have been cited in the literature, but there is generally limited information regarding how these were justified. More studies on optimal cutoffs for the SHAI are needed.

Illness Attitude Scales

The Illness Attitude Scales (IAS) (Kellner, 1986a) were developed based on statements by patients with high levels of illness behavior or a conviction of being ill. It covers a broad scope of symptoms and has 29 items rated 0–4 and a total scale range of 0–108 (only 27 items are used for the sum score). The IAS has nine subscales: (I) worry about illness, (II) concerns about pain, (III) health habits, (IV) hypochondriacal beliefs, (V) thanatophobia (fear of death), (VI) disease phobia, (VII) bodily preoccupations, (VIII) treatment experience, and (IX) effects of symptoms. As described by Sirri, Grandi, and Fava (2008), these scales represent different aspects of health anxiety, but should not be regarded as factors in a conventional psychometric sense. Several studies investigating the structure of the IAS using factor analysis have found that the scale is composed of two broad factors representing (I) the cognitive and emotional components of health anxiety and (II) illness behavior (e.g., Speckens, Spinhoven, Sloekers, Bolk, & van Hemert, 1996). In contrast to most other measures of health anxiety, there is also a version of the IAS—the Childhood Illness Attitude Scales—that is adapted for children in the ages 8–15 (Wright & Asmundson, 2003). This is important, given the recent research indicating that health anxiety is prevalent also in youth (see Chapter 10).

Reliability

Although the IAS was developed to have good clinimetric properties rather than high internal consistency, several studies have reported Cronbach αs >0.85 (Hedman, Ljótsson, et al., 2015; Hiller & Janca, 2003; Hiller, Rief, & Fichter, 2002), indicating high internal consistency. The IAS has also been shown to have high test-retest reliability, especially in clinical populations. In a sample of patients with functional somatic problems, the test-retest reliability over 30 days was $r=0.89$ (Hiller & Janca, 2003). In samples of patients with health anxiety, studies have shown test-retest reliability rs $=0.80$–0.96 over ≤ 4 weeks (Bouman & Visser, 1998; Hedman, Ljótsson, et al., 2015).

Validity

There is strong evidence supporting the convergent and discriminant validity of the IAS. The scale is more strongly correlated with other measures of health anxiety than to other psychiatric constructs (e.g., Hedman, Ljótsson, et al., 2015). The IAS also discriminates between persons with health anxiety and persons high in somatization but without health anxiety (Hiller et al., 2002; Speckens, Spinhoven, et al., 1996). Further indication of the external validity of the scale is that it has been found to predict health-care utilization in medical outpatient clinics (Kapur et al., 2004; Speckens, Van Hemert, Spinhoven, & Bolk, 1996) and that it is associated with heightened somatosensory sensitivity and negative interpretation of ambiguous somatic sensations (for a review, see Sirri et al., 2008).

Clinical Cut-offs

A study by Hiller et al. (2002) showed that a score of 45 or higher was the most accurate in discriminating persons with health anxiety (DSM-IV hypochondriasis) from nonsomatoform controls. This cutoff yielded a sensitivity of 73% and a specificity of 79%. Weck, Bleichhardt, and Hiller (2010) studied cutoff scores in a large study that combined a representative general population sample ($n = 1575$) and individuals with DSM-IV hypochondriasis ($n = 61$). A cutoff of 50.9 yielded high sensitivity (95%) and specificity (90%). Hedman, Lekander, et al. (2015) found that a similar cutoff score, 47 or higher, was the most optimal in discriminating persons with health anxiety (DSM-IV hypochondriasis) from persons with obsessive-compulsive disorder and healthy controls. This cutoff yielded a sensitivity of 96% and a specificity of 95%, suggesting that the IAS can be an effective tool for correctly identifying persons with or without health anxiety.

In many contexts, it is highly important to use brief and efficient screening measures that require little time to fill out. To this end, some studies have investigated whether a reduced set of items of the IAS can be used to detect persons with health anxiety. In one study, it was shown that the bodily preoccupation subscale of the IAS, which consists of only three items (subscale range 0–12), could be used to efficiently screen for health anxiety in a combined general population and DSM-IV hypochondriasis sample (Weck et al., 2010). A cutoff score of 5.5 yielded high sensitivity (92%) and specificity (90%). In a subsequent study, Hofling and Weck (2013) again tested the discriminative ability of the bodily preoccupation subscale of the IAS and found that the best cutoff score was 6.5. This yielded a sensitivity of 88% and a specificity of 83% in discriminating between individuals with health anxiety and individuals with other anxiety disorders. This brief subscale can thus be an efficient method to screen for health anxiety.

Whiteley Index

The Whiteley Index (Pilowsky, 1967) was one of the first scales developed to measure symptoms associated with health anxiety, and its items were based on clinicians' written definitions of hypochondriasis. The original version of the Whiteley Index is composed of 14 items, but Fink et al. (1999) showed that a reduced version of the scale with only 7 items seemed to yield improved psychometric properties. The original version of the scale had dichotomous scoring, that is, each item was rated yes/no that resulted in a total scale range of 0–14. Recent research has however shown that scoring the items on a 5-point Likert-type scale increases the total scale variance, which might be an advantage due to increased sensitivity to change (Welch, Carleton, & Asmundson, 2009). The factor structure of the 14-item Whiteley Index has been investigated in several studies that have largely come to conflicting results (Veddegjaerde, Sivertsen, Wilhelmsen, & Skogen, 2014). The 7-item Whiteley Index appears to be unidimensional but with two intercorrelated subscales, illness conviction and illness worrying (Conradt, Cavanagh, Franklin, & Rief, 2006; Fink et al., 1999).

Reliability

The 14-item Whiteley Index with dichotomous response options has demonstrated high test-retest reliability ($r = 0.80$–81) over a mean of 2.4 weeks in a combined sample of individuals with health anxiety and healthy controls (Hedman, Ljótsson, et al., 2015) and over a mean of 18.4 weeks in a combined sample of psychiatric patients with and without health anxiety (Pilowsky, 1967). Both the 7- and 14-item versions of the Whiteley Index have also demonstrated adequate internal consistency ($\alpha = 0.73$–80) in several studies (e.g., Hiller et al., 2002; Laferton et al., 2017; Lee, Ng, Ma, Tsang, & Kwok, 2011). As noted by Conradt et al. (2006), it is not surprising that the 7-item Whiteley Index has a lower alpha coefficient compared with the 14-item version as Cronbach's alpha is partly a function of the number of items (Tavakol & Dennick, 2011).

Validity

Studies have shown that the 14-item Whiteley Index is highly correlated with other measures of health anxiety (Hedman, Ljótsson, et al., 2015; Hiller et al., 2002) and that both the 14- and 7-item versions predict future health-care use (Lee et al., 2011; Tomenson et al., 2012). The 14-item Whiteley Index has been shown to discriminate between persons with health anxiety and those without (Hedman, Lekander, et al., 2015; Hiller et al., 2002), and the 7-item scale has also been found to discriminate between health anxiety and somatoform disorder without health anxiety (Hiller et al., 2002). In the original study by Pilowsky (1967), it was also shown that patients' self-reported scores on the 14-item Whiteley Index were significantly correlated with spouses' ratings of the patients' health anxiety.

Clinical Cut-offs

Several studies have investigated how well the Whiteley Index can identify persons with health anxiety. Weck et al. (2010) used the 7-item version with dichotomous scoring of items (scale range of 0–7) and found that a score of ≥ 4.8 yielded the best combined sensitivity (79%) and specificity (83%) when discriminating health anxiety (DSM-IV hypochondriasis) from other anxiety disorders. When discriminating health anxiety from healthy controls, the optimal cutoff was ≥ 2.5, which yielded a specificity of 97% and a specificity of 99%. Conradt et al. (2006) also used the 7-item version with dichotomous scoring and found that a cutoff of ≥ 3 was optimal and yielded a sensitivity of 82% and a specificity of 81%. Speckens, Van Hemert, et al. (1996) used the 14-item Whiteley Index with dichotomous scoring (scale range of 0–14) in a medical outpatient sample and found that a cutoff of ≥6 yielded a sensitivity of 87% and a specificity of 72%. In a study by Hedman, Lekander, et al. (2015) using the same version of the Whiteley Index, it was found that the optimal cutoff for discriminating persons with health anxiety from persons with obsessive-compulsive disorder and healthy controls was ≥5, which yielded a sensitivity and specificity of 99%. Hiller et al. (2002) found that a slightly higher cutoff of 8 was optimal when discriminating health anxiety from nonsomatizing clinical controls, which gave a sensitivity of 71% and a specificity of 80%. It thus seems as the optimal cutoff for detecting health anxiety is somewhere between 5 and 8 when using the 14-item version with dichotomous scoring and between 2.5 and 5 when using the shorter 7-item version. Of course, one central methodological aspect that determines the adequacy of cutoffs is the type of control group used. So when choosing cutoff, irrespective of measure, it is important to consider the context in which it will be used.

The studies above generally used DSM-III or DSM-IV hypochondriasis as diagnostic marker, and it should be noted that there is little information about cutoffs when using the relatively new DSM-5 disorders somatic symptom disorder and illness anxiety disorder as criterion variable. However, in one recent study where participants were randomly selected from the general population, it was found that a cutoff of ≥1 was the best to identify persons with a diagnosis of somatic symptom disorder, which yielded a sensitivity of 69% and a specificity of 74% (Laferton et al., 2017).

Administering Measures Via the Internet

Using the Internet to administer measures of health anxiety confers several important advantages compared with the paper-and-pencil format. These include that the patient can access the measures from any computer, tablet, or mobile phone with Internet connection, that storing of data is easy and secure (no risk of losing paper forms), and that one can reduce internal dropout to 0% (i.e., one can design the forms so that it is impossible to skip items). Furthermore, Internet administration of health anxiety measures makes it possible for the clinician to monitor the patient's symptom course also between sessions, and it is possible to have built-in feedback messages to the clinician to alert if the patient is deteriorating or shows an increase in other risk markers, for example, suicidal ideation. When using the Internet, it is also possible to use automatic reminders to the patient if he or she has forgotten to complete the assessment. The relative ease of administration means that the patient can fill out forms with relatively tight intervals. For example, our experience from both clinical trials and routine practice is that the primary outcome can be administered with at least once per week with good completion rates (e.g., Hedman et al., 2011). Repeated assessments are an important strength from a research perspective, as this renders increased statistical power and enables better estimation of symptom status at post treatment, not least should the patient not complete the intended symptom forms after treatment has ended. Last but not least, Internet administration of health anxiety measures is highly likely an environmentally friendly option that yields a net reduction of CO_2 emissions compared with using paper forms.

Of course, all these advantages are little worth if psychometric properties would be compromised when measures are administered online. Nearly all commonly used self-reported symptom measures in the psychiatric field have been developed using a paper-and-pencil format, which means that the reevaluation of online versions is important before implementing internet administration. Several studies have conducted psychometric evaluations of Internet-administered symptom measures and have generally found that they are equally reliable and valid as their paper-and-pencil equivalents (van Ballegooijen, Riper, Cuijpers, van Oppen, & Smit, 2016). As for health anxiety, it has been shown that the Health Anxiety Inventory, the Illness Attitude Scales, and the Whiteley Index can be administered via the Internet with high reliability and good convergent and discriminant validity (Hedman, Ljótsson, et al., 2015).

Dimensional Measures Administered by a Clinician

Whereas most dimensional measures of health anxiety are self-rated (see above), there also exist a few continuous scales intended to be administered by a clinician or researcher. A recurrent pattern in many studies has been that this measurement format tends to result in slightly higher standardized effect sizes, as compared with self-rated scales (e.g., Cuijpers et al., 2014). One instrument intended to be completed by a clinician or researcher is the rating scale of hypochondriacal beliefs (Kellner, 1986c), a one-item scale to measure health anxiety from 1 ("Absent—No concerns about physical symptoms or illness.") to 9 ("Extremely severe—Persistent and continuous belief that he/she suffers from a physical illness; reassurance by a physician does not alter the belief."). The interrater reliability of this scale, as estimated with two raters and a sample of patients with health anxiety, has been demonstrated to be excellent ($r = 0.92$) (Kellner, 1986b), and the scale is also responsive to change (Kellner, 1983). Another clinician-administered one-item scale is the Heightened Illness Concern Severity Scale (Fallon, 2001). This scale ranges from 1 ("No heightened illness concern.") to 7 ("Extreme heightened illness concern. Among the most ill of all heightened illness concern patients, causing extreme distress and significant social and occupational impairment.") and has also been demonstrated to be sensitive to change (Fallon et al., 2003). A more comprehensive dimensional measure of health anxiety is the modified Yale-Brown Obsessive-Compulsive Scale for Hypochondriasis (H-YBOCS-M) (Skritskaya et al., 2012), which is based on the gold standard scale for assessment of obsessive-compulsive disorder and comprises 19 items intended to survey thoughts, behaviors, and avoidance typical of health anxiety. Based on factor analysis in a sample with health anxiety, the H-YBOCS-M is believed to incorporate the five dimensions (I) avoidance, (II) compulsive behaviors, (III) interference, (IV) worry control, and (V) worry frequency. The scale has adequate internal consistency ($\alpha = 0.85$) and is sensitive to change. It is also moderately correlated with the self-rated Whiteley Index ($r = 0.45$), with lower associations with measures of general anxiety ($r = 0.17$–0.28) indicating construct validity (Skritskaya et al., 2012).

Diagnostic Assessment of Health Anxiety

Although dimensional measures of health anxiety are critical for establishing symptom severity and monitoring change over time, the foundation of evidence-based medicine is the diagnosis. In this section, we give an overview of diagnostic instruments to assess psychiatric disorders primarily characterized by health anxiety.

Assessment of DSM-5 Somatic Symptom Disorder and Illness Anxiety Disorder

With the advent of the DSM-5 (American Psychiatric Association, 2013), there has been substantial changes of relevance for health anxiety diagnostics. Hypochondriasis has been replaced by two new diagnoses: somatic symptom disorder and illness anxiety disorder. The somatic symptom disorder diagnosis is intended for those who experience distress over at least one marked somatic symptom, whereas illness anxiety disorder is a diagnosis for persons who have excessive health anxiety but no or only mild somatic symptoms. According to DSM-5, it is expected that about 75% of those who meet criteria for DSM-IV hypochondriasis will be diagnosed with somatic symptom disorder and 25% with illness anxiety disorder (American Psychiatric Association, 2013). Designed specifically for the assessment of these new diagnoses, The Health Preoccupation Diagnostic Interview (Axelsson, Andersson, Ljótsson, Wallhed Finn, & Hedman, 2016) is a structured clinical interview that comprises 42 items, of which 24 are questions to the patient and 18 are items rated by the clinician. In a psychometric evaluation, this instrument was used in conjunction with the structured assessment of common differential diagnoses in a combined sample of individuals with health anxiety and healthy controls. The overall interrater reliability of the diagnostic procedure was Cohen's $\kappa = 0.85$, indicating high reliability in the discrimination of individuals with SSD, individuals with IAD, and individuals without any of these disorders. The Health Preoccupation Diagnostic Interview is free to use and provided in the original publication (Axelsson et al., 2016).

Recently, modules for somatic symptom disorder and illness anxiety disorder have also been included in the Anxiety and Related Disorders Interview Schedule for DSM-5 (ADIS-5) (Brown, Bourgeois, & Rutter, 2017), the Diagnostic Interview for Anxiety, Mood, and OCD and Related Neuropsychiatric Disorders (DIAMOND) (Tolin et al., 2018), and the Structured Clinical Interview for DSM-5 (SCID-5) (First, Williams, Karg, & Spitzer, 2015). The ADIS-5, like the Health Preoccupation Diagnostic Interview, has been found to possess adequate interrater reliability in the assessment of somatic symptom disorder and illness anxiety disorder in one study (Newby, Hobbs, Mahoney, Wong, & Andrews, 2017). To our knowledge, no published study has however established that the modules of DIAMOND and SCID-5 can be used to reliably discriminate between somatic symptom disorder and illness anxiety disorder.

Assessment of DSM-IV Hypochondriasis

There are several structured interviews developed for the assessment of DSM-IV hypochondriasis. One of the first interviews to be psychometrically evaluated was the structured diagnostic interview for hypochondriasis developed by Barsky et al. (1992). This 12-item interview was shown to have high interrater reliability (96%) in the decision to code hypochondriasis in a pooled sample of 88 general medical patients with high levels of health anxiety and 100 patients with low levels of health anxiety. The interview also showed external validity in the sense that cases identified as having hypochondriasis had higher health-care consumption and were more disabled (Barsky et al., 1992). Two other structured diagnostic interviews commonly used to aid the assessment of hypochondriasis are the Anxiety Disorders Interview Schedule for DSM-IV (ADIS-IV) (Di Nardo, O'Brien, Barlow, Waddell, & Blanchard, 1983) and the Structured Clinical Interview for DSM-IV (SCID-IV) (First, Spitzer, Gibbon, & Williams, 2002). These both include hypochondriasis modules that cover all the criteria listed for the disorder in DSM-IV (18 questions in total in ADIS-IV and 5 in SCID-IV), but there is limited research on the reliability of these modules in the assessment of hypochondriasis.

Summary and Conclusion

To assess symptom severity and follow the course of health anxiety over time, dimensional symptom measures are crucial. Three self-report measures that are well used and have been shown to be both reliable and valid are the Health Anxiety Inventory, the Illness Attitude Scales, and the Whiteley Index. These instruments can also be used as screening tools to detect health anxiety, but suggested cutoffs vary to some degree between studies, in part explained by differences in clinical samples. The clinician should therefore consider the context in which the screening will take place before deciding on clinical cutoff. A promising dimensional measure that can be administered by a clinician or researcher is the H-YBOCS-M. As for assessment of the new DSM-5 diagnoses somatic symptom disorder and illness anxiety disorder, the Health Preoccupation Diagnostic Interview and the ADIS-5 are two structured diagnostic tools that have been psychometrically evaluated specifically for the purpose of surveying these disorders. There is an urgent need for psychometric studies of the modules covering somatic symptom disorder and illness anxiety disorder in the DIAMOND and SCID-5.

References

Abramowitz, J. S., Olatunji, B. O., & Deacon, B. J. (2007). Health anxiety, hypochondriasis, and the anxiety disorders. *Behavior Therapy*, *38*(1), 86–94. https://doi.org/10.1016/j.beth.2006.05.001.

Alberts, N. M., Hadjistavropoulos, H. D., Jones, S. L., & Sharpe, D. (2013). The Short Health Anxiety Inventory: A systematic review and meta-analysis. *Journal of Anxiety Disorders*, *27*(1), 68–78. https://doi.org/10.1016/j.janxdis.2012.10.009.

American Psychiatric Association (2013). *Diagnostic and statistical manual of mental disorders* (5th ed.). Arlington, VA: American Psychiatric Publishing.

Axelsson, E., Andersson, E., Ljótsson, B., Wallhed Finn, D., & Hedman, E. (2016). The health preoccupation diagnostic interview: inter-rater reliability of a structured interview for diagnostic assessment of DSM-5 somatic symptom disorder and illness anxiety disorder. *Cognitive Behaviour Therapy, 45*, 259–269. https://doi.org/10.1080/16506073.2016.1161663.

Barsky, A. J., Cleary, P. D., Wyshak, G., Spitzer, R. L., Williams, J. B., & Klerman, G. L. (1992). A structured diagnostic interview for hypochondriasis. A proposed criterion standard. *Journal of Nervous and Mental Disease, 180*(1), 20–27.

Boston, A. F., & Merrick, P. L. (2010). Health anxiety among older people: an exploratory study of health anxiety and safety behaviors in a cohort of older adults in New Zealand. *International Psychogeriatrics, 22*(4), 549–558. https://doi.org/10.1017/s1041610209991712.

Bouman, T. K., & Visser, S. (1998). Cognitive and behavioural treatment of hypochondriasis. *Psychotherapy and Psychosomatics, 67*(4-5), 214–221.

Brown, T., Bourgeois, M., & Rutter, L. (2017). *Anxiety and related disorders interview schedule for dsm-5. In A. Wenzel (Ed.), The sage encyclopedia of abnormal and clinical psychology.* Thousand Oaks, CA: SAGE Publications, Inc. Retrieved from *http://sk.sagepub.com/reference/the-sage-encyclopedia-of-abnormal-and-clinical-psychology* doi: 10.4135/9781483365817.

Clark, D. M. (2011). Implementing NICE guidelines for the psychological treatment of depression and anxiety disorders: the IAPT experience. *International Review of Psychiatry, 23*(4), 318–327. https://doi.org/10.3109/09540261.2011.606803.

Conradt, M., Cavanagh, M., Franklin, J., & Rief, W. (2006). Dimensionality of the Whiteley Index: assessment of hypochondriasis in an Australian sample of primary care patients. *Journal of Psychosomatic Research, 60*(2), 137–143. https://doi.org/10.1016/j.jpsychores.2005.07.003.

Cuijpers, P., Sijbrandij, M., Koole, S., Huibers, M., Berking, M., & Andersson, G. (2014). Psychological treatment of generalized anxiety disorder: a meta-analysis. *Clinical Psychology Review, 34*(2), 130–140. https://doi.org/10.1016/j.cpr.2014.01.002.

Di Nardo, P. A., O'Brien, G. T., Barlow, D. H., Waddell, M. T., & Blanchard, E. B. (1983). Reliability of DSM-III anxiety disorder categories using a new structured interview. *Archives of General Psychiatry, 40*(10), 1070–1074.

Fallon, B. A. (2001). Pharmacologic strategies for hypochondriasis. In V. Starcevic & D. R. Lipsitt (Eds.), *Hypochondriasis: Modern perspectives on an Ancient Malady*. New York: Oxford University Press.

Fallon, B. A., Qureshi, A. I., Schneier, F. R., Sanchez-Lacay, A., Vermes, D., Feinstein, R., ... Liebowitz, M. R. (2003). An open trial of fluvoxamine for hypochondriasis. *Psychosomatics, 44*(4), 298–303. https://doi.org/10.1176/appi.psy.44.4.298.

Fink, P., Ewald, H., Jensen, J., Sorensen, L., Engberg, M., Holm, M., & Munk-Jorgensen, P. (1999). Screening for somatization and hypochondriasis in primary care and neurological in-patients: a seven-item scale for hypochondriasis and somatization. *Journal of Psychosomatic Research, 46*(3), 261–273.

First, M. B., Spitzer, R. L., Gibbon, M., & Williams, J. B. W. (Eds.), (2002). *Structured clinical interview for DSM-IV-TR axis I Disorders, research version, patient edition.* New York: Biometrics Research, New York State Psychiatric Institute.

First, M. B., Williams, J. B. W., Karg, R. S., & Spitzer, R. L. (2015). *Structured clinical interview for DSM-5, research version.* Arlington, VA: American Psychiatric Association.

Hedman, E., Andersson, G., Andersson, E., Ljótsson, B., Rück, C., Asmundson, G. J., & Lindefors, N. (2011). Internet-based cognitive-behavioural therapy for severe health anxiety: randomised controlled trial. *The British Journal of Psychiatry, 198*, 230–236. https://doi.org/10.1192/bjp.bp.110.086843 198/3/230 [pii].

Hedman, E., Lekander, M., Ljótsson, B., Lindefors, N., Rück, C., Andersson, G., & Andersson, E. (2015). Optimal cut-off points on the health anxiety inventory, illness attitude scales and whiteley index to identify severe health anxiety. *PLoS ONE, 10*(4), e0123412. https://doi.org/10.1371/journal.pone.0123412.

Hedman, E., Ljótsson, B., Andersson, E., Andersson, G., Lindefors, N., Rück, C., … Lekander, M. (2015). Psychometric properties of Internet-administered measures of health anxiety: An investigation of the Health Anxiety Inventory, the Illness Attitude Scales, and the Whiteley Index. *Journal of Anxiety Disorders, 31C*, 32–37. https://doi.org/10.1016/j.janxdis.2015.01.008.

Hiller, W., & Janca, A. (2003). Assessment of somatoform disorders: a review of strategies and instruments. *Acta Neuropsychiatrica, 15*, 167–179.

Hiller, W., Rief, W., & Fichter, M. M. (2002). Dimensional and categorical approaches to hypochondriasis. *Psychological Medicine, 32*(4), 707–718.

Hofling, V., & Weck, F. (2013). Assessing Bodily Preoccupations is sufficient: clinically effective screening for hypochondriasis. *Journal of Psychosomatic Research, 75*(6), 526–531. https://doi.org/10.1016/j.jpsychores.2013.10.011.

IAPT (2011). *The IAPT data handbook. http://www.healthcare-today.co.uk/doclibrary/documents/pdf/636_the_iapt-data-handbook.pdf.*

Kapur, N., Hunt, I., Lunt, M., McBeth, J., Creed, F., & Macfarlane, G. (2004). Psychosocial and illness related predictors of consultation rates in primary care—a cohort study. *Psychological Medicine, 34*(4), 719–728. https://doi.org/10.1017/s0033291703001223.

Kellner, R. (1983). Prognosis of treated hypochondriasis. A clinical study. *Acta Psychiatrica Scandinavica, 67*(2), 69–79.

Kellner, R. (1986a). Illness Attitude Scales. In *Somatization and hypochondriasis* (pp. 319–324). New York: Praeger Publishers (Appendix A).

Kellner, R. (1986b). Psychological tests and observer-rating and self-rating scales. In *Somatization and hypochondriasis* (pp. 196–210). New York: Praeger Publishers.

Kellner, R. (1986c). Rating scale of hypochondriacal beliefs. In *Somatization and hypochondriasis* (pp. 196–210). New York: Praeger Publishers (Appedix B).

Laferton, J. A. C., Stenzel, N. M., Rief, W., Klaus, K., Brahler, E., & Mewes, R. (2017). Screening for DSM-5 Somatic Symptom Disorder: Diagnostic Accuracy of Self-Report Measures Within a Population Sample. *Psychosomatic Medicine, 79*(9), 974–981. https://doi.org/10.1097/psy.0000000000000530.

Lee, S., Ng, K. L., Ma, Y. L., Tsang, A., & Kwok, K. P. (2011). A general population study of the Chinese Whiteley-7 index in Hong Kong. *Journal of Psychosomatic Research, 71*(6), 387–391. https://doi.org/10.1016/j.jpsychores.2011.05.013.

Olatunji, B. O., Deacon, B. J., Abramowitz, J. S., & Valentiner, D. P. (2007). Body vigilance in nonclinical and anxiety disorder samples: structure, correlates, and prediction of health concerns. *Behavior Therapy, 38*(4), 392–401. https://doi.org/10.1016/j.beth.2006.09.002.

Olatunji, B. O., Etzel, E. N., Tomarken, A. J., Ciesielski, B. G., & Deacon, B. (2011). The effects of safety behaviors on health anxiety: an experimental investigation. *Behaviour Research and Therapy, 49*(11), 719–728. https://doi.org/10.1016/j.brat.2011.07.008.

Newby, J. M., Hobbs, M. J., Mahoney, A. E. J., Wong, S. K., & Andrews, G. (2017). DSM-5 illness anxiety disorder and somatic symptom disorder: Comorbidity, correlates, and overlap with DSM-IV hypochondriasis. *Journal of Psychosomatic Research, 101*, 31–37. https://doi.org/10.1016/j.jpsychores.2017.07.010.

Pilowsky, I. (1967). Dimensions of Hypochondriasis. *The British Journal of Psychiatry, 113*(494), 89–93. https://doi.org/10.1192/bjp.113.494.89.

Salkovskis, P. M., Rimes, K. A., Warwick, H. M., & Clark, D. M. (2002). The Health Anxiety Inventory: development and validation of scales for the measurement of health anxiety and hypochondriasis. *Psychological Medicine, 32*(5), 843–853.

Sirri, L., Grandi, S., & Fava, G. A. (2008). The Illness attitude scales. *Psychotherapy and Psychosomatics*, 77, 337–350.

Skritskaya, N. A., Carson-Wong, A. R., Moeller, J. R., Shen, S., Barsky, A. J., & Fallon, B. A. (2012). A clinician-administered severity rating scale for illness anxiety: development, reliability, and validity of the H-YBOCS-M. *Depress Anxiety*, *29*(7), 652–664. https://doi.org/10.1002/da.21949.

Speckens, A. E. M., Spinhoven, P., Sloekers, P. P., Bolk, J. H., & van Hemert, A. M. (1996). A validation study of the Whiteley Index, the Illness Attitude Scales, and the Somatosensory Amplification Scale in general medical and general practice patients. *J Psychosom Res*, *40*(1), 95–104.

Speckens, A. E., Van Hemert, A. M., Spinhoven, P., & Bolk, J. H. (1996). The diagnostic and prognostic significance of the Whiteley Index, the Illness Attitude Scales and the Somatosensory Amplification Scale. *Psychol Med*, *26*(5), 1085–1090.

Tavakol, M., & Dennick, R. (2011). Making sense of Cronbach's alpha. *International Journal of Medical Education*, *2*, 53–55.

Tolin, D. F., Gilliam, C., Wootton, B. M., Bowe, W., Bragdon, L. B., Davis, E., ... Hallion, L. S. (2018). Psychometric properties of a structured diagnostic interview for DSM-5 Anxiety, Mood, and Obsessive-Compulsive and Related Disorders. *Assessment*, *25*(1), 3–13. https://doi.org/10.1177/1073191116638410.

Tomenson, B., McBeth, J., Chew-Graham, C. A., MacFarlane, G., Davies, I., Jackson, J., ... Creed, F. H. (2012). Somatization and health anxiety as predictors of health care use. *Psychosomatic Medicine*, *74*(6), 656–664. https://doi.org/10.1097/PSY.0b013e31825cb140.

van Ballegooijen, W., Riper, H., Cuijpers, P., van Oppen, P., & Smit, J. H. (2016). Validation of online psychometric instruments for common mental health disorders: a systematic review. *BMC Psychiatry*. *16*, 45https://doi.org/10.1186/s12888-016-0735-7.

Veddegjaerde, K. E., Sivertsen, B., Wilhelmsen, I., & Skogen, J. C. (2014). Confirmatory factor analysis and item response theory analysis of the Whiteley Index. Results from a large population based study in Norway. The Hordaland Health Study (HUSK). *Journal of Psychosomatic Research*, 77(3), 213–218. https://doi.org/10.1016/j.jpsychores.2014.06.011.

Weck, F., Bleichhardt, G., & Hiller, W. (2010). Screening for hypochondriasis with the Illness Attitude Scales. *Journal of Personality Assessment*, *92*(3), 260–268. https://doi.org/10.1080/00223891003670216.

Welch, P. G., Carleton, R. N., & Asmundson, G. J. (2009). Measuring health anxiety: moving past the dichotomous response option of the original Whiteley Index. *Journal of Anxiety Disorders*, *23*(7), 1002–1007. https://doi.org/10.1016/j.janxdis.2009.05.006.

Wright, K. D., & Asmundson, G. J. (2003). Health anxiety in children: Development and psychometric properties of the Childhood Illness Attitude Scales. *Cognitive Behaviour Therapy*, *32*(4), 194–202. https://doi.org/10.1080/16506070310014691.

CHAPTER SIX

Cognitive Behavioral Therapy for Health Anxiety

Erik Hedman-Lagerlöf and Erland Axelsson
Department of Clinical Neuroscience, Karolinska Institutet, Stockholm, Sweden

Cognitive behavioral therapy (CBT) is the most well-studied psychological treatment for health anxiety (e.g., Cooper, Gregory, Walker, Lambe, & Salkovskis, 2017) and the first-line treatment for anxiety according to the National Institute for Health and Care Excellence (NICE) guidelines (National institute for health and clinical excellence, 2011). This chapter gives an overview of the most important components of CBT for health anxiety and how this treatment can be used in clinical care. The aim of this chapter is to give the reader an understanding of both the theoretical model underlying CBT and how to practically adapt it to the patient's needs. The focus of this chapter is on clinical applications; please see Chapters 1 and 4 for a comprehensive account of knowledge regarding mechanisms of health anxiety.

The Concept of CBT

Despite it being a well-researched treatment, CBT is a relatively young therapeutic approach. On a broad level, it is a treatment with roots in both learning and cognitive theory. In media, CBT is often described as if it were one specific treatment, and headlines such as "New study shows that CBT is effective" are not uncommon. CBT is however an overarching label for a wide range of treatments whose contents, supposed mechanisms, and therapeutic focal points may differ substantially. However, most scholars would probably agree that all forms of CBT share the following:

- The assumption that behaviors, cognitions, physiological reactions, and context are dynamically interrelated, and that change in any of these domains is like to affect the others.
- The treatment focuses on changing that which maintains the clinical problem, rather than understanding the etiology of the problem. This means that the central question of therapy becomes "What should we change to reduce health anxiety?" or "What needs to be done in order

The Clinician's Guide to Treating Health Anxiety
https://doi.org/10.1016/B978-0-12-811806-1.00006-8

for the patient to live a better life?" rather than "Why did this specific patient develop health anxiety?"

- The treatment is specific and concrete. That is, in CBT, both the goals of therapy and the way to achieve them are made explicit to both the patient and therapist, and in order to reach these goals, the patient typically works with hands-on strategies in his or her daily life throughout the treatment.
- The treatment is marked by collaboration between the therapist and patient. This means that treatment is viewed as a process where therapist and patient work together to achieve the same, shared goal.
- CBT takes a hypothesis-testing empirical approach to psychological treatment and assumes that the therapist and patient work together to create hypotheses regarding how the patient can improve and then test these hypotheses empirically. In CBT, the value of therapeutic analyses ultimately depends on if they lead to interventions that improve the patient's health.

In the following, we describe how the analysis of the patient's problems can be conducted in the context of CBT and how empirically supported interventions for health anxiety are best used. The emphasis of this chapter will be on exposure-based techniques, which have been found to be highly efficacious for individuals with health anxiety.

Clinical Analysis of the Patient's Problems

An essential part of treatment is to analyze the patient's presenting problems. Although behavior analysis is often emphasized during the initial stage of treatment, this is a process that is ongoing throughout the treatment. This means that the analysis of the individual patient's health anxiety can be regarded as a constant testing of hypotheses. As more information is collected, the therapist might revise the analysis. An analysis of health anxiety broadly contains two elements: a descriptive summary of the patient's presenting problems, that is, a descriptive case formulation, and an analysis of maintaining factors, that is, a functional analysis. The former constitutes answers to the question "What is the problem?", while the latter attempts to answer the question "Why does the problem persist?" The purpose of conducting a behavior analysis is to help the clinician to make effective choices of intervention.

Descriptive Case Formulation

A descriptive case formulation is a way of efficiently describing information of potential clinical value. This part of the case formulation should contain an overview of all difficulties that the patient is struggling with, as it is common that persons with health anxiety also have other problems, such as depressed mood, sleep difficulties, or relationship problems. Information about the duration of the problems; the circumstances of the debut of health anxiety; and the basic demographic information, such as age, gender, family, and occupational status, are also part of the descriptive case formulation.

The use of psychiatric diagnoses is one of the most common ways to summarize the patient's problems. As mentioned in Chapter 1, health anxiety can be a feature of several different disorders, for example, panic disorder or obsessive-compulsive disorder, and is the dominating feature of ICD-10 hypochondriasis. For the clinician working with DSM-5, somatic symptom disorder and illness anxiety disorder are the prototypical health anxiety disorders, where the former describes patient with marked somatic symptoms and the latter those with health anxiety but who have no or minimal somatic symptoms. It should be noted that somatic symptom disorder is a broad diagnosis that is indicated in several types of clinical problems, for example, pain problems, where excessive behaviors and emotional responses to somatic symptoms dominate the clinical picture. This means that the somatic symptom disorder diagnosis contains less exact clinical information compared with, for example, DSM-IV hypochondriasis. Whereas DSM-IV hypochondriasis gave a relatively clear hint as to which treatment that might be suitable, this is to a lesser extent the case with somatic symptom disorder. See Chapter 5 for an introduction to structured interviews to facilitate the assessment of hypochondriasis, somatic symptom disorder, and illness anxiety disorder.

Another useful piece of information in the descriptive case formulation is the patient's rating of his or her health anxiety on validated symptom inventories (see Chapter 5 for details). One of the most widely used instruments is the Health Anxiety Inventory (HAI) (Salkovskis, Rimes, Warwick, & Clark, 2002), which is based on a cognitive behavioral model of health anxiety. The patient's rating gives an idea of the severity of the health anxiety, and information from such a scale can be used in several ways. Empirically derived cutoffs for a health anxiety diagnosis (hypochondriasis) can give a crude estimate of whether the patient is expected to meet diagnostic criteria. An instrument like HAI cannot replace a structured diagnostic interview, but information from self-rating scales can deepen the understanding of the patient's problems. If, for example, a patient seems to meet diagnostic criteria for a health anxiety diagnosis but has a low total summed score on the HAI, this might indicate that there are relatively few specific situations that trigger the health anxiety but these few situations might cause all the more problems. It is usually a good idea to discuss this type of information as openly as possible with the patient, as this can lead to a clarifying discussion of the nature of the patient's symptoms. Checking the responses to individual items might be of high value to get a quick picture of the health anxiety. It is, for example, likely a patient who ticks the response options "I always avoid situations which trigger thoughts of death or dying (HAI item 13)" and "I don't usually examine my body" (HAI item 15) has a rather different type of health anxiety than the person who responds "I do not avoid situations which trigger thoughts of death or dying" and "I examine my body constantly." Table 1 displays an example of a summarized descriptive case formulation for a patient seeking help for health anxiety.

Functional Analysis of Health Anxiety

As mentioned above, the goal of a functional analysis is to create an understanding of how the patient's problems are maintained and to effectively guide the clinician's interventions. When used correctly, this is a powerful tool not only for behavior change but also for creating a shared view between patient and therapist as to why the problems persist.

The ABC of Health Anxiety

The underlying assumption of the functional analysis is that health anxiety behaviors do not occur randomly, but are influenced by contextual factors that precede and follow on the behavior. In this type of analysis, A stands for "antecedent" and refers to factors that signal that a given behavior is likely to be reinforced. B is the behavior under analysis, and C is the consequence that follows on a behavior. When analyzing excess behaviors (behaviors that are so frequent, intense, or long lasting that they cause suffering or impairment), C denotes factors that reinforce a behavior, that is, that increase the probability that the behavior will be repeated when A is present. It is often of pedagogical value to add distal effects (DE) to the ABC analysis, that is, ABC-DE, where DE is the long-term nongoverning negative effects of the behavior. DE is thus not something that reinforces the behavior, but is a description of the negative effects of the behavior in the longer run. Oftentimes, DE is what makes the patient seek professional help.

Table 1 Summary of a Descriptive Case Formulation
Name of the patient: Jim Jones

Gender	Male
Age	56
Family	Widower, two sons (ages 22 and 19)
Education	9 years of primary school, 2 years vocational school (construction)
Work situation	Construction worker, unemployed since 4 months
Referral	From GP
Clinical problems (current)	Health anxiety Sleep problems Depressed Worried about unemployment and financial situation
Debut of health anxiety	3 years ago, shortly after his wife died of cancer
Psychiatric disorders	Somatic symptom disorder, principal problem (also meets criteria for DSM-IV hypochondriasis) Depression, secondary problem
Ratings on self-report measures	Health Anxiety Inventory, 119 Patient Health Questionnaire (PHQ-9) (depression), 14 Insomnia Severity Index, 12 Sheehan Disability Scales, 12
Medication	SSRI (fluoxetine) since about 2 years Anxiolytics when needed
Previous psychiatric contact	None. Psychotropic medication prescribed by GP for "mixed anxiety and depression"
Previous psychological treatment	5–6 sessions of counseling when the patient's wife died. No previous experience of CBT
Alcohol consumption	AUDIT rating, 7 (threshold for hazardous use is 8 or higher)

Case Example: Cathy

Cathy, 46, has always been a bit more worried than others but seeks help because she feels that her anxiety has become unmanageable. Six years ago, she had stomachaches that persisted for a long time, which eventually led her to visit her GP. She was referred to a gastroenterological clinic where exams were conducted and that showed that she had an uncommon form of tumor in her stomach and that the tumor had to be removed. Cathy was terrified from hearing that she had a potentially deadly disease, and at times during this period, she just knew that "this was it"; she would soon be dead and wouldn't see her children grow up and wouldn't grow old with her husband John. The fear was so intense that she hardly ate or slept the week before the surgery. The surgery however went well. The tumor could be entirely removed and had not spread. Since then, Cathy has had two follow-ups per year (which all indicted no signs of tumors), and her doctor has reassured her that she is no more likely than anybody else to have a new form of cancer.

For a few months after the surgery, Cathy was so relieved and felt as she had been given a second chance. "It was almost joy that I felt in that time," Cathy says. After a while, however, Cathy noted that she started getting anxious again. Could the doctors be really sure that the tumor had been completely removed? She became increasingly preoccupied with thoughts about becoming ill again and noticed that she became very sensitive to bodily signals. In the recent year, she has had panic-like attacks when she's had sensations from her stomach, especially if these sensations couldn't be attributed to some clear cause, such as being full after eating.

When experiencing an unexplained sensation from the bowel tract, Cathy typically becomes very anxious and monitors the sensation closely, and if it hasn't subsided after 20–30 min, she becomes certain that the cancer is back. Sometimes, she gets clear images of herself being back in the hospital and sees the doctor explaining to her that the cancer is back. When this happens, she starts feeling dizzy and feels her heart pounding. Cathy often calls her husband John when this happens (she has told him that it is extremely important that she always can reach him). Sometimes, John manages to calm Cathy down by reminding her what the doctors have said, that is, that it is perfectly normal to have stomach pains and that they can be triggered by all sorts of things, such as stress, hunger, or having had too much to eat. Occasionally, this helps but mostly just for a short period of time. If the pain is still there, Cathy can't tolerate not knowing what it means and mostly ends up calling her doctor and books an appointment. Once she has had her checkup and the medical exam indicates that Cathy is well, she can feel her anxiety and thoughts about dying subsiding gradually. But as sure as day follows night, the process starts all over again the next time that Cathy experiences a stomach sensation that "shouldn't be there."

Cathy has noticed not only how she has become more sensitive to bodily signals but also that there are some things that she just cannot stand. When people start talking about diseases at work during coffee breaks, she often excuses herself and goes back to her office. Hearing other talk about someone getting sick always leads to her thinking about her own risk of dying, and walking away is often the best way to avoid getting into a severe anxiety spiral. Watching TV series about hospitals and people falling ill is out of the question.

Cathy now seeks help because she is starting to lose all control over her health anxiety. It is difficult to work; her job requires that she can concentrate in front of the computer, but when she gets worried over a symptom, it's nearly impossible. Everything takes much longer, and instead of being a person that takes initiatives at work, she now struggles doing what's absolutely necessary in order to do her job. Sometimes, she discovers that she hasn't worked for about an hour, but that she has been caught up in worrying about the future. Sometimes, it's just so hard not to, but thinking about bad things that might happen often leads to a sense that she to some extent is less uncertain. And even if she becomes convinced that she will soon die, it's better to be sure about it than not knowing. She constantly feels that she is behind at work, as if she is a fraud that tries to appear as if she is working effectively but doesn't.

Cathy's health anxiety also puts a great deal of strain on her relationship with John. While he understands that she was shaken up by the cancer and treatments, Cathy's worries have started to make John increasingly irritated. A couple of weeks ago, he shouted at her saying "all we ever talk about is your anxieties; you have to see someone about this; it is clear that I'm not the therapist that you need." John has started to work late more and more, and Cathy feels as if he is trying to avoid her. But what's worst is that Cathy feels that her health worries have started to spread to their children who are 10 and 12 years old. She constantly fears that they will become severely ill and often checks that they are ok. She has read that cancer might be hereditary and that early signs in children are that they become more tired than usual. In the last year, Cathy has taken them to the doctor at least eight times. Even though she knows that she might make them more worried, it is so hard not to do it. If the children would be really sick, Cathy would never be able to forgive herself given that she hadn't done something about it at an early stage.

So, how are Cathy's problems to be understood from a functional analytic perspective? First, it is important to identify which behaviors that are of relevance to analyze. What constitutes relevance can be defined in different ways, but basic selection criteria are that the behavior in question is likely to be causing suffering for the patient, and that it maintains health anxiety. In Cathy's case, a relevant behavior seems to be reassurance seeking, that is, gaining more information about her health. Reassurance seeking is however a relatively broad label, and it might be that there are several behaviors that are relevant within this definition and it isn't certain that they are all controlled by the same antecedents and consequences. For example, it doesn't seem as it is the exact same factors that trigger Cathy to call John as it is for calling her doctor, so for our purposes, we have to be more specific. Considering that Cathy mentions that a major negative effect of her calling John to talk about her health worries is that it is bad for her relationship with John,

Table 2 Example of Functional Analysis of Health Anxiety Behavior

Antecedent	Behavior	Consequence	Distal Effects
Situation: At work. Stomach pain for at least 20 min *Thoughts*: "The cancer is back," mental images of being back at the hospital *Physiological response*: Tense, sweating, heavy breathing	Calls John and talks about symptoms	Thoughts about cancer subside as John provides reassurance (neg. reinforcement) Tension, sweating, and heavy breathing subside (neg. reinforcement)	Strain on relationship with John Thoughts about not being able to handle the situation, self-criticism Maintained fear of bodily symptoms

this is a good candidate to start with. Table 2 presents an overview of how an ABC analysis can look like.

As shown in Table 2, the ABC analysis provides a concise overview of factors that affect the health anxiety behavior, and the inclusion of DE gives a pedagogical description of the unwanted side effects of the behavior. Importantly, each of the factors listed in the antecedent should have a unique contribution to the probability that the behavior will occur; if they don't, they shouldn't be included. Trying to obtain as specific antecedents as possible is imperative because later in treatment the therapist and Cathy must know which stimuli to approach while attempting to refrain from seeking reassurance. Of course, all factors listed as negative reinforces under consequences must also be part of the antecedent, following the simple rule that if a reduction of X reinforces behavior, then X must first be increased.

Although not explicit in Table 2 in this type of ABC analysis, the excessive health-anxiety-related thoughts and feelings are presented as respondent processes in the antecedent.

That is, stomach pain (conditioned stimulus) triggers thoughts about cancer and anxiety (conditioned response), which in turn trigger the operant behavior to call John. In an ABC analysis, thoughts can also be the operant behavior of interest. Such an example, again based on Cathy's health anxiety, is presented Table 3.

Table 3 Functional Analysis of Health Anxiety Thoughts as Operant Behavior

Antecedent	Behavior	Consequence	Distal Effects
Situation: At work. Overheard a conversation about someone's mother being maltreated by health care *Thoughts*: "What if my doctors have missed something?" *Physiological response*: Tense muscles and light-headedness	Ruminates about treatment history, tries to determine how likely it is that the doctors have done something seriously wrong	Uncertainty reduced because convinced of being maltreated (neg. reinforcement) Tension and light-headedness eventually reduced (neg. reinforcement)	Increased anxiety and fear of death Less concentrated on work, struggles with meeting basic demands Unnecessary and time-consuming health-care visits

As shown in Table 3, worry behavior, which is common in persons with health anxiety, can be viewed as an operant. As in Cathy's case, the antecedent of that type of behavior is often not intense panic-like anxiety but more likely a lower-key sense of uncertainty. This type of behavior is often a bit more tricky to analyze, because it is not always the case that the reinforcing consequences are of the type typically seen in anxiety disorders, that is, a fast reduction of anxiety. In fact, more anxiety is not seldom the direct effect of worry behavior because it can lead to the person being convinced that they are really sick (or as in this case that they have been maltreated by health care). At first glance, this might appear to be illogical (Why would anyone engage in behaviors that increase anxiety?), but the governing consequence is often that the individual becomes less uncertain. So, the increased anxiety can be viewed as a nongoverning distal effect, and the consequence that really controls the behavior is a reduced sense of uncertainty. Of course, it is the rule rather than the exception that the effect of the worry behavior, for example, in Cathy's case the conviction that she has been maltreated, becomes part of the antecedent of subsequent health anxiety behavior, such as calling one's doctor. In other words, the ABC elements of the functional analysis are often a selected part of a longer behavioral chain.

Behavior Diary

Important to underscore is that a detailed description of antecedents, behaviors, and consequences is not always possible for the patient to provide simply through discussions with the therapist. Many patients actively try not to think about what happens in situations that are of potential clinical relevance, or have avoided those situations for such a long time that they are unsure of what would happen if they were exposed to them. This means that in order to be able to conduct a meaningful behavior analysis, it is often necessary to have the patient collecting data about his or her own health anxiety in a structured fashion. One practical way of doing this is to use a health anxiety behavior diary. The purpose of this type of diary is to obtain a comprehensive picture of all the patient's health anxiety behaviors and the antecedents and consequences that control them. As not all these behaviors occur with regular intervals, we recommend that the patient uses this diary for at least 3 weeks in the beginning of the treatment. The instruction to the patient is to record all potential health anxiety behaviors on a daily basis. It is often practical for the patient to try to look out for health anxiety behaviors in four overarching domains: *avoidance behaviors* (e.g., changing channels if there are reports about disease on TV), *checking behaviors* (e.g., daily checks of one's body), *reassurance-seeking behaviors* (e.g., calling one's doctor), and *preventive behaviors* (e.g., adopting an extremely healthy diet to avoid disease). When starting to use the health anxiety diary, it is often helpful to ask the patient to have the following questions in mind:

- What am I doing to reduce my health anxiety or keep it in check?
- What am I doing to determine if I am suffering from a severe disease?
- What am I doing or how am I preparing in order to "feel safe"?
- What am I doing in order not to worry about my health?

Below is an example of a filled in behavior diary after about 1 week's usage.

Worksheet—Behavior Diary *Example*: Peter Smith

Date and time	Situation	Behavior	Consequence
When was it?	*What situation were you in? What went through your mind? What were your bodily sensations?*	*What did you do? Did you avoid something because of your fear? Did you seek reassurance? Did you do anything not to get symptoms or become ill?*	*What happened just after your health anxiety behavior? Did it affect your anxiety? Did you feel safer or less uncertain?*
12th October Just woken up		Stretched my back to see how it felt	Almost no pain, I was relieved

	In bed. Worried that my back pain would still be there		
12th October In the morning	Nothing specific I think. Routine habit	Checked my molds in the bathroom mirror	Found nothing that worried me, always a good start of the day
12th October Lunch time	At work. Don't want to eat junk food; it causes heart disease	Declined the offer to go with some colleagues to eat pizza	A bit boring to miss out on lunch with the rest. But I would have felt miserable had I eaten pizza
13th October Lunch time	Lunch with a work client. He started talking about a relative who just found out she has MS	I changed the topic as soon as possible	I felt bad that I showed no interest; I could see he was a bit hurt that I didn't seem to care. But good that I prevented becoming obsessed with MS
13th October 8 PM	At home. My back pain was worse. Can't figure out where this pain is coming from	Called my neighbor, who is a doctor and asked him if this is normal	He sounded very uninterested, just said I worry too much. Felt good to hear
15th October Most of the night	At home. Had watched a TV program about kidney cancer. Worried that my back pain might be cancer	Spent all night searching the Internet for articles about back pain and cancer	Just got more nervous instead of calmer. Decided to call my GP the next day. Couldn't sleep
16th October 9 AM	At work, had canceled an appointment to be able to call when telephone hours start	Called my GP	Haven't seen my GP yet, but it makes me less nervous knowing that I will be examined
17th October All day	My right leg trembled constantly, especially in the morning. Worried that it was MS or something similar	Stretched my leg about 100 times	The tremor subsided at about 4 PM. Less worried about MS

As shown in the example work sheet, the patient does not typically come back with a "perfect" functional analysis, but nonetheless, these registrations can be extremely helpful for the therapist. After 3 weeks of registration, it is likely that most of the important health anxiety behaviors have come to both the patient's and the therapist's attention. This information is highly valuable in later parts of the treatment when focus is on approaching situations, somatic sensations, and thoughts about illness. When discussing what steps to take, the therapist and patient can use this bank of health anxiety behaviors to decide what to do.

Identifying Obstacles for Treatment

Before starting a treatment that typically lasts for about 3 months and that requires a lot of work for the patient, it is important to assess whether treatment is suitable. The literature about predictors of treatment effects in CBT is inconclusive. The most stable finding seems to be that health anxiety at baseline predicts treatment outcome in the sense that more health anxiety before treatment is associated not only with more health anxiety after treatment, but also with larger reductions of health anxiety over the course of treatment (e.g., Hedman et al., 2013). Demographic variables such as age and gender have not been consistently shown to be related to treatment outcome. At least one study has shown that treatment credibility predicts better treatment outcome (Hedman, Andersson, Lekander, & Ljótsson, 2015), that is, believing that a treatment is credible, and that it will be helpful, seems to lead to better outcomes. In that study, it was shown that the combination of having high levels of health anxiety (above 104 on the HAI) and a score below 39 on the treatment credibility scale (C-scale) (Borkovec & Nau, 1972) was associated with a poor treatment response (only 12% clinically significantly improved). Conversely, of the participants with a treatment credibility score of 39 or higher who had a HAI score of 109 or lower, as many as 83% were clinically significantly improved. This suggests that a patient who is skeptical toward the treatment is at risk of not responding to treatment, especially if he or she has high levels of health anxiety. Of course, the clinician should make an effort to make the treatment as credible as possible and at the same time take hints of the patient not believing in treatment seriously. Some studies have also shown that treatment adherence is a predictor of better outcome in CBT (e.g., Hedman et al., 2015; Hedman et al., 2013). This is however of limited value for the clinician when making treatment decisions since this information is not available before starting treatment.

It does however suggest that motivating the patient to go through the entire treatment once it has started is an important task of the therapist.

One limitation in the predictor literature is that most clinical trials use exclusion criteria in order not to include patients at high risk of not responding to treatment. Most of these criteria have not been empirically evaluated but are based on clinical judgment and therefore of interest for most clinicians. If one takes the inverse of these exclusion criteria, there seems to be a relatively broad consensus that the following factors seem to be beneficial for CBT in health anxiety:

- Health anxiety should be the principal clinical problem.
- The patient should not have a comorbid bipolar or psychotic disorder.
- If comorbid depression is present, the symptom severity should be mild to moderate including low perceived risk of suicide.
- The patient should not undergo other psychological treatments simultaneously.
- The patient should have sufficient language skills to understand and communicate with the therapist.

These listed factors are of course broad and probably the same for most anxiety disorders. In a regular clinical setting, it might be however not be possible or desirable to use these variables as rigid criteria for starting treatment (it might also be unethical). The point here is that if a given patient does not meet these criteria, it is important for the therapist to make an assessment as to whether it is likely that the patient will be able to go through with the treatment and if there is anything that the therapist can do to augment the treatment to ensure that the treatment can be successfully conducted. When assessing if it is suitable to start CBT, our experience is that it is very important that the patient knows what to expect, that is, that CBT is an intensive treatment that requires at least an hour's work per day for about 3 months. Practical obstacles should not be underestimated, for example, if a patient says that they have a really hectic period at work or that they are planning to go abroad on vacation for 2–3 weeks in the middle of the treatment. The decision to start treatment should not be made in haste, and if the patient is hesitant, we suggest that the therapist takes a step back and gives the patient room to think over if he or she is willing to make the commitment to start treatment. Put differently, "persuading" a patient to start treatment should be avoided.

Before starting with structured behavior change, we find it useful to see that we haven't missed important information by using a behavior analysis checklist (see below). If all questions are answered with a clear "yes," then the job has been done correctly.

Clinician's Checklist for Health Anxiety Behavior Analysis

Descriptive case formulation
Has demographic information been collected, for example, age, gender, family status, and occupational status?
Has information about the onset of health anxiety been collected?
Has a comprehensive problem list been generated?
Has a structured interview, such as the Health Preoccupation Diagnostic Interview (HPDI), been used to assess the presence of health anxiety diagnoses?
Has it been established that health anxiety is the patient's principal clinical problem?
Has a valid measure of health anxiety, such as the HAI, been used to assess the severity of health anxiety?
Has potential obstacles for starting treatment been assessed?
Functional analysis
Has a behavior diary been used to collect information about potential clinically relevant behaviors?
A—antecedent
Do the factors described under A increase the probability of the behavior?
Is the situation specified?
Is the cognition specified?
Is the somatic sensation specified?
Does each of the variables under A make a unique contribution to the probability of B? That is, is the probability of the behavior reduced if the variables under A are removed?
B—behavior
Is the behavior specific enough?
Does the analyzed behavior reduce the patient's quality of life?
Does the analyzed behavior contribute to persistent health anxiety because it maintains the stimulus-response relationship?
C—consequence
Is the type of reinforcer described (negative or positive)?
Is the reinforcer described in sufficient detail?
If the reinforcer is negative, is that which is reduced also described under A?
DE—distal effect
Is DE idiosyncratically described, that is, does it describe the suffering of this particular patient?
Clinical usefulness
Does the analysis generate clear ideas about suitable and individually tailored interventions?

Psychoeducation

Psychoeducation refers to interventions in health-care services that aim to give the patient knowledge about his or her disorder. This knowledge, which is often based on a theoretical model of the problem (e.g., a cognitive behavioral conceptualization), is in turn intended to empower the patient and to lead to effective coping strategies.

In the case of health anxiety, psychoeducation typically involves learning patients about the nature of health anxiety, which includes that it is common to misinterpret harmless bodily sensations as signs of serious disease and that there are plenty of normal bodily processes that can give rise to symptoms that the patient associates with serious disease (e.g., tense muscles can lead to aches and pains, and a stressful day at work can lead to bowel symptoms). Psychoeducation also often includes explaining to patients how excessive health anxiety behaviors, such as checking one's pulse with tight intervals or asking one's spouse if a bodily sensation is indicative of disease, can lead to increased health anxiety in the long run, as these behaviors increase the focus on symptoms and prevent the patient from learning that both bodily sensations and anxiety can subside without the patient acting on them.

There are, broadly speaking, two types of psychoeducation: One is when psychoeducation is one component in a multicomponent treatment (e.g., CBT or problem-solving therapy), and the other type is when it constitutes the entire intervention. In both instances, there are at least two potential ways through which psychoeducation achieves its effects. First, there might be a direct anxiety-reducing effect of gaining more information about health anxiety (e.g., learning that our bodies are noisy and that numerous sensations are perfectly normal). Second, psychoeducation might be effective by creating a coherent context for subsequent behavior change. By explaining to patients, using a credible theoretical model, why safety behaviors can maintain health anxiety and why it can be an efficient strategy to engage in behaviors that are aversive to the patient, the patient's motivation can be enhanced. Concisely put, psychoeducation can be used to make aversive—but helpful—behaviors appetitive.

In our experience, it is of high value not only to provide psychoeducation within sessions but also to use self-help texts throughout the treatment. Considering that there are large and complex pieces of information that the therapist wants to convey to the patient, there is a substantial risk that the patient, shortly after the session, has forgotten some central aspect of the psychoeducation. This is however much less of a problem if the therapist has prepared a written summary of the take-home messages of the psychoeducation. If this has been done, the patient can, in peace and quiet, go through the written psychoeducation after the session, which increases the chance that he or she will understand the rationale for treatment as soon as possible and reduces the risk of misconceptions. Most patients appreciate such support material, and there is, in our experience, little risk that the patient experiences that reading self-help texts is burdening. A good example of a comprehensive text material that can be used as psychoeducation in adjunct to CBT for health anxiety is the self-help book *It's Not All in Your Head* by Asmundson and Taylor (2005).

As most cognitive behavioral treatments entail psychoeducation as one part of many, it is difficult to determine its specific therapeutic effect. However, judging from symptom trajectories in some clinical trials where symptom assessment has been done with short intervals during treatment, it seems that patients start to improve already during the first couple of weeks (e.g., see Fig. 1 from Hedman et al., 2011), that is, when psychoeducation is the focal point of treatment. This might indicate that just the process of learning about health anxiety and beginning to understand the treatment rationale can in itself trigger the start of recovery.

At least one randomized controlled trial has investigated the effect of pure cognitive behavioral psychoeducation (Buwalda, Bouman, & van Duijn, 2007). In that study, CBT psychoeducation was delivered in a group format and composed of six sessions. The results of the study showed that patients after CBT psychoeducation made large within-group improvements in terms of health anxiety reduction (Cohen's $d=1.01$). This observed effect was larger than for the control group who received

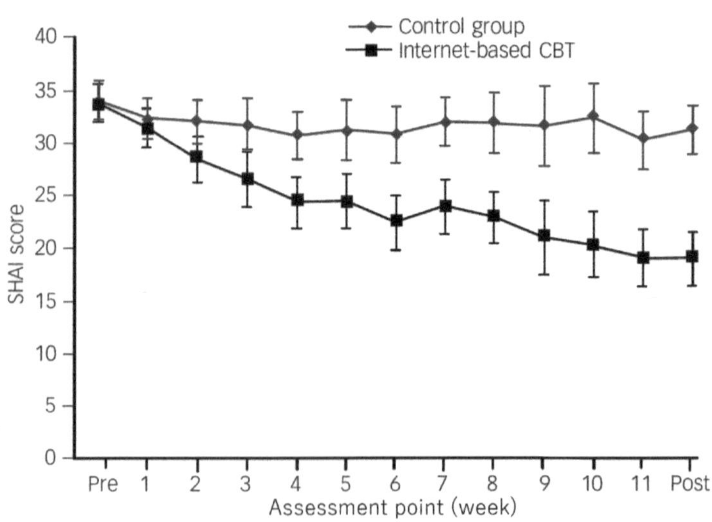

Fig. 1 Example of improvement trajectory in CBT for health anxiety (Hedman et al., 2011). Note that symptom improvement starts early in treatment, where psychoeducation is the main part of the treatment.

psychoeducation based on problem-solving (Cohen's $d = 0.54$). There were however no significant differences between treatments, which might be explained by low statistical power (there were less than 30 participants in each treatment group). Psychoeducation based on CBT thus seems to be promising as stand-alone treatment when it comes to reducing health anxiety, but the evidence is so far too limited for this type of treatment to be regarded as a firsthand choice.

Cognitive Restructuring Techniques

As described in Chapter 1, an assumption of the cognitive behavioral model of health anxiety is that health anxiety at least in part results from misinterpretations of benign bodily sensations or external events. A commonly used technique in CBT that aims to directly alter these misinterpretations pertaining health and disease is cognitive restructuring (e.g., Salkovskis & Warwick, 1986; Warwick & Salkovskis, 1990). The hypothesized mechanism of cognitive restructuring is that if the patient obtains information that is inconsistent with the misinterpretations or negative thoughts associated with health anxiety, then he or she will develop a more realistic perception of health-related stimuli, which in turn will lead to reduced health anxiety (e.g., Taylor & Asmundson, 2004). The first step of cognitive restructuring is always to identify the threatening thought so that it is clear to both therapist and patient what the feared outcome is. This is essential because quite different forms of information are needed to test thoughts such as the following: "The pain I'm sensing is a sign of cancer"; "if I die, my family won't make it"; or "if I don't have this symptom checked up before Christmas, the holidays will be ruined." This is followed by data collection that can test the validity of the patient's threatening thought. As described by Abramowitz and Braddock (2008), the cognitive restructuring should preferably yield information that disconfirms the negative thought and simultaneously provide support for an alternative explanation (e.g., the meaning of a physical sensation).

Broadly speaking, there are two types of cognitive restructuring techniques. One is based on logical reasoning, that is, the therapist challenges the patient's appraisals by asking questions that point to information that is in conflict with the patient's negative thoughts. The long-term goal is that the patient should acquire the skill to challenge his or her own negative thoughts without the guidance of the therapist. The other type of cognitive restructuring technique is to test the validity of the patient's thoughts through behavioral experiments, which probably has become the dominant method of cognitive restructuring. The idea here is to collect empirical data, as opposed to using logical reasoning, that disconfirm the patient's faulty appraisal. This is done by testing the negative thought in a carefully designed experiment that has the potential to yield information that questions the validity of the thought. For a patient who fears that his or her heart will cease functioning under stress, a behavioral experiment might be to do jumping jacks until exhaustion and see if it leads to acute heart failure. For a patient who thinks that he or she would not sleep for a second without calling the doctor and asking about a newly developed bodily sensation, a behavioral experiment might be to refrain from seeking health care and see if the worry leads to complete sleep loss.

As has been previously described (Hedman & Axelsson, 2017), there are great similarities between behavioral experiments and classical forms of exposure, and from the patient's perspective, they are probably often perceived as the same type of exercise.

At least two randomized trials have compared cognitive therapy, where cognitive restructuring is the main component, with exposure-based treatment for health anxiety (Visser & Bouman, 2001; Weck, Neng, Richtberg, Jakob, & Stangier, 2014). Both trials showed no significant differences between the two CBT forms on the primary health anxiety outcome. One study however showed that exposure therapy was significantly more effective than cognitive therapy in reducing safety behaviors. In a 3-year follow-up study, the effects had further improved in both treatments, but there was a trend toward higher rates of deterioration in cognitive therapy compared with exposure treatment (Weck, Nagel, Hofling, & Neng, 2017). Interestingly, a study investigating potential mediators found that both types of treatment changed dysfunctional appraisals of bodily symptoms to the same extent (Weck, Neng, Schwind, & Hofling, 2015).

Exposure-Based Techniques

As in the treatment of most anxiety disorders, a potent component of CBT for health anxiety is exposure to aversive stimuli, such as feared physical sensations and health-related information. A patient who fears developing multiple sclerosis may, for example, be encouraged to watch an anxiety-inducing documentary about a person suffering from this disorder, and a patient who worries about having a heart disease may be encouraged to engage in physical activity while refraining from pulse checking. As pointed out above, some clinicians and theorists see exposure primarily as a tool to conduct powerful behavioral experiments where the patient's negative thoughts and health-related beliefs are submitted to empirical investigation (e.g., Bennett-Levy et al., 2004). Others emphasize that the primary aim of exposure should be to allow the patient to gradually reduce anxiety (e.g., Foa & Kozak, 1986) and/or develop more fruitful behaviors in situations perceived as threatening (e.g., Craske et al., 2008). As with most psychological interventions, the exact mechanisms contributing to the effects of exposure are yet to be revealed.

Any patient with health anxiety will have experienced the negative short-term effects of confronting what he or she fears. Many are therefore understandably skeptical of exposure as a means to achieve therapeutic effects. Some clinicians also shy away from using exposure-based techniques, not least out of fear of causing harm or premature treatment termination (Deacon & Farrell, 2013). We therefore wish to emphasize that the common fear that the patient will deteriorate or easily drop out of treatment as a consequence of exposure is likely to be largely unfounded (Hembree et al., 2003) and that the choice of exposure exercises should always be tailor-made to the patient, and grounded in functional analysis. If done right, few techniques (if any) are as effective in the treatment of anxiety, including health anxiety, as exposure (Olatunji, Cisler, & Deacon, 2010; Visser & Bouman, 2001). An advantage of exposure-based techniques is also that these are relatively easy to understand and put to practice, both for the therapist and the patient. In order to ensure that the patient realizes the benefits of exposure, it is important to educate the patient about the detrimental effects of avoidance and that there are important differences between exposure within the context of CBT and spontaneous confrontation with aversive stimuli in everyday life. Here follows a typical introduction to exposure:

> *"Therapist: As you now know, behavioral strategies such as symptom checking and avoidance of the things that make you scared are not going to take away your health anxiety in the long run. The more you engage in such strategies, the more your life will center around your health and the possibility of developing a serious disease. The very same strategies that lower your anxiety in the short term also ensure that you minimize your time spent with uncertainty about your health. If, for example, every time you discover a vague new symptom you do your best to quickly 'rule out' that it is something serious, you also prevent yourself from experiencing how it is to live with unfamiliar symptoms for a longer period of time. Since you take away the very situation that you want to learn how to master, you also take away your opportunities to work through your fears and become more apt at tackling the things that you worry about. Once you find yourself in a similar situation, the next time and discover another vague symptom, this is likely to be just as difficult for you as the last time.*

Managing health anxiety with avoidance or reassurance seeking is perfectly normal and understandable, especially when one has worried as much about one's health as you have. But it is simply an unfortunate fact that if your fear has grown out of proportion, this type of strategy ultimately serves to reinforce the problem rather than solve it. Again, the more you try to keep your fear under control and avoid the things that you fear, the less experience you will have in dealing with the things you fear, and the more your health anxiety will grow over time. It might not always feel that way, but that's how health anxiety works. Chances are that if you don't strive to revert this pattern, you will gradually become even more worried about your health. This might lead to even more avoidance, more fear, and so on. At the very least, the use of such behavioral strategies will ensure that your fear returns time and time again.

This is why it is important that we start to work with exposure, which is a technique to make it easier for you to handle the things that trigger your fear and will enable you to live your life more freely. In a nutshell, exposure is the opposite of avoidance and keeping your symptoms under control. Instead of avoiding what you fear, you confront something that you find triggers your health anxiety, so as to change the way you can manage similar things in the future. Working with exposure is a process that takes time and that can be challenging, but once we make it through, you will see that it can be extremely effective.

Now, you have already told me that all sorts of things, everything from your own physical sensations to public health campaigns, can trigger health anxiety. I also get the impression that you encounter these things pretty often in your daily life. In that sense, it might seem as if you're doing exposure nearly every day, right? Even if it seems that way, in order for exposure to work, we need to follow certain principles that go well above and beyond the way you typically encounter triggers for your health anxiety in your daily life. In other words, there is a very large difference between merely scaring yourself senseless and working systematically with exposure.

Say, for example, that you decide to watch some sort of video about a person suffering from a serious disease as a form of exposure exercise. First, if you want to see any sort of effect, it is important that you do not immediately leave the situation or use any sort of strategy to make it less frightening. You will have to do your best not to pause the video, distance yourself from your emotions, or anything like that. Second, you need to work with repetition. Without repetition, you will simply not be able to achieve the training effect that we are striving for here. It is a little bit like being unfit, making it to the gym, and lifting weights once or twice. This might of course make you sore, but without repetition, you won't be able to build your muscles. Last but not least, you will need to have a plan and actively provoke your fear rather than to wait for it to be spontaneously triggered. Planning your exposure is the only way to really achieve the sort of repeated training that will get you somewhere."

Although exposure may be conducted in an infinite number of ways, we suggest that it can be helpful to think of exposure exercises for health anxiety as belonging to one of four categories: exposure to one's own physical sensations (interoceptive exposure), exposure to things and situations outside of one's own body (exposure in vivo), exposure to one's own thoughts and mental images (imaginal exposure), and exposure accomplished through the reduction of safety behaviors (response prevention). In the following, we describe how exposure can be conducted within each of these categories. Please note that even though we present the four types of exposure for health anxiety separately, there is no reason not to mix these up and, for example, work with interoceptive exposure, in vivo exercises, and response prevention in parallel. The choice of exposure exercises should always be tailor-made for the patient at hand, and we would advise that exposure is made as varied as possible in the sense that different types of exercises are used so as to maximize the probability of generalization of new learning.

Interoceptive Exposure

A majority of patients with health anxiety are continuously bothered by physical sensations such as aches and pains or dizziness, and fear that these may be symptoms of a serious disease. In these cases, an obvious target for exposure exercises is the patient's feared bodily symptoms and inner sensations. Interoceptive exposure—that is, exposure to one's own physical sensations—is typically achieved through the repetition of exercises that give rise to physical sensations associated with autonomic arousal. It is, for example, common to have the patient hyperventilate so as to induce alkalinity of the blood and symptoms such as palpitations, sweating, and dizziness. Table 4 contains a list of interoceptive exposure exercises that we have found are useful for a large proportion of patients with health anxiety.

For many patients, interoceptive exposure is experienced as very frightening. There is however also a large group of patients who do not primarily fear their own bodily symptoms but instead typically worry about either future ill health (e.g., gradually developing cancer) or disease states that cannot be easily verified through bodily symptoms (e.g., having HIV). Some patients might also say that this type of exposure triggers no anxiety because the cause of the physical sensations is so clear. While these individuals usually have little to gain from interoceptive exposure, we have also experienced several cases where patients initially voiced a strong concern that interoceptive exposure "was not for them," but where the patient nevertheless later reported high levels of anxiety in response to common interoceptive

Table 4 Common Interoceptive Exposure Exercises

Exercise	Instruction
Hyperventilating	For 90 s, without pausing, stand up and breathe heavily (deep and with force) through your mouth. Breathe as if you just had finished a marathon or run up a long flight of stairs
Holding your breath	Breathe out all the way and then immediately, for 30 s or as long as you can, hold your breath
Spinning on the spot	For 1 min, stand up and spin around (rotate your body)
Breathing through a straw	For 2 min, breathe through a drinking straw
Tensing your muscles	For 1 min, sit down and tense all your muscles as much as possible. At the same time, tense your feet and calves, thighs, bottom, back, breast muscles, throat, shoulder muscles, face, arms, and hands as much as possible
Running up stairs	For 1 min, without pausing, run up and down a flight of stairs as fast as you can
Pressing your throat	For 1 min, press your fingers against your throat. Press hard enough for it to be noticeable, but do not use any sort of tool (such as a belt) or prevent the air passage
Swallowing quickly	Four times, without pausing, swallow as quickly as you can
Rising quickly	For 90 s, sit down and lower your head between your legs and heart. Then, quickly rise your head and sit still
Taking a sauna or hot bath	For 15 min, take a sauna or hot bath
Staring at a light source	For 30 s, stare at a light source
Wearing tight clothing	For a day, wear something that intensifies your physical sensations. For example, if you dislike heat, try and wear something warm; if you dislike pressure against your chest, try and wear a tight shirt or underwired bra, and if you dislike pressure against your throat, try and wear a tie or turtleneck
Observing your body	For 10 min, sit down in a chair and observe the physical sensations in your body without attempting to distract or reason with yourself. Do your best to "let the symptoms be" and observe them without taking any particular action

exercises. Given that individuals with health anxiety often interpret physical sensations as signs of disease, it is not so surprising that they also may have difficulties in determining whether interoceptive exposure could be of relevance or not.

In most cases, we would recommend that an attempt at going through the interoceptive exposure exercises listed in Table 4 is made at least once, so as to establish if these are worth pursuing further. Preferably, it should be made clear to the patient that this attempt at interoceptive exposure may be seen as a test of the extent to which a hypersensitivity to physical sensations plays a part in exacerbating the patient's anxiety. So as to forego common misunderstandings, it should also preferably be made clear that if it turns out that no form of interoceptive exposure gives rise to anxiety, this does not mean that the patient does not suffer from health anxiety, or that the patient will be resistant to therapy. All that it means is that other forms of exposure are likely to be more suitable. A typical rationale for interoceptive exposure would be the following:

> *"Therapist: Most who suffer from health anxiety experience their own physical sensations as distressing, and it is therefore important for us to address this in your treatment. As we have talked about, a powerful tool to come to grips with your health anxiety is exposure. Interoceptive exposure is a particular form of exposure, where the thing that you are confronting is your own physical sensations. The point of this is to change the way you react to such sensations, lower the risk of intense anxiety, and enable you to find new and more effective ways to tackle similar feelings in your body.*
>
> *This part of the treatment may or may not be relevant for you, but it is difficult to tell without having given it a try. Therefore, my suggestion is that we work through a short list of standardized interoceptive exercises as a sort of test. If it so happens that you experience a strong reaction to any of these exercises, this is a good thing, since you will be able to repeat the exercises to gradually change the way you react to certain bodily cues.*
>
> *If, on the other hand, it turns out that you don't find that these exercises provoke your anxiety, we will put them aside and instead focus on other forms of exposure. This, of course, is not a problem. It only means that we might need to look elsewhere to find those exposure exercises that are best suited for your particular needs."*

Of course, if the functional analysis indicates that the patient fears physical sensations that are better triggered by other exercises than the ones listed in Table 4, the therapist and patient should be creative and try out other exercises that are more well tailored to the patient's problems.

Exposure In Vivo

A key aim of CBT for health anxiety is to ensure that the patient becomes better equipped to deal also with triggers of health anxiety other than physical sensations. Since in most cases a strong fear can be evoked by anything from health-related media alerts to the sight of hospitals or medical information leaflets, the initial question with regard to exposure in vivo is often not "Is there anything to expose to?" but rather "Where do we start?" A good place to start is usually to consult the behavior diary for examples of frequent avoidance behaviors and to ask the patient about which situations that have been most difficult to tackle in the past. Here are some typical examples of in vivo exercises for health anxiety:

- Reading health- or illness-related texts such as newspaper articles, information from medical authorities, blogs, or medical information leaflets
- Viewing health- or illness-related films such as documentaries about someone falling ill, full-length movies, TV series, interviews, or short online clips
- Listening to health- or illness-related audio clips such as documentaries, interviews, or online podcasts
- Visiting health- or illness-related places such as hospitals or places with poor access to health care (e.g., taking a walk in the countryside without a mobile phone)
- Physical activity such as running or lifting weights
- Consuming things feared to have negative effects, for example, medicines, nuts, seafood, or particular drinks (this type of exercise is of course done with caution)
- Doing something "magical" (e.g., wearing a cancer awareness pin) feared to increase the risk of developing a serious disease
- Touching one's own body, for example, while conducting a breast self-exam
- Taking a blood pressure test on a "good day," without double-checking afterwards
- Talking or writing about symptoms or disease (e.g., repeatedly saying "cancer" aloud)
- Reading texts, for example, obituaries, which relate to death or dying
- Viewing films or listening to audio clips that relate to death or dying
- Visiting places, such as graveyards or crematoriums, which relate to death or dying
- Writing a legally binding last will

Typically, the therapist would introduce exposure in vivo by saying something like as follows: "As you know firsthand, a problem with health anxiety is that a very large number of situations and things may trigger or increase your health-related fear. From what you have told me, I get the impression that everything from newspaper articles to TV shows or everyday discussions about disease can make you worry about your health and the possibility of having a serious disease. That sounds really awful, and I want to assure you that you are far from alone in having this problem. Unfortunately, if we don't find a way to make it easier for you to face these types of situations, we can be almost certain that your health anxiety will return time and time and time again. Fortunately, exposure in vivo—or exposure to things and situations outside of your own body—is a highly effective technique to deal with this problem. As with all types of exposure, from now on, instead of avoiding the things and situations that you fear, what you need to strive for here is to actively pursue and engage the things you fear. If you do this repeatedly, you will gradually discover that your health anxiety is not evoked as easily, and that your fears do not affect your life as much as they used to do. This, of course, is a long-term process."

As with all forms of exposure, it is of crucial importance that the choice of exercises is grounded in needs of the individual patient. Some patients with a fear of stomach cancer may, for example, use repeated checking for lumps as a means to reduce anxiety and "keep in control," whereas others may cope with a very similar fear by instead refraining from touching their body. It is only in the latter case that touching one's own stomach would be a suitable exposure exercise; in the former case, the "exposure" would in fact be a form of safety behavior likely to produce an increase in health anxiety over time.

It is also important to realize that the function of the patient's behavior may differ over time and over different conditions. To build on our previous example, a common pattern is for the patient to avoid touching his or her stomach so as to not evoke a strong fear of cancer during "good" periods, but once something resembling a lump is found, the very same patient may resort to intensive symptom checking as a strategy to "get to grips with what the symptom is." If this is the case, it would be a good idea for the patient not to avoid touching his or her stomach during "good" periods while also refraining from frequent symptom checks if a new symptom is found. Our experience is that overly simplistic advice, and the failure to recognize patterns similar to this, is one of the most common pitfalls in CBT for health anxiety. We have, for example, met numerous patients who reported being told by their therapist or doctor never to read about symptoms or disease, despite having only used this as a safety behavior under very specific circumstances or even not at all. While it is understandable that such advice is given, because the very same behavior may serve different functions for different people and in different situations, it is important for the therapist to instruct the patient to analyze the function of his or her own behavior and to make distinctions between specific situations. Here follows a list of common examples from CBT for health anxiety where the same behavior serves different functions in different situations:

- Repeated checking of newfound symptoms but avoidance of getting in contact with one's own body where new symptoms could be found
- Intensive information seeking related to current symptoms or feared diseases but avoidance of media feared to contain information about "new" symptoms or diseases
- Use of painkillers to relieve feared stomachache sometimes feared to be cancer but avoidance of painkillers to relieve a headache feared to be an emerging stroke
- Use of physical activity on "good days" so as to prevent cardiovascular disease but avoidance of training in the presence of chest pain so as to avoid a heart attack
- Use of repeated blood pressure tests in the presence of dizziness and nausea but avoidance of blood pressure tests on "good days" so as to not "get a bad result"
- High intake of sweets in order to relieve anxiety when there are no bodily symptoms but strict avoidance of sweets in the presence of numb limbs so as to not develop diabetes
- Careful reading of certain obituaries in an attempt to persuade oneself that people generally live long and healthy lives but avoidance of obituaries where the deceased was in one's own age

As with interoceptive exposure, a key element of in vivo exposure is repetition. It is relatively common, especially if online media is used for exposure, that the patient musters up the courage to confront numerous feared texts and video clips but never takes the time to revisit them. Suppose, for example, that the patient begins the first week of exposure in vivo by reading an entire online blog written by someone who died from a neurological disorder and by watching an entire season of a TV reality series about a hospital intensive care unit. Given that the patient previously avoided such stimuli, this attempt at exposure is certainly a substantial step in the right direction. But it is also important to realize that both the blog and the episodes from the reality series are likely to contain a very large number of triggers for health anxiety. While engaging in exposure is never in and of itself a problem, for many patients, working through these many triggers each week is simply too demanding, and the risk that the patient will drop out of treatment prior to experiencing any beneficial effects is—in our clinical experience—relatively high. In conducting exposure in vivo, we would therefore advise most patients to start small and focus on repetition so as to achieve a sense of progress and change. The patient in the text above could, for example, be encouraged to partition the blog into small text segments that are then repeatedly read over several days so that they become less difficult to handle. In the same way, the patient could be encouraged to consider watching each of the TV episodes as an exposure exercise in its own right and to repeatedly watch each of those episodes that give rise to health anxiety.

Therapists unfamiliar with health anxiety may, like many patients, carry with them a preconceived notion that the aim of in vivo exposure should be to "curb" a current episode of health anxiety by having the patient abstain from everyday avoidance of triggers that frequently show up in the patient's daily life. While this is an excellent place to start, what is easily forgotten is that many typical triggers for health anxiety, such as written information and unfamiliar physical sensations, do not show up very often. It is therefore important for the therapist to ensure that the patient, by engaging in exposure, not only finds a way to abstain from his or her most frequent avoidance behaviors but also engages in exposure to triggers that would otherwise elicit an episode of health anxiety in the future. In metaphoric terms, in vivo exposure for health anxiety may thus oftentimes be compared with the methodical clearance of a minefield, where it is only a matter of time before triggers for health anxiety (e.g., a newspaper article about a "new" serious disease) are activated. If these triggers are dealt with in the context of systematic exposure, there are good chances that the patient quickly learns that they can be handled without long-lasting suffering or loss of control.

As with all anxiety disorders, in working with exposure, it is our experience that it is best to raise the bar as high as possible and encourage the patient to overcompensate in breaking free from avoidance. Just like a patient with snake phobia might be encouraged to let a snake crawl inside his or her shirt and a patient with obsessive-compulsive disorder might be encouraged to purposely make his or her hands dirty, a patient with health anxiety should preferably be instructed to confront situations that would evoke some degree of discomfort for almost anyone. A patient with a fear of having a hidden heart disease and long-standing avoidance of physical activities might, for example, be instructed to ingest a caffeine pill before engaging in heavy physical activity followed by voluntary overbreathing. Similarly, a patient with a fear of having motor neuron disease might be encouraged to deliberately sleep poorly and watch an emotionally gripping documentary about a young person dying from this disease. In other words, exposure should not merely be seen as a way for the patient to "be able to do what most people do," but the patient should be encouraged to actively seek out situations that evoke those emotions and thoughts deemed related to health anxiety.

Imaginal Exposure

Imaginal exposure, or exposure to one's own thoughts and mental images, is an important element of CBT for health anxiety because many of the things most feared by the patient are typically hypothetical scenarios that are unlikely to ever materialize. Common examples include vivid mental images of a tumor growing inside one's head, being told that one has a brain tumor, having to go through chemotherapy, and dying without the opportunity to see one's own children grow up. While it is important to realize that interoceptive or in vivo exposure also includes an integral component of exposure to thoughts (a patient with a fear of contracting a heart attack and that engages in physical activity may, for example, have mental images of the coronary arteries being blocked), these thoughts are often fleeting and not the focal point of the exposure. Imaginal exposure allows the patient to confront his or her most feared thoughts more fully, and may thereby contribute substantially to the overall treatment effect. Sometimes, imaginal exposure could also be used as a first step toward a strongly feared in vivo exercise. A patient with a strong fear of going to the doctor might, for example, first practice by imagining going to the doctor, before actually doing so.

As described by Furer and Walker (2005), a powerful approach to imaginal exposure is to have the patient write a short text where the things that he or she fears the most eventually come true. A patient with an excessive fear of developing dementia may, for example, write a story about gradually losing touch with reality, being diagnosed with Alzheimer's disease, having to rely on others for personal hygiene, eventually becoming weaker, and ultimately dying. Such an "illness story" may then be repeatedly edited and read so as to allow for the patient to get in contact with his or her most feared thoughts and mental images as fully as possible.

> *A typical rationale for imaginal exposure would be as follows: "From what you have told me, it seems as if you fear not only your symptoms in themselves, but also your thoughts about your health and what might happen in the future. This is a common problem, and most persons with health anxiety try to deal with this problem by doing everything to get away from the thoughts and inner images that they fear. But as you now know, this simply won't work in the long run, but instead ensures that these thoughts remain very strongly emotionally charged. In*

other words, in order for you to become less worried about your health, we need to find a way for you to confront the thoughts and mental images that you fear the most. This is what we usually refer to as 'imaginal exposure'."

In our experience, it is best to encourage the patient to write as realistic as possible in the sense that even though the illness story represents "the worst-case scenario," the patient gets a feeling that the scenario described in the text could really happen. For example, we always advise our patients to write in present or future tense, to vividly describe their own physical and emotional reactions, and to use the real everyday names of their friends and family members.

An obvious strategy to optimize the effect of working with an illness story is to ask the patient what he or she fears the most and then ensure that this is represented in the text. Here, the so-called "downward arrow" technique could be of use, where the patient is methodically asked to express the meaning of or identify the ultimate and most unwanted consequences of having or developing a disease (Salkovkskis, 2007). Another technique that is often helpful in increasing the usefulness of the illness story is to have the patient read a first draft of the story and then encourage the patient to expand those parts of the text that are experienced as most emotionally charged. For example, if the patient reports being most shaken up by the phrase "Claire is crying," the therapist could suggest that the illness story is revised so that Claire's reaction is described in more detail.

Sometimes, the thing that the patient finds most disturbing about writing an illness story is not the catastrophic beliefs expressed therein, but rather that the act of writing them down might somehow make the catastrophic scenarios more likely to materialize in real life. Although this is often a distressing prospect, it should not be considered as a proper reason to abstain from writing an illness story. On the contrary, in these cases, imaginal exposure may be seen as particularly suitable, since this strategy will allow the patient to disprove key dysfunctional assumptions about the thoughts themselves (e.g., that thinking about having a particular illness will increase the risk of acquiring it). In these cases, it might be helpful for the patient if the therapist models imaginal exposure by creating an own illness story and reading it to the patient.

Individuals with health anxiety typically have a high, in some cases extreme, intolerance of uncertainty or inability to cope with situations where the outcome is unclear (Deacon & Abramowitz, 2008). For some, this problem is so pronounced that the distress from *not knowing* whether or not one has a particular disease far exceeds the imagined distress from actually being diagnosed with this disease. Many who fall under this category also use planning or "thinking through what could happen" as a strategy to cope with and try to reduce the uncertainty in their lives. In these cases, the risk is that by writing an illness story about being diagnosed with a feared disease, the patient may not achieve the sought-after exposure effect, but may instead temporarily reduce the feeling of uncertainty about the future and thereby reinforce his or her fear. A patient with a recurrent fear of having contracted HIV/AIDS may, for example, find it remarkably comforting to imagine being told that he or she indeed has this disease ("at least then, I will be able to do something about it, and I know modern medications are effective") or even dying from its complications ("as long as I would know in advance, I'm sure that I would manage"). Such a patient may, for example, instead find it almost unbearable to imagine having to wait for a medical test result that is accidentally lost, without ever being given a diagnosis or knowing anything about the future. As with all forms of exposure, it is important that imaginal exposure exercises are tailor-made for the patient and grounded in functional analysis.

Response Prevention

As described in Chapters 1 and 4, safety behaviors or behaviors that serve to reduce health anxiety in the short term exacerbate health anxiety over time. There are probably several reasons for this. For example, safety behaviors may lead to an increased focus on bodily functions and health, they may lead to a priming effect where illness-related thoughts are more easily evoked, they may prevent the patient from disproving dysfunctional health-related beliefs, and they may keep the patient from learning more adaptive behavioral responses. They may also directly cause or worsen bodily symptoms, such as when pinching and scratching leads to inflammation of the skin or dietary changes lead to disturbances in the bowel functions. Due to the detrimental effects of safety behaviors, response prevention is an integral part of CBT for health anxiety, and we advise that response prevention is applied whenever safety behaviors are identified. Safety behaviors typically fall into one of the three following categories:

1. *Checking behaviors related to symptoms, physical sensations, or bodily functions*

   These are behaviors that aim to monitor bodily processes or to determine the cause behind—or characteristics of—physical sensations or bodily symptoms.

Examples include pulse checking, blood pressure checks, visual inspection of the body (e.g., skin lesions or eyes), repeated touching and pinching, comparison of body halves, physical exercise as a way to assess bodily functions, inspection of feces and urine, neurological tests, evaluation of muscle strength, evaluation of visual disturbances, coughing or taking deep breaths to evaluate throat soreness or lung capacity, use of a journal to record symptoms, and repeated weight checks.

2. *Reassurance-seeking behaviors*

   These are behaviors that serve to collect information from others pertaining to bodily processes, physical sensations, bodily symptoms, health, or disease states.

   Examples include going to the doctor, discussing symptoms or diseases with friends or family members, comparing one's symptoms with those of others, calling medical services, and reading about symptoms or diseases on the Internet or in books.

3. *Preventive behaviors*

   These are behaviors that aim to prevent future health anxiety, illness, or bad health.

   Examples include reading up on "health tips" (e.g., with regard to food intake or training), taking unnecessary supplements, avoiding particular foods or drinks, carrying medical equipment or personal medical information, planning trips and researching destinations so as to minimize the risk of not being able to access health care, always ensuring that someone else is present, informing friends or relatives about one's whereabouts, leaving doors open or unlocked so that help can arrive in time, using or carrying anxiolytic medicine, and always carrying a mobile phone.

Since most individuals with health anxiety have relied on numerous safety behaviors for a long period of time, reaching an acceptable level of response prevention is likely to take at least a couple of months of hard work. We would therefore advise that response prevention is introduced as early in treatment as possible, and that it is maintained for the duration of the treatment as well as after treatment termination. In other words, response prevention is meant to be a long-term commitment, rather than something that the patient "tries out" for a limited period of time.

The therapist may introduce response prevention by saying something like the following: "As we have already talked about, the more you rely on short-term strategies to keep your anxiety under control and try to prevent or rule out the possibility of being ill, the more your health anxiety will increase over time. It is therefore

> *important that you find a way to gradually reduce and abstain from your safety behaviors. This is a process known as 'response prevention', and something that we will work with every time that we meet for the remainder of the treatment. You will also continue with response prevention long after this treatment is complete.*
>
> *So, what we will have to do is first to write a list of your safety behaviors. Once we have this preliminary overview, you will get the opportunity to set your own goals for how to gradually, step by step, get rid of these behaviors that maintain your anxiety over time. So each time we meet, the idea is that we will check up on how well you are able to reach your goals and you will be able to revise them if you want. In most cases, what we will have to aim for is that you reach a point where you simply don't do the behavior anymore. There are of course important exceptions, such as health-care seeking, but this is the general rule of thumb. I will try my best to support you in your work and encourage you to take the next step whenever you are ready to do so."*

Setting short-term goals is arguably the most important and challenging element of response prevention, and we would like to stress three aspects of this process. First, our experience is that it is of crucial importance that the patient understands the purpose of response prevention and takes an active role in the choice and continuous revision of short-term goals. Not only is this likely to make response prevention more meaningful for the patient, but this is also likely to increase the chances of beneficial long-term effects. Given that most individuals with health anxiety fear different diseases for different periods of time, it is only natural that they also engage in different sets of safety behaviors for different periods of time (depending on which symptom or disease that they worry about). For example, the same person may first primarily be scared of having rectal cancer and check his or her feces for blood and then primarily be scared of having multiple sclerosis and perform multiple neurological tests. Therefore, having the patient understand the general principle of response prevention rather than merely instructing the patient to abstain from particular behaviors is important because this allows the patient to identify new safety behaviors and abstain from these also after treatment termination.

Second, all short-term goals for response prevention should be as specific and mood-independent as possible. Many patients intuitively prefer to abandon their safety behaviors "little by little," without any particular short- or even long-term goals in mind. Others intuitively propose the use of different goals depending on their level of anxiety (e.g., to wait 5 days before calling the doctor on good weeks, while waiting only 15 min before calling the doctor on weeks with high levels of health anxiety). While such approaches might work for some, the risk is that patients may revert to safety behaviors when their health anxiety is most pronounced and that they will be more inclined to give in to the urge to perform safety behaviors if there is no clearly decided "least acceptable level" of response prevention to strive toward. Setting different goals for "high-anxiety" versus "low-anxiety" periods of time is of course also a subtle safety behavior that ultimately needs to be challenged. In other words, it is usually best to set very clear short-term goals, for example, to "wait at least 1 week before acting on the urge to ask someone about the pain in my elbow," which also apply regardless of anxiety level.

Third, short-term goals should always be challenging but yet possible for the patient to reach. To ensure that the patient continuously "pushes the boundaries" for what he or she can handle, it is important to routinely encourage the patient to take the next step in response prevention. If the patient is reluctant to refrain from engaging in safety behaviors, this should be openly discussed in an objective manner that does not leave the patient with a feeling of guilt, but that nevertheless makes it clear that a reduction in safety behaviors is necessary so as to achieve a substantial treatment effect. Our experience is that it is usually best to leave with the patient the decision to go further or not. Just like the patient not being willing to abstain from safety behaviors may become a problem, it is likewise of no use to stick with ambitious goals if these are not met in practice. In such cases, we advise that the therapist and patient work together to find new goals that are challenging but yet acceptable to the patient, and possible for the patient to meet also under the most difficult circumstances.

In the case of most safety behaviors, the patient could be encouraged either to abstain from the behavior altogether, to reduce the frequency of the behavior (e.g., maximum of three pulse checks per day), or to wait for a particular period of time from intuitively wanting to perform the behavior to actually doing so (e.g., wait 2 h before every pulse check). Ultimately, the goal should be to achieve a very high level of response prevention, which then, as already mentioned, is maintained also after treatment termination. For example, our experience is that it is typically not sufficient to reduce checking behaviors without ever reaching the point where the patient abstains from these entirely. Therefore, we advise that the overarching goal of "total response prevention" should be clearly conveyed to the patient as a mere matter of course, as early as possible. There are, however, important exceptions. One such exception is medical consultations, where patients with this as a safety behavior may be encouraged to always wait for a particular period of time (e.g., 3 weeks) before contacting medical care due to vague new symptoms. Other common exceptions include women's breast and men's testicular self-exams, which are usually recommended by medical agencies to be performed about once a month.

In many cases, the most potent safety behaviors are processes in the patient's head, rather than behaviors in the everyday sense. These mental strategies can typically be understood as corresponding to one of the three types of safety behaviors already presented or constitute some other types of avoidance. In other words, attempts at monitoring physical sensations may be thought of as "internal" checking behavior, repeated attempts to persuade oneself that the risk of developing a severe disease is small may be seen as a special case of reassurance seeking, carefully thinking through the best travel route and planning how to best get in contact with medical care may be regarded as a mental form of preventive behavior, and distraction from frightening thoughts may be seen as a special case of avoidance. Totally abstaining from such "mental safety behaviors" is usually not a feasible goal, but it is usually possible for the patient to abstain to some degree. Through the use of proper exposure exercises, the patient's catastrophic fears will also become less emotionally charged, which gradually makes it easier for the patient not to worry about his or her health.

Another common challenge to response prevention is that the patient may be so used to performing certain safety behaviors that it, simply due to the "force of habit," becomes very difficult to abstain from these. Typical examples of this would be patients who frequently check their pulse, patients who regularly examine their skin in the mirror, and patients who have fallen into the habit of examining their feces. Our experience is that it is usually best to keep encouraging the patient to meet the intended goals insofar as this is possible, but yet acknowledge that it is common to perform certain behaviors without any conscious intent or purposeful effort. The patient may also be instructed to act in ways that make it more difficult to perform certain safety behaviors or that is incompatible with performing these. A patient who regularly performs pulse checks may, for example, initially be encouraged to purposely place his or her hands on the thighs rather than in the lap while sitting, so as to make it more difficult to perform pulse checks. Similarly, a patient who regularly examines his or her skin in the mirror may be encouraged to—for a period of time—use smaller mirrors and wear clothes that cover the skin so as to not make it so easy to check himself or herself for signs of skin cancer. Another strategy to get to grips with "impulsive" safety behaviors is to conduct exposure exercises that target the same type of fears and emotions that forego the behavior. It is, for example, often much easier to abstain from pulse checks after having properly worked through interoceptive exposure.

Getting the Most Out of Exposure Treatment

Determining the Length of the Treatment

It is typically necessary to work with exposure—that is, response prevention in conjunction with interoceptive, in vivo, and/or imaginal exercises—on a daily basis for at least 2 or 3 months to achieve the maximum effects. In general terms, research suggests that longer treatments (i.e., treatments with more sessions) give better results (Olatunji et al., 2014) but the time needed to respond and the trajectory of change vary substantially from patient to patient (e.g., Hedman et al., 2014). While some patients report "feeling like a whole new person" after a mere couple of weeks of CBT, others struggle for months with making the necessary behavior changes and feel highly distressed by doing so before eventually improving gradually. Still others, do not improve at all. As pointed out above, we know little about predictors of long-term treatment effect, and it is not uncommon to be surprised (either positively or negatively) at how a particular patient approaches the treatment and tries to tackle common challenges as these arise. Given the difficult nature of predicting precisely what the patient has to gain from carrying on with CBT, we advise that determining the length of treatment should be a collaborative process, where it is important to take heed of not only symptom levels and health anxiety behaviors but also the contextual factors, the history and resources, and the goals and wishes of the patient. While there might be many justifiable reasons to impose a time limit on the treatment (e.g., financial), in general, we see no reason to decide the length of treatment a priori. Because research suggests that longer treatments give better results, we would however advise therapists to remember and to convey to patients that CBT for health anxiety is a long-term venture that cannot be evaluated prior to at least couple of months of working with the treatment strategies. We would expect 3 months to suffice for most, such as in one study where we saw that 12 weeks of CBT were enough for 80% of patients with DSM-IV hypochondriasis to not meet diagnostic criteria at 6-month follow-up (Hedman et al., 2011). But, again, the length of the treatment should ideally be determined in collaboration with the patient over the course of the treatment.

Preparing for Exposure and Increasing the Motivation for Change

Our experience is that most patients are willing and able to conduct exposure, including interoceptive exercises, on their own and not merely together with the therapist. But for this to work, it is necessary to plan ahead and always be very explicit about the direction and focus of the treatment and to convey to the patient that the beneficial effects of exposure will be seen over time. Exposure exercises should preferably be planned in a collaborative manner, so that the patient feels involved and is as likely as possible to work with the treatment, regardless of short-term fluctuations in mood and motivation. The patient should also be encouraged to evaluate progress based on long-term changes in behavior, rather than fluctuations in mood from day to day or week to week.

In order to determine which exposure exercises are worth pursuing, we suggest the use of the subjective units of distress (SUD) scale. In plain language, this is the straightforward practice of having the patient rate his or her momentary level of anxiety on a scale from 0 to 10 or 0 to 100. As a rule of thumb, we encourage our patients to work with exposure exercises that have an SUD score of 20/100 or higher and to repeat these exercises until they have an SUD score below 20. Even though recent studies suggest that habituation to triggers for anxiety may in and of itself be a poor predictor of treatment effect (Craske, Treanor, Conway, Zbozinek, & Vervliet, 2014), we argue that the common practice of using SUD scores and habituation rationales serves the function of keeping the patient focused on working with exercises and seeking out situations that has some relevance to their anxiety disorder. Having the patient predict how strongly he or she will react to particular exposure exercises may also evoke thoughts about possible outcomes of these exercises and thereby induce more pronounced violations of the patient's expectancies, which in turn may increase the effect of exposure (Craske et al., 2014). In some cases, the patient may however have great difficulty in using numbers to quantify the intensity of his or her emotional response. An alternative to the SUD could be to use a simplified scale (e.g., with short words or labels, colors, or happy and sad faces) so as to make it possible to compare exercises and determine which of these are worth prioritizing.

Whereas most clinicians and researchers have traditionally recommended that in CBT for anxiety disorders, putative exposure exercises should initially be ranked by SUD score to form a hierarchy where the least anxiety-inducing exercises are done first (i.e., graded exposure), recent studies suggest that the order in which exercises are done may not be important for the treatment effect (e.g., Kircanski et al., 2012). We would nevertheless typically advise that exposure is approached in a graded manner, if only to prevent treatment attrition. At the same time, our experience is that the pacing of the treatment is often best left with the patient and that he or she should generally not be discouraged from conducting challenging exposure exercises early on if he or she wishes to do so. Dissuading the patient from confronting key triggers for anxiety may in unfortunate cases signal to the patient that these are worth avoiding or being cautious of, reinforce patient's dysfunctional assumptions about health or disease, and also lower the patient's commitment to, and sense of self-efficacy with regard to working with, exposure in general. Knowing when to "push the patient forward" (e.g., by suggesting more difficult goals for response prevention) and when to "stand back" and give the patient time to recover or adapt is one of the most difficult aspects of exposure-based CBT for health anxiety.

The Importance of a Good Therapeutic Relationship

A relatively common misconception about exposure-based CBT, not least among patients, is that the treatment is characterized by heavy discipline, brute correction, and a long series of forceful instructions from the therapist. Nothing could be further from the truth. While it is certainly the case that exposure can be challenging at times and that it is oftentimes helpful to be organized in confronting triggers for anxiety, the ideal therapeutic relationship is one of compassion, truthfulness, and collaboration. As previously suggested, the relationship should as much as possible be built on mutual trust, not least so that the patient feels comfortable with discussing his or her innermost fears. The therapist should strive to meet the patient as an equal, and it is our experience that the common challenges of exposure are easiest overcome when there has been a strong emphasis on "working as a team" in the early phase of treatment. Although, as pointed out, studies on predictors of treatment effect in CBT for health anxiety have come to contradictory results, at least two studies have investigated the role of the therapeutic alliance and indicated that stronger alliance is associated with larger treatment effects (Hedman et al., 2015; Weck, Richtberg, Jakob, Neng, & Hofling, 2015).

Refraining from Reassuring the Patient

Prior to seeking psychological treatment, patients with health anxiety have usually devoted a large amount of time and effort to determining the cause of their symptoms, and it is common that the patient repeatedly asks the therapist to decide if his or her physical sensations are "only psychological" or not. We would argue that the ideal way of managing these situations is generally not to reassure the patient, but rather to abstain from answering the question and instead validate the patient's sense of distress and to acknowledge that the cause of the patient's symptoms can never be determined with absolute certainty. There are three main reasons for us suggesting this approach. First, strictly speaking, it is simply true that one can never know with 100% certainty that the patient does not suffer from a serious disease. It could therefore be argued to be unethical—especially in cases where the therapist lacks proper medical training—to insinuate otherwise. Second, while in many cases a plausible explanation for the patient's symptoms may be given—for example, that they arise from autonomic arousal, long-term stress, or a temporary infection—the way that a particular symptom is experienced always depends on both psychological processes and physiological changes. That is, even in cases of severe disease states such as lung cancer and neurological disorders, psychological factors such as the attention given to symptoms may affect how a symptom (e.g., aches and pains or shortness of breath) is perceived. Likewise, even in cases of common psychiatric disorders such as depression and panic disorder, the patient's symptoms are of course very much related to changes in the brain and other physical processes. The third and most important reason for us suggesting that the therapist should not reassure the patient about symptoms being "psychological" or "all in the head" is that reassurance seeking typically serves as a safety behavior that, like other safety behaviors, is likely to exacerbate the patient's health anxiety over time. If the therapist instead empathically reiterates that the cause of the patient's symptoms strictly speaking *could* be a serious disease and reminds the patient about the detrimental effects of reassurance seeking, this is more likely to help the patient in breaking free from health anxiety and getting to grips with his or her symptoms over time.

Worry About Others and the Fear of Death

It is not uncommon that individuals who fear having or acquiring a severe disease also worry about the health of their friends and family members. It is, for example, not uncommon for patients with health anxiety to closely monitor the symptoms of their children or persuade their partners to seek health care faster and more often. While some patients do not see this as a problem, others consider their fear for the health of their loved ones to equal or even overshadow their fear for their own medical status. This is of course important to address in therapy, and can be addressed with the same strategies that are used in the treatment of fear for one's own health.

Another topic that we always make an attempt to address is the fear of death and dying. Whereas some with health anxiety see their fear of dying as the most significant aspect of their problem, others do not fear death at all (but rather other outcomes, such as severe functional impairment). As suggested above, a method to deal with a fear of dying is to conduct in vivo exposure exercises such as reading obituaries or visiting cemeteries. Another possibility is to work with imaginal exposure, for example, by writing about dying from a serious disease. In finding the proper exposure exercises, it is important to realize that different thoughts and aspects related to death and dying may be frightening to different people. Some patients primarily fear not knowing how dying will be like, some do not want to leave their family members without support, others may have strong spiritual understanding of what it means to die, and still others may react with strong emotion to the thought of being physically disintegrated or to thoughts of infinity and the idea that "everything goes black."

Addressing Comorbid Anxiety Disorders

Approximately 30% of individuals with health anxiety also meet criteria for at least one other anxiety disorder or obsessive-compulsive disorder (Sunderland, Newby, & Andrews, 2013). It is our clinical impression that in routine clinical care and at least in cases of comorbid panic disorder or obsessive-compulsive disorder, exposure-based therapy for health anxiety can be pursued in a seamless fashion in the sense that it is possible to address both disorders (e.g., health anxiety and panic disorder) without the need to use separate rationales or make a big issue about the patient meeting criteria for two disorders. There is some evidence in support of this approach (Noyes, Reich, Clancy, & O'Gorman, 1986), which has the advantage of making it easier for the patient to take in the psychoeducative segment of the treatment. This, in turn, may lead to more time being spent with exposure, and may increase the chances that the patient will generalize the principles of exposure with response prevention to more situations.

Mindfulness as a Method of Enhancing Exposure

As already mentioned, it is common that mental strategies function as safety behaviors in that they maintain the patient's health anxiety over time. In other words, in engaging in exposure, it is beneficial for the patient to, as much as possible, abstain from such mental strategies as distraction, attempts at convincing oneself that there is "nothing to worry about," and "thinking through" the causes of somatic symptoms. One way of facilitating this process is to incorporate secularized mindfulness training in the early phase of the treatment. We usually encourage the patient to practice mindfulness for at least 10 min per day through a basic exercise where the aim is to increase the skill of observing thoughts and somatic sensations without trying to alter them. In the beginning, the patient is instructed to practice mindfulness when feeling relatively calm, but as the treatment progresses, mindfulness practice is used during exposure, that is, when the patient feels highly anxious.

Relapse Prevention and Booster sessions

Given that health anxiety typically has a tendency to wax and wane, it is very much advisable to devote the last segment of the treatment to planning for the future, decreasing the risk of a possible relapse, and ensuring that the patient is comfortable with continuing the treatment without further support by the therapist. Given that beneficial effects of relapse prevention and booster components have been convincingly demonstrated in the case of obsessive-compulsive disorder (Andersson et al., 2014; Hiss, Foa, & Kozak, 1994), it is also likely that this pattern would generalize to health anxiety. Relapse prevention should ideally be integrated into CBT for health anxiety from day one in the sense that a long-term perspective on exposure and health anxiety is adopted, and that the patient takes an active role in the treatment so that it follows naturally for the patient to continue working independently with the treatment strategies also after treatment termination. In the final phase of CBT, it is also helpful to discuss possible future challenges and encourage the patient to imagine different scenarios that could arise over the following weeks or months, so as to prepare for these. For each likely future obstacle to carrying on with the treatment strategies, it is advisable to develop some sort of concrete plan. It is, for example, common to consider the possibility of discovering some new type of unfamiliar physical sensation, and a common plan to handle this situation is to keep a bundle of work sheets for planning response prevention and to instruct a family member to help with remembering the long-term benefits of exposure with response prevention. In the later stages of treatment, it is also advisable to expand on exposure by systematically varying establishing operations (i.e., the conditions that determine the difficulty of particular attempts at exposure with response prevention). A patient who reports feeling especially prone to worrying about health if being hungry could, for example, deliberately abstain from eating lunch and instead conduct some sort of exposure exercise, so as to become better at tackling this also under the most difficult of conditions. This may then contribute to protect the patient against future relapse under similar conditions (starting to worry partly as a consequence of being hungry) in his or her everyday life. In other words, oftentimes, working with exposure in a creative manner is also the best form of relapse prevention.

Summary and Conclusion

CBT, which is based in learning and cognitive theory, is the most well-researched psychological treatment for health anxiety, and its efficacy has been established in at least 15 randomized controlled trials. A thorough assessment in the form of a descriptive case formulation and functional analysis of the patient's idiosyncratic health anxiety behaviors is a foundation for successful treatment. The most commonly used components of CBT for health anxiety are psychoeducation, cognitive restructuring, and exposure with response prevention. Through psychoeducation, the patient learns about the mechanisms of health anxiety, and this part of the treatment also sets the stage for subsequent behavior change. Cognitive restructuring techniques are used to correct faulty appraisals related to health and are typically done either through logical reasoning or by behavioral experiments in which the validity of the negative thoughts is tested. Exposure, which is the main focus of this chapter, can broadly be categorized into interoceptive, in vivo, or imaginal. Interoceptive exposure means that the patient systematically approaches feared bodily sensations, whereas in vivo exposure refers to confronting external situations or events, such as visiting a cemetery or reading about disease or death. Imaginal exposure is to actively trigger and stay in contact with feared thoughts or images related to health anxiety. In order for exposure exercises to yield the desired effect, it is essential that they are rooted in the functional analysis of the individual patient. This is because a given behavior might be effective exposure for one patient but constitute a counterproductive avoidance behavior for another. It is important to combine exposure with response prevention, that is, to refrain from safety behaviors, such as checking one's body for symptoms and reassurance seeking. Mindfulness practice could be used to increase the motivation for and efficiency of exposure as it provides a means for coping with aversive emotional experiences. Exposure-based CBT is a demanding treatment that requires the patient to confront their fears in a systematic fashion for about 3 months. However, exposure can also be highly rewarding and lead to the remission of symptoms and increased quality of life.

References

Abramowitz, J. S., & Braddock, A. E. (2008). *Psychological treatment of health anxiety and hypochondriasis: A biopsychological approach*. Cambridge, MA: Hogrefe & Huber Publishers.

Andersson, E., Steneby, S., Karlsson, K., Ljótsson, B., Hedman, E., Enander, J., & Rück, C. (2014). Long-term efficacy of internet-based cognitive behavior therapy for obsessive-compulsive disorder with or without booster: a randomized controlled trial. *Psychological Medicine*, *44*(13), 2877–2887. https://doi.org/10.1017/s0033291714000543.

Asmundson, G. J. G., & Taylor, S. (2005). *It's not all in your head: How worrying about your health could be making you sick—and what you can do about it*. New York: The Guilford Press.

Bennett-Levy, J., Westbrook, D., Fennell, M., Cooper, M., Rouf, K., & Hackmann, A. (2004). Behavioural experiments: Historical and conceptual underpinnings. In J. Bennett-Levy, G. Butler, M. Fennell, A. Hackmann, M. Mueller, & D. Westbrook (Eds.), *Oxford guide to behavioural experiments in cognitive therapy* (pp. 1–20). Oxford, UK: Oxford University Press.

Borkovec, T. D., & Nau, S. D. (1972). Credibility of analogue therapy rationales. *Journal of Behavior Therapy and Experimental Psychiatry*, *3*(4), 257–260.

Buwalda, F. M., Bouman, T. K., & van Duijn, M. A. (2007). Psychoeducation for hypochondriasis: A comparison of a cognitive-behavioural approach and a problem-solving approach. *Behaviour Research and Therapy*, *45*(5), 887–899. https://doi.org/10.1016/j.brat.2006.08.004.

Cooper, K., Gregory, J. D., Walker, I., Lambe, S., & Salkovskis, P. M. (2017). Cognitive behaviour therapy for health anxiety: A systematic review and meta-analysis. *Behavioural and Cognitive Psychotherapy*, *45*(2), 110–123. https://doi.org/10.1017/s1352465816000527.

Craske, M. G., Kircanski, K., Zelikowsky, M., Mystkowski, J., Chowdhury, N., & Baker, A. (2008). Optimizing inhibitory learning during exposure therapy. *Behaviour Research and Therapy*, *46*(1), 5–27. https://doi.org/10.1016/j.brat.2007.10.003.

Craske, M. G., Treanor, M., Conway, C. C., Zbozinek, T., & Vervliet, B. (2014). Maximizing exposure therapy: An inhibitory learning approach. *Behaviour Research and Therapy*, *58*, 10–23. https://doi.org/10.1016/j.brat.2014.04.006.

Deacon, B., & Abramowitz, J. S. (2008). Is hypochondriasis related to obsessive-compulsive disorder, panic disorder, or both? An empirical evaluation. *Journal of Cognitive Psychotherapy*, *22*(2), 115–127.

Deacon, B. J., & Farrell, N. R. (2013). Therapist barriers to the dissemination of exposure therapy. In *Handbook of treating variants and complications in anxiety disorders*. New York: Springer.

Foa, E. B., & Kozak, M. J. (1986). Emotional processing of fear: Exposure to corrective information. *Psychological Bulletin*, *99*(1), 20–35.

Furer, P., & Walker, J. R. (2005). Treatment of hypochondriasis with exposure. *Journal of Contemporary Psychotherapy*, *35*(3), 251–267.

Hedman, E., Andersson, G., Andersson, E., Ljótsson, B., Rück, C., Asmundson, G. J., & Lindefors, N. (2011). Internet-based cognitive-behavioural therapy for severe health anxiety: Randomised controlled trial. *The British Journal of Psychiatry*, *198*(3), 230–236. https://doi.org/10.1192/bjp.bp.110.086843.

Hedman, E., Andersson, E., Lekander, M., & Ljótsson, B. (2015). Predictors in internet-delivered cognitive behavior therapy and behavioral stress management for severe health anxiety. *Behaviour Research and Therapy*, *64*, 49–55. https://doi.org/10.1016/j.brat.2014.11.009.

Hedman, E., & Axelsson, E. (2017). Severe health anxiety in the treatment of somatic symptoms and related disorders. In J. S. Abramowitz, E. Storch, & D. McKay (Eds.), *Empirically supported treatments* (pp. 345–359). Chichester, UK: Wiley Press.

Hedman, E., Lekander, M., Ljótsson, B., Lindefors, N., Rück, C., Hofmann, S. G., & Schulz, S. M. (2014). Sudden gains in internet-based cognitive behaviour therapy for severe health anxiety. *Behaviour Research and Therapy*, *54*, 22–29. https://doi.org/10.1016/j.brat.2013.12.007.

Hedman, E., Lindefors, N., Andersson, G., Andersson, E., Lekander, M., Rück, C., & Ljótsson, B. (2013). Predictors of outcome in internet-based cognitive behavior therapy for severe health anxiety. *Behaviour Research and Therapy*, *51*(10), 711–717. https://doi.org/10.1016/j.brat.2013.07.009.

Hembree, E. A., Foa, E. B., Dorfan, N. M., Street, G. P., Kowalski, J., & Tu, X. (2003). Do patients drop out prematurely from exposure therapy for PTSD? *Journal of Traumatic Stress*, *16*(6), 555–562. https://doi.org/10.1023/B:JOTS.0000004078.93012.7d.

Hiss, H., Foa, E. B., & Kozak, M. J. (1994). Relapse prevention program for treatment of obsessive-compulsive disorder. *Journal of Consulting and Clinical Psychology*, *62*(4), 801–808.

Kircanski, K., Mortazavi, A., Castriotta, N., Baker, A. S., Mystkowski, J. L., Yi, R., & Craske, M. G. (2012). Challenges to the traditional exposure paradigm: Variability in exposure therapy for contamination fears. *Journal of Behavior Therapy and Experimental Psychiatry*, *43*(2), 745–751. https://doi.org/10.1016/j.jbtep.2011.10.010.

National institute for health and clinical excellence. (2011). *Generalised anxiety disorder and panic disorder (with or without agoraphobia) in adults.*

Noyes, R., Reich, J., Clancy, J., & O'Gorman, T. W. (1986). Reduction in hypochondriasis with treatment of panic disorder. *The British Journal of Psychiatry*, *149*, 631–635.

Olatunji, B. O., Cisler, J. M., & Deacon, B. J. (2010). Efficacy of cognitive behavioral therapy for anxiety disorders: A review of meta-analytic findings. *The Psychiatric Clinics of North America*, *33*(3), 557–577. https://doi.org/10.1016/j.psc.2010.04.002.

Olatunji, B. O., Kauffman, B. Y., Meltzer, S., Davis, M. L., Smits, J. A., & Powers, M. B. (2014). Cognitive-behavioral therapy for hypochondriasis/health anxiety: a meta-analysis of treatment outcome and moderators. *Behaviour Research and Therapy*, *58*, 65–74. https://doi.org/10.1016/j.brat.2014.05.002.

Salkovkskis, P. M. (2007). Psychological treatment of obsessive-compulsive disorder. *Psychiatry*, *8*, 229–233.

Salkovskis, P. M., Rimes, K. A., Warwick, H. M., & Clark, D. M. (2002). The health anxiety inventory: development and validation of scales for the measurement of health anxiety and hypochondriasis. *Psychological Medicine*, *32*(5), 843–853.

Salkovskis, P. M., & Warwick, H. M. (1986). Morbid preoccupations, health anxiety and reassurance: A cognitive-behavioural approach to hypochondriasis. *Behaviour Research and Therapy*, *24*(5), 597–602.

Sunderland, M., Newby, J. M., & Andrews, G. (2013). Health anxiety in Australia: prevalence, comorbidity, disability and service use. *The British Journal of Psychiatry*, *202*(1), 56–61. https://doi.org/10.1192/bjp.bp.111.103960.

Taylor, S., & Asmundson, G. J. G. (2004). *Treating health anxiety: A cognitive-behavioral approach*. New York: Guilford Press.

Visser, S., & Bouman, T. K. (2001). The treatment of hypochondriasis: exposure plus response prevention vs cognitive therapy. *Behaviour Research and Therapy*, *39*(4), 423–442.

Warwick, H. M., & Salkovskis, P. M. (1990). Hypochondriasis. *Behaviour Research and Therapy, 28*(2), 105–117.
Weck, F., Nagel, L. C., Höfling, V., & Neng, J. M. B. (2017). Cognitive therapy and exposure therapy for hypochondriasis (health anxiety): a 3-year naturalistic follow-up. *Journal of Consulting and Clinical Psychology, 85*(10), 1012–1017. https://doi.org/10.1037/ccp0000239.
Weck, F., Neng, J. M., Richtberg, S., Jakob, M., & Stangier, U. (2014). Cognitive therapy versus exposure therapy for hypochondriasis (health anxiety): a randomized controlled trial. *Journal of Consulting and Clinical Psychology*. https://doi.org/10.1037/ccp0000013.
Weck, F., Neng, J. M., Schwind, J., & Höfling, V. (2015). Exposure therapy changes dysfunctional evaluations of somatic symptoms in patients with hypochondriasis (health anxiety). A randomized controlled trial. *Journal of Anxiety Disorders, 34*, 1–7. https://doi.org/10.1016/j.janxdis.2015.05.008.
Weck, F., Richtberg, S., Jakob, M., Neng, J. M., & Höfling, V. (2015). Therapist competence and therapeutic alliance are important in the treatment of health anxiety (hypochondriasis). *Psychiatry Research, 228*(1), 53–58. https://doi.org/10.1016/j.psychres.2015.03.042.

CHAPTER SEVEN

Acceptance and Commitment Therapy for Health Anxiety

Ditte Hoffmann*, Charlotte U. Rask† and Lisbeth Frostholm*
*The Research Clinic for Functional Disorders and Psychosomatics, Aarhus University Hospital, Aarhus, Denmark
†Research Unit, Department of Child and Adolescent Psychiatry, Aarhus University Hospital, Skejby, Denmark

The Rationale of Acceptance and Commitment Therapy

Acceptance and commitment therapy (ACT) is a so-called "third wave" behavioral therapy, which is part of the cognitive behavioral tradition, but differs from it in at least two important areas (Pielech, Vowles, & Wicksell, 2017): First, there is a strong focus on value-based actions in ACT. While this is not unique for ACT, the centrality is distinctive. Second, in ACT, there are specific assumptions regarding the leading role of human language and cognition for the development and perpetuation of mental health problems. Overall, ACT poses two questions: What do you want your life to be about? And what is stopping you?

ACT is based on the philosophy of *pragmatism* and a scientific theoretical approach called *functional contextualism* (Fox, 2006; Hayes, Strosahl, & Wilson, 2012). Contextualism emphasizes that human behaviors (including thoughts, feelings, and bodily sensations) are conditioned in a specific historical and personal context. Therefore, to understand a given behavior, the context should always be considered. Pragmatism emphasizes that the workability of a given behavior should be evaluated against what works, which in ACT is operationalized as the ability of the behavior to move the individual *toward* a better life.

ACT theory distinguishes between clean pain and dirty pain. Clean pain relates to the universal experience of pain in life such as separation, conflict, illness, and loss of loved ones etc. Dirty pain relates to humans' tendency to, if possible, seek immediate relief from clean pain by the use of various control and avoidance strategies. ACT focuses on increasing workable actions from the before-mentioned pragmatic stance, when pain is present, as inner experience is not directly controllable. In other words, ACT aims at a

The Clinician's Guide to Treating Health Anxiety
https://doi.org/10.1016/B978-0-12-811806-1.00007-X

behavioral shift from control and avoidance of inner pain to value-based actions even when aversive experiences are present.

Case example

Thirty-four-year-old Peter has become increasingly worried that he is seriously ill after his father died from a brain tumor 1 year ago. Especially, he worries that he has cancer and that the cancer will be diagnosed too late. He has consulted his general practitioner several times due to concerns about various physical symptoms, most recently headaches and visual disturbances. He has been referred to several specialist doctors who all conclude that he is healthy. Still, he is not reassured that his bodily sensations are benign.

To begin with, he sought information online but learned that the extensive information about various types of cancer worsened his symptoms and increased the anxiety. He now avoids health-related programs on TV and increasingly withdraws from social interactions to avoid possible talk about illness. Before, he enjoyed playing football, but since he experienced tingling sensations in his legs during a training session, he has reduced exercising to a minimum.

He is now continually checking his sight and the sensitivity of his legs. Sometimes, he has panic attacks induced by vivid scenarios about dying from a brain tumor including intrusive images of his own funeral and the hardships his children and wife must endure.

The case exemplifies common control and avoidance behaviors, such as seeking medical advice and examinations, displayed by clients with health anxiety. The purpose of these strategies is to alleviate the unpleasant experiences induced by worries about illness, and often, they only work short term. In the long run, the bodily sensations and the worries are maintained and even exacerbated with negative consequences for the clients' quality of life.

Thus, persons with health anxiety struggle to get 100 % reassured that they are not medically ill. This battle is hard to win, because no medical reassurance can provide such certainty. The focus in ACT is therefore to change the client's relationship to uncertainty by nurturing a broader and value-based behavioral repertoire. It follows that from an ACT perspective, symptom reduction is not necessarily a goal. The focus is on helping the individual lead a valued and meaningful life rather than making him/her feeling less anxious, depressed, and so forth. However, as described in the next sections, symptom reduction will often occur as a "positive side effect."

ACT Model of Psychological Flexibility

The overarching goal of ACT is to increase psychological flexibility. Psychological flexibility is the ability to stay in contact with the present moment regardless of unpleasant thoughts, feelings, and bodily sensations, while choosing one's behaviors based on the situation and personal values. Studies show that psychological flexibility is associated with quality of life and mental well-being and may mediate symptom reduction (Eilenberg, Hoffmann, Jensen, & Frostholm, 2017; Forman et al., 2012; Hayes, Luoma, Bond, Masuda, & Lillis, 2006; Wicksell, Olsson, & Hayes, 2011). It is worth noticing that psychological flexibility is not a state of happiness or ease but an ability to flexibly navigate through changing demands of life, also when difficult thoughts and feelings arise. Thus, the metric from which psychological health is evaluated is broadened from symptom reduction to include how the individual as a whole functions with respect to valued life domains as stated by Kashdan and Rottenberg (2010): "after all, a healthy person is someone who can manage themselves in the uncertain, unpredictable world around them, where novelty and change are the norm rather than the exception" (p. 875) (Kashdan & Rottenberg, 2010).

ACT targets unhelpful control and avoidance behaviors while empowering psychological flexibility through six interrelated core processes. Theoretically, these six core processes are defined separately, but in practice, they are always intertwined. Further, they can be unified in three pillars (see Fig. 1).

The three pillars that constitute the overarching process of psychological flexibility are as follows: (1) open up with acceptance and defusion, (2) be present with contact to the present moment and self-as-context, and (3) do what matters with value clarity and committed action (Harris, 2009). They are based on the following six core processes:

Acceptance originally means an "action of taking or receiving what is offered." It is often misunderstood as passive tolerance or resignation. Instead, acceptance refers to actions entailing a choice and thus willingness.

Defusion is the opposite of fusion. Fusion is when a person identifies oneself with the content of thoughts, feelings, and memories; for example, "I am sick." Defusion identifies the content of inner experiences as such and not as the truth; for example, "I have the thought that I am sick" or "I notice that I have the thought that I am sick." This promotes a greater distance to the thought.

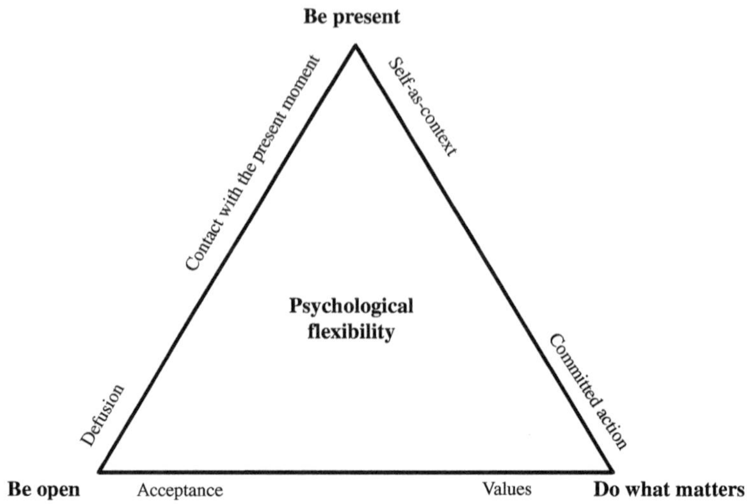

Fig. 1 The six core processes unified in three pillars of the triflex (Harris, 2009).

Contact with the present moment is a nonjudgmental awareness of inner and outer experiences in the present moment. This does not imply that the present moment is necessarily comfortable; it may be unpleasant. It means that the person does not resist what is present but trains an attitude toward every moment that "this is it."

Self-as-context is opposite to self-as-content. Instead of identifying oneself with the changing content of one's thoughts, feelings, and bodily sensations, self-as-context is the experience that you are not the content of your thoughts, but the one experiencing it. Therefore, it is more a constant sense of self-containing the flux of thoughts, feelings, and sensations.

Values clarify what is most important for a person and creates a direction in life. Therefore, values guide and motivate actions but are superior to concrete goals, because values cannot be reached like a goal. A value is more like a direction on a compass and not the destination. Lacking clarity of one's values may entail more rule-governed or avoidance behaviors.

Committed action is a concrete step or action toward a goal guided by the values. Committed action underlines the willingness to carry through even though there may be unpleasant experiences such as anxiety, thoughts, feelings, and bodily sensations. The opposite may be actions determined by control and avoidance.

According to an ACT conceptualization, the cause of psychological distress is psychological inflexibility (see Fig. 2). This pertains to both clients

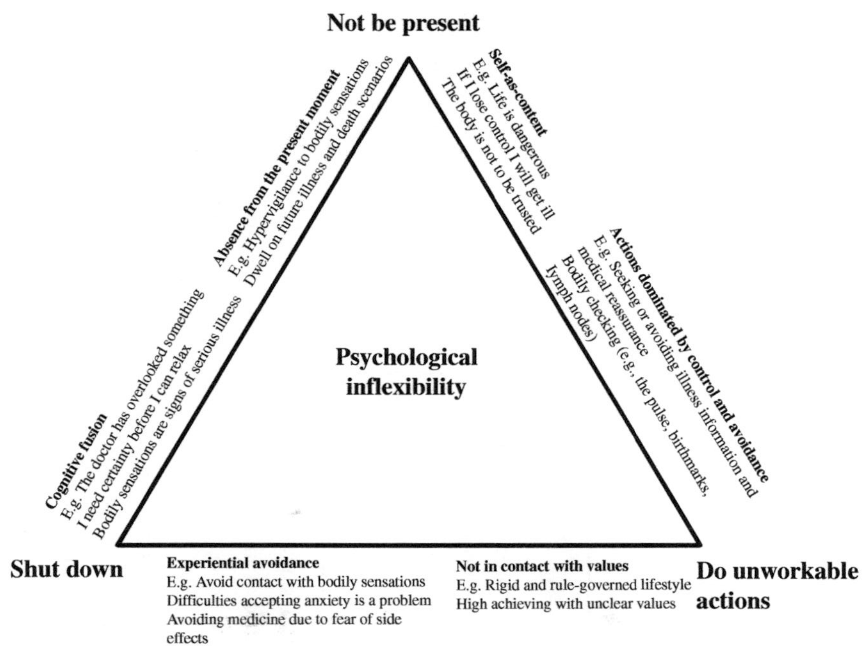

Fig. 2 Conceptualization of health anxiety using the triflex.

with health anxiety and people with other mental health problems. The pathological processes involved are presented in Figure 2 specifically exemplified in relation to health anxiety.

These pathological processes will naturally be the focus for treatment with ACT. Clinically, the triflex can be used for case conceptualization to identify both skills and limitations within one or more processes, which can guide the further treatment planning. For example, our case person Peter may be aware of his personal values and live a meaningful life with his family but still feel disconnected because he constantly thinks about illness and death. From the outside, everything looks fine, but on the inside, he is not present and misses out on his life. In treatment, he would typically be encouraged to train present-moment awareness and defusion from thoughts and images. How to work with the different core processes will be described in more detail in the next section.

Treatment Progression

In ACT treatment, each session often begins with a mindfulness exercise, then homework experience is discussed, and a new ACT theme (defusion, being present, and so forth) is introduced, after which new homework is assigned. Due to the assumed central role of language and cognition in human suffering, there is an emphasis on experiential exercises such as metaphors and mindfulness exercises in order to access experience more directly.

In the initial stages, priority is often on exploring the workability of existing control and avoidance strategies using functional analysis, which aims to undermine psychological inflexibility. At the same time or a bit later, value work is introduced as a larger context against which existing strategies are appraised. Processes aimed at being present and opening up are then used to help the client cope with barriers as he or she commits to take steps (goals) informed by chosen values. Most importantly, however, the therapist should flexibly employ the processes from the triflex as they relate best to the client's actual problems.

As the treatment progresses, it is also helpful to align the rationale of the treatment directly to the client in relation to his/her own problem presentation. For this purpose, some use the triflex described above. However, one may also introduce simpler models such as the lifeline model (see Fig. 3).

The lifeline model can serve several purposes in treatment. It may help clarify the overall treatment rationale for the client at the beginning of treatment and help identify his/her main problem behaviors. It can be used to

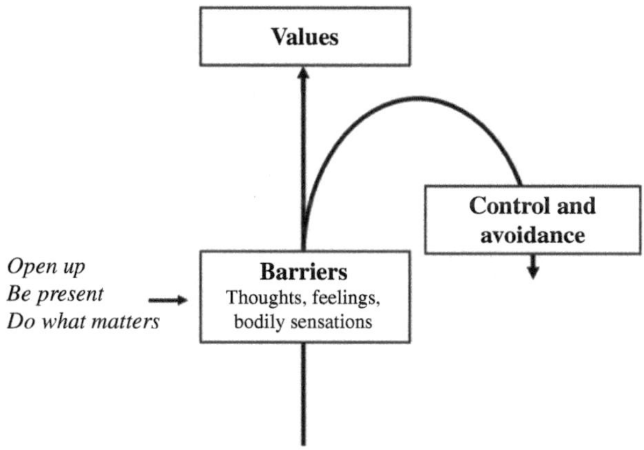

Fig. 3 The lifeline model shows how internal barriers in the form of thoughts, feelings, and bodily sensations stop us from pursuing what really matters (values), because of a tendency to employ short-term control and avoidance strategies to distance oneself from painful inner experience (Dahl, Plumb Vilardaga, Stewart, & Lundgren, 2009).

establish homework assignments in line with a valued direction or for summarizing at the end of each session. The model can be drawn on a whiteboard and used as a psychoeducational tool, or it may be used as an experiential exercise where the client is guided by the therapist through the processes. In the latter format, the values may be written on a piece of paper placed at a distance from the client, and the therapist takes the role as an instructor guiding the client to get in touch with a painful situation leading the client away from value-based behaviors to control or avoidance. These processes are demonstrated physically where the therapist, with the consent of the client, moves him/her around on the floor, that is, away from the posted values. Usually, this physical demonstration is easily comprehensible and the consequences tangible for the client. As a next step, the therapist may model how to open up, stay present, and move toward the values with the unpleasant inner experiences. In this context, the therapist might act out the thoughts or feelings in different ways to enhance the client's learning of the new skills. Finally, the model is also helpful in relating separate treatment processes such as mindfulness or defusion work to the overall rationale.

Functional Analysis

The treatment usually begins with a functional analysis to examine the workability of the client's actions in response to the health anxiety. Do they bring the client closer to living a valuable and rich life? The stance of the therapist in this process is that whatever the client has done is understandable and reasonable because all actions serve a function. At the same time, the therapist helps the client to analyze the short-term and long-term workability of the actions, given the client's own life goals/values and aspirations (see Table 1).

Case example continued

When treating patients like Peter, it is important to understand whether a behavior such as reducing exercise is an avoidance behavior or could be a value-based action. Peter has previously enjoyed physical activity, so reducing this could be one of his avoidance strategies in order not to provoke bodily sensations and thereby anxious thoughts. For another person with health anxiety who has started doing excessive exercise as a way of checking the body's function, reducing this behavior could actually be a step toward a sensitive life balance and value-based direction.

Typically, the functional analysis is presented in four columns: A (antecedents), B (behavior), and C (consequences, short-term and long-term). An antecedent is here understood as an internal "trigger" that elicits a behavior (B). Often, external stimuli or situations seem to "trigger" anxiety, but given that the same situation may entail different responses in different individuals, you need as a therapist also to understand the internal cues or triggers within the person. Typically, the client and therapist will work out that it is the internal reaction (thoughts and feelings) that causes the problematic behavior, not the situation itself.

The therapist tries to help clients identify triggers in the form of thoughts, feelings, and/or bodily sensations. Column B for behavior is everything the client does in relation to the antecedents. These actions will, as previously illustrated, often be dominated by control and avoidance strategies in the natural attempt to reduce the anxiety. Often, there is emphasis on disentangling triggers and coping efforts (behavior) because these often happen automatically and without the client really being aware of what he/she is avoiding. The short-term and long-term consequences (C) are analyzed separately and aim to investigate the behavioral function and workability of the client's actions. In general, control and avoidance behaviors relieve anxiety immediately; if not, they would not be repeated and become a strategy. Subsequently, the long-term effect of these behaviors is analyzed and will often reveal negative consequences where the anxiety has only been maintained or even exacerbated.

Table 1 Functional Analysis

A: Antecedents Sensations, Thoughts, Feelings	B: Behavior What Do You Do?	C: Consequence (Short-Term)	C: Consequence (Long-Term)
Visual disturbances Thought: "This is a brain tumor!" Anxiety	Call my doctor for an acute appointment	Anxiety goes down	Anxiety rises again shortly after leaving the consultation Feel hopeless and lonely Fear everybody will get tired of me
Bodily sensations after physical activity: pain, dizziness, tingling sensations in legs Thought: "This is a sign of a serious illness" Anxiety	Seek medical information on the internet	Feel relief while actively engaging in finding a cause for my symptoms	New symptoms, more anxiety Spending more and more time reading and thinking about symptoms Not present with my friends, family, and on work Irritable and restless
Irregular heart palpitations Thought: "I am dying" Panic	Immediate reaction: call an ambulance. Remote reactions: staying close to hospitals. Stop running and exercising	Immediate relief after medical examination Less worries while not exercising	Increased attention on the heart Physically unfit Miss social contact through exercising Stop traveling Feeling lonely and stuck
Hears about a seriously ill relative Thought: "I could have the same disease and die in the near future" Anxiety	Finds excuse for not paying a visit	Anxiety dampens Relief here and now	Anxiety increases when the pressure from family to visit increases Feeling shame, sadness, isolation

The first two examples are based on the case example with Peter.

As shown in the examples in Table 1, the client is likely during the process to discover that the old solutions have not worked very well and may also have come at considerable costs in the long run. Different metaphors such as "The tiger cub" can be used to underline the point of unworkable actions and the long-term consequences:

Metaphor: The Tiger Cub

Imagine one day you come home to find a small tiger cub in your kitchen. It is cute and cuddly but starts to purr and snarl after some time, like he wants something from you. You look in the fridge and find some minced meat for him, because you know tigers eat meat. This satisfies the tiger for a short while, and he falls asleep. The next day, the tiger is hungry again and starts to snarl at you, you feed him, and this continues day after day... and each time, he demands a little more from you. After a year, it is no longer minced meat but half a cow that is required to calm and satisfy the tiger. He no longer purrs at you but roars impatiently. Eventually, you may discover that you have no more meat to feed him. When you turn around to look at him, you realize that he is no longer a cub, but a full-grown tiger staring hungrily at you.

This experiential realization is in ACT terms called "creative hopelessness" and may naturally lead the client to feel frustrated and sad. However, it is not the same as mere hopelessness, even though it may feel like that in the beginning. It is actually a stance of self-validation that can be a motivational stepping stone for the client to let go of unworkable strategies and for him/her to begin to open up to entirely new possibilities and repertoires of responses to his/her anxiety. The therapist can use this or another metaphor to develop creative hopelessness in the moment of a session by connecting verbal knowledge to a powerful image. This can help clients in remembering and understanding the long-term consequences experientially. The images linked to such a metaphor can then be referenced again when the client is caught up in another unhelpful control or avoidance strategy.

Open Up—With Acceptance and Defusion

Opening up to aversive experiences such as health anxiety is an act of willingness. Acceptance is often misunderstood as a passive stance. On the contrary, it is a deliberate choice to confront anxiety-provoking situations and allow thoughts, feelings, and bodily sensations to be as they are, knowing that they are a normal part of life. This will enable the client to act more freely on values and what is important in life. Furthermore, human language and cognition enable a verbal trap called fusion where clients get enmeshed with the content of thinking; for example, "I have cancer." The process of defusion is changing the relationship with thoughts by realizing they are part of normal human verbal processing and not a precise description of reality. When clients are fused with their thoughts, they lose contact to important here-and-now sensory perceptions and information. The body typically reacts as if the thought is real, and behaviors will be controlled by the thoughts.

Case example continued

Peter is aware that his thoughts about illness may be exaggerated. On the other hand, he has a hard time accepting that he has an anxiety problem and that he cannot get 100 % certainty from his doctor that he will stay well. Therefore, as soon as he experiences a strange feeling in the body, he cannot stop thinking about cancer symptoms, that his doctor may have overlooked something, and that he needs to get a new appointment very soon.

The opposite of acceptance in ACT is *experiential avoidance*, which underlines that the behavioral function is to avoid the internal *experience*. Frequently, clients hold the external situation responsible and therefore start to avoid certain places or situations such as going to the hospital. However, there are only few things that are dangerous in themselves, such as speeding cars. A hospital is only bricks and bits and not dangerous. Therefore, from an ACT stance, the problematic core is the inability to accept and "open up" to the inner experiences when going to the hospital. Experiential avoidance can have multiple expressions and is often, as previously mentioned, introduced to the client as control and avoidance strategies. Common strategies, especially pertaining to health anxiety, are listed below (see Table 2).

If a client shows up for treatment, this is the first sign of willingness to open up (and a committed action). Often, clients with health anxiety feel ashamed about the inability to control their thoughts and behaviors. Therefore, starting to disclose their diverse control and avoidance strategies is in itself an acceptance exercise. Generally, the extensive strategies have served their function to keep thoughts, feelings, and bodily reactions in the outskirts of consciousness. To support the client's process of opening

Table 2 Examples of Control and Avoidance Strategies in Clients Suffering From Health Anxiety

Control Strategies	Avoidance Strategies
Checking bodily functions (pulse rate, blood pressure, and weight)	Avoiding places and situations that may trigger anxiety
Seeking medical reassurance	Avoiding the doctor, health checks, and examinations
Observing bodily symptoms and sensations	Avoiding medicine and food subjects due to fear of side effects
Checking body parts (lymphs, feces, and birth marks)	Not visiting sick friends or relatives
Staying close to hospitals and emergency rooms	Avoiding information about illness (newspapers, television, and WebMD)
Excessive control of health (food, vitamins, and diets)	Avoiding exercising and getting the heart rate up
Exercise to check whether the body is healthy and well	

up to the avoided experience, behavioral exercises should be tailored to match his/her specific unhelpful strategies. For example, if the client checks his heart rate five times a day, an exercise could be to minimize the checking behavior.

Working with cognitive fusion in treatment pertains to a shift in perspective, where the client is training to be able to take a different perspective on his/her thinking. Often, "the thinker" and "the thinking" are fused. For example, the client may train to verbalize "I have the thought that I have cancer." This is already a bit more defused from the thought "I have cancer." The client may further play with the perspective by formulating "I am noticing that I have the thought that I have cancer."

Be Present—With Contact to the Present Moment and Self-as-Context

Being present refers to a nonjudgmental moment-to-moment awareness with fewer struggles to change the present experiences and a sense of a stable self that is the context of all experiences, as opposed to an unstable sense of self-as-content where the person identifies him-/herself with the changing experiences themselves (Hayes, Levin, Plumb-Vilardaga, Villatte, & Pistorello, 2013). Self-as-context can be defined as the observing self, that is, the perspective from where noticing happens.

Case example continued

Sometimes, Peter becomes so anxious due to his thoughts about cancer that he starts thinking about his own funeral and how his children and wife will manage without him. He can especially find himself ruminate about this scenario in the middle of joyful activities with his family and find it difficult to engage fully in these. Peter feels very guilty about this as he would like to be an engaged father and husband. At the same time, he is convinced that he needs to be in control and that others (especially health professionals) are not to be trusted. As a consequence, he feels it is ultimately his own responsibility to react in time on his bodily sensations in order to prevent his premature death due to a progressed cancer, too late to treat.

Being present is challenging for our case person Peter, especially in the initial phase of treatment, because the here and now is absorbed with anxious thoughts about illness and bodily sensations, which provokes control and avoidance behaviors. He is quite motivated to work with his ability to stay present because he realizes the amount of suffering it causes him to disconnect from his family and joyful activities. Peter spends a lot of time debating in his mind whether he can trust his doctor and the recent medical results. In treatment, he is asked to redirect his attention from verbal problem solving (am I sick?) to examining his bodily sensations and thoughts about illness and death. While staying with the numerous inputs pertaining to the senses long enough, he experiences that the anxiety and symptoms are fluctuating. Gradually, he is able to tolerate more distress before he begins to withdraw from the situation. In this form, in vivo exposure can be applied numerous times within a single session. Present moment exercises in ACT are not a new way to control symptoms and bring relief. Rather, the aim is to decrease the urge to control or alter present-moment experience. When the client begins to experience how present-moment awareness can increase value-based and purposeful living, the willingness to be with unpleasant thoughts, feelings, and sensations often increases as well.

Being present in ACT thus somewhat resembles mindfulness defined as taking contact with the present moment in a compassionate and nonjudgmental way (Baer et al., 2008). When training being present, various mindfulness and visualization exercises may be applied. Visualizations are often created to illustrate a treatment process or point in therapy such as self-as-context illustrated in "The sky and the weather" exercise (see below) (Stoddard & Afari, 2014).

Metaphor: The Sky and the Weather

The part of you that notices and observes is like the sky. Thoughts and feelings and bodily sensations are like the weather. The weather changes all the time, sometimes slowly like the seasons and sometimes like a tropical cyclone. But no matter how bad the weather gets, the weather cannot harm the sky in any way. The mightiest thunderstorm, the most turbulent hurricane, or the most severe winter blizzard cannot hurt or harm the sky. And no matter how bad the weather, the sky always has room for it. And sooner or later, the weather always changes.

Sometimes, we forget the sky is there, but it is still there. Sometimes, we cannot see the sky because it is obscured by clouds. But if we rise high enough above those clouds—even the thickest, darkest thunderclouds—we will reach clear sky, stretching in all directions, boundless and pure.

In ACT, formal mindfulness exercises such as awareness of the breath and body scan are often used in shorter versions compared with pure mindfulness-based therapies. It is paradoxical in a way to train clients with health anxiety to feel their bodies, because in a way they are constantly aware of their bodies. But this awareness is often quite selective and focusing on bodily areas where they fear having a tumor, suffering from heart failure, etc. This means that the bodily awareness is colored by anxiety and that clients actually do not have a pure awareness of their body in itself.

Training the ability to have and observe painful or distressing thoughts and bodily sensations facilitates the realization that *you* are different from the thoughts and that *you* can have these thoughts about illness without spiraling into panic and thereby strengthen the self-as-context: When *you* are observing the thoughts, *you* are different from the thoughts. *You* are the context of your experience. Hence, you are not equal to your experience. From this stance, greater acceptance and nonjudgment of inner experiences may develop, and inner experiences may become less aversive.

Do What Matters—With Values Clarity and Committed Action

To do what matters, you need to know your values and priorities in life—what makes life rich and meaningful for you (Plumb, Stewart, Dahl, &

Lundgren, 2009). Knowing your values is not enough; you also need to take committed actions toward your values. A clear valued direction in life can help guide behaviors when difficult things arise. Values can be described as a compass pointing west. West is then the direction, but not the destination. In the same way, values differ from specific goals because values cannot be obtained and accomplished definitively. But values can change during life and in different periods, and they may also be mutually competing. Values are always personal and therefore not the same as societal rules or norms. Furthermore, they are not things you should have, could have, or would have; they are personally meaningful and do not depend on reinforcement from other.

The value compass is a common tool to investigate the importance of values in different life domains (see Fig. 4). In therapy, the client may rate how important a given value is in one or more domains and how close or far away he/she is from living according to this value. Thereby, this exercise clarifies the potential discrepancy between his/her actual behaviors and

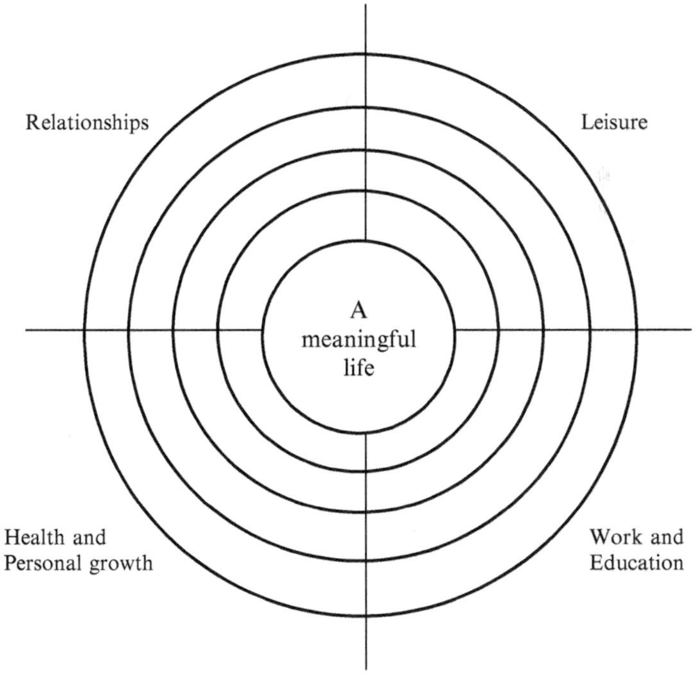

Fig. 4 The values compass (Dahl et al., 2009).

values and may help clients to choose to work with value-based actions within a specific area.

Case example continued

Peter identifies that the most important value for him is being in close and rewarding relationships. During the treatment process, he realizes that his health anxiety often triggers avoidance and control behaviors that only moves him longer away from this value as he has stopped many social activities with his friends and often finds himself isolated and emotionally detached from his family when he is occupied with thoughts about symptoms and illness. In order to move in a more valued direction, he decides with support from his therapist that a first committed action will be to just recognize the most dominant illness thoughts he has for a day and try not to react with usually unworkable strategies such as checking behavior or calling his doctor. The long-term goal is to be able to participate in a football match arranged by his work place.

Each session is ended with homework, which often encompasses a committed action in one of the four value domains. Working to increase value-based actions is similar to classical graded exposure exercises; only here the goal is value-driven. The therapist helps the client to choose a life domain and get in contact with values within the area. The client may decide on a long-term goal and subsidiary goals or just commit to one step for the next week. The staircase can be used as a tool for committed action (see Fig. 5).

Research and Future Perspective

This section briefly reviews the evidence and presents some of the challenges and future directions for ACT in becoming a mainstream treatment for health anxiety. Currently, one RCT examines the effect of group-based ACT for severe health anxiety (Eilenberg, Fink, Jensen, Rief, & Frostholm, 2016). This study showed promising results with large reductions in health anxiety symptoms. Additionally, mediation analysis confirmed that psychological flexibility was an important intervening variable supporting the ACT model (Eilenberg et al., 2017). An internet-delivered ACT program has recently been developed and is currently being evaluated in a larger RCT (Hoffmann, Rask, Hedman-Lagerlof, Ljotsson, & Frostholm, 2018). Thus, ACT for clients with health anxiety must be

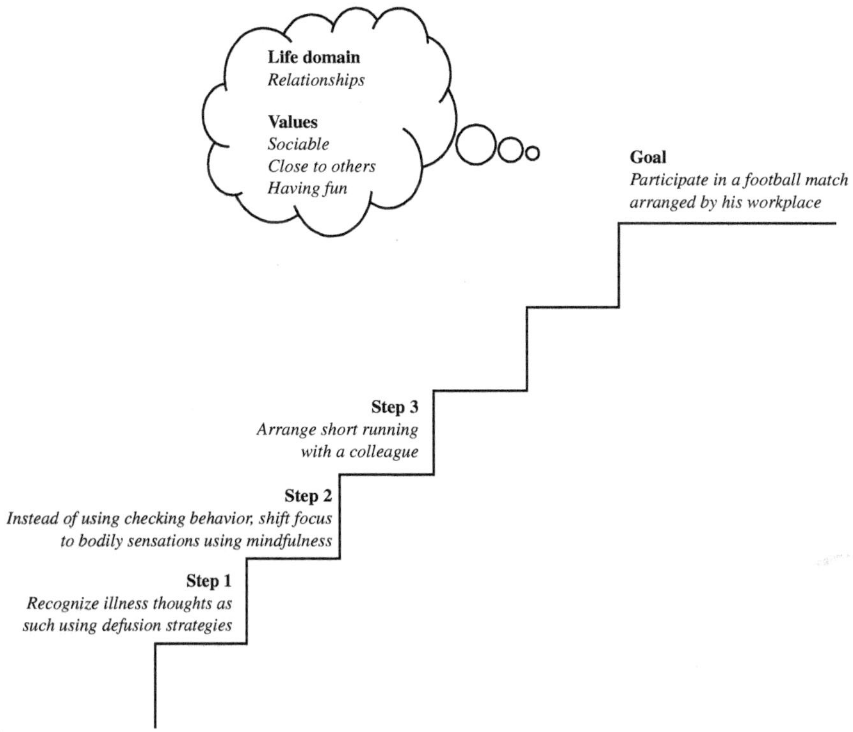

Fig. 5 The value-based staircase used for committed action.

categorized as work in progress. The overall empirical support of ACT has increased substantially in recent years for various mental health disorders such as anxiety disorders, depression, obsessive-compulsive disorder, psychosis, and chronic pain (Arch et al., 2012; Bach & Hayes, 2002; Forman, Herbert, Moitra, Yeomans, & Geller, 2007; Hayes-Skelton, Roemer, & Orsillo, 2013; Roemer, Orsillo, & Salters-Pedneault, 2008; Twohig et al., 2010). A recent metaanalysis included 39 RCTs on mental disorders and somatic health problems and found that ACT outperformed treatment as usual, waitlist control, and psychological placebo with moderate to large effect sizes (A-Tjak et al., 2015). In addition, preliminary metaanalytic results indicate that ACT seems to be equally effective as cognitive behavioral therapy (CBT) in treating various anxiety disorders (Bluett, Homan, Morrison, Levin, & Twohig, 2014). Though there is growing support for the general use of ACT as a new treatment approach, there is still a need for more methodologically rigorous studies (Hacker, Stone, &

MacBeth, 2016; Ost, 2014; Swain, Hancock, Hainsworth, & Bowman, 2013). Future studies should include larger samples and randomized controlled trials and explore different formats with ACT, both face-to-face and internet-delivered treatment in comparison with "gold-standard treatment" or CBT for health anxiety. Moreover, investigations of mediators, moderators, and mechanisms of treatment are warranted. Further work exploring the feasibility and acceptability of ACT besides its efficacy would also strengthen its evidence base and wider implementation as a standard treatment of health anxiety.

Summary and Conclusion

In this chapter, we have described how ACT, one of the so-called third-wave behavior therapies, can be applied for health anxiety. With respect to health anxiety, an important issue is that even though CBT is the most well-established treatment for the disorder (Thomson & Page, 2007), some clients decline participation, and some do not benefit from CBT. Thus, new treatment programs are warranted because different approaches may apply to clients with different needs and preferences. Even though CBT and ACT both draw on cognitive behavioral principles, there are distinct differences such as the value-based focus in ACT and the approach to cognitions. Overall, ACT poses two questions: What do you want your life to be about? And what is stopping you? ACT aims to increase engagement in activities that bring meaning and vitality to the clients' lives even when discomfort or distress is present. Furthermore, rather than changing the unpleasant inner experience (thoughts, feelings, and bodily sensations), the focus is on changing the way in which the client relates to and reacts to these events. Where CBT works to change or replace problematic thoughts, ACT aims to increase the experiential acceptance of thoughts and feelings in the body here and now. This is especially relevant when these aversive experiences cannot be effectively avoided or when avoidance efforts risk their exacerbation as is often the case in health anxiety. Furthermore, even though ACT does not deliberately aim to decrease symptoms, symptom reduction is just as welcomed as in CBT. Thus, ACT provides a different treatment model and may be highly relevant to clients with health anxiety since possible illness and death cannot be avoided and therefore need to be accepted while reinvesting time and energy into living a valuable life.

References

Arch, J. J., Eifert, G. H., Davies, C., Plumb Vilardaga, J. C., Rose, R. D., & Craske, M. G. (2012). Randomized clinical trial of cognitive behavioral therapy (CBT) versus acceptance and commitment therapy (ACT) for mixed anxiety disorders. *Journal of Consulting and Clinical Psychology*, *80*(5), 750–765 doi: 2012-12071-001. pii.

A-Tjak, J. G., Davis, M. L., Morina, N., Powers, M. B., Smits, J. A., & Emmelkamp, P. M. (2015). A meta-analysis of the efficacy of acceptance and commitment therapy for clinically relevant mental and physical health problems. *Psychotherapy and Psychosomatics*, *84* (1), 30–36. https://doi.org/10.1159/000365764.

Bach, P., & Hayes, S. C. (2002). The use of acceptance and commitment therapy to prevent the rehospitalization of psychotic patients: a randomized controlled trial. *Journal of Consulting and Clinical Psychology*, *70*(5), 1129–1139.

Baer, R. A., Smith, G. T., Lykins, E., Button, D., Krietemeyer, J., Sauer, S., … Williams, J. M. (2008). Construct validity of the five facet mindfulness questionnaire in meditating and nonmeditating samples. *Assessment*, *15*(3), 329–342. https://doi.org/10.1177/1073191107313003.

Bluett, E. J., Homan, K. J., Morrison, K. L., Levin, M. E., & Twohig, M. P. (2014). Acceptance and commitment therapy for anxiety and OCD spectrum disorders: An empirical review. *Journal of Anxiety Disorders*, *28*(6), 612–624. https://doi.org/10.1016/j.janxdis.2014.06.008.

Dahl, J., Plumb Vilardaga, J. C., Stewart, I., & Lundgren, T. (2009). *The art & science of valuing in psychotherapy: Helping clients discover, explore, and commit to valued action using acceptance and commitment therapy*. Oakland, CA: New Harbinger Publications.

Eilenberg, T., Fink, P., Jensen, J. S., Rief, W., & Frostholm, L. (2016). Acceptance and commitment group therapy (ACT-G) for health anxiety: A randomized controlled trial. *Psychological Medicine*, *46*(1), 103–115. https://doi.org/10.1017/S0033291715001579.

Eilenberg, T., Hoffmann, D., Jensen, J. S., & Frostholm, L. (2017). Intervening variables in group-based acceptance & commitment therapy for severe health anxiety. *Behaviour Research and Therapy*, *92*, 24–31 doi: S0005-7967(17)30016-5 [pii].

Forman, E. M., Chapman, J. E., Herbert, J. D., Goetter, E. M., Yuen, E. K., & Moitra, E. (2012). Using session-by-session measurement to compare mechanisms of action for acceptance and commitment therapy and cognitive therapy. *Behavior Therapy*, *43*(2), 341–354. https://doi.org/10.1016/j.beth.2011.07.004.

Forman, E. M., Herbert, J. D., Moitra, E., Yeomans, P. D., & Geller, P. A. (2007). A randomized controlled effectiveness trial of acceptance and commitment therapy and cognitive therapy for anxiety and depression. *Behavior Modification*, *31*(6), 772–799 doi: 31/6/772 [pii].

Fox, E. J. (2006). Constructing a pragmatic science of learning and instruction with functional contextualism. *Educational Technology Research and Development*, *54*(1), 5–36. https://doi.org/10.1007/s11423-006-6491-5.

Hacker, T., Stone, P., & MacBeth, A. (2016). Acceptance and commitment therapy—do we know enough? Cumulative and sequential meta-analyses of randomized controlled trials. *Journal of Affective Disorders*, *190*, 551–565. https://doi.org/10.1016/j.jad.2015.10.053.

Harris, R. (2009). *ACT made simple: An easy-to-read primer on acceptance and commitment therapy*. Oakland, CA: New Harbinger Publications.

Hayes, S. C., Levin, M. E., Plumb-Vilardaga, J., Villatte, J. L., & Pistorello, J. (2013). Acceptance and commitment therapy and contextual behavioral science: examining the progress of a distinctive model of behavioral and cognitive therapy. *Behavior Therapy*, *44*(2), 180–198. https://doi.org/10.1016/j.beth.2009.08.002.

Hayes, S. C., Luoma, J. B., Bond, F. W., Masuda, A., & Lillis, J. (2006). Acceptance and commitment therapy: Model, processes and outcomes. *Behaviour Research and Therapy*, *44*(1), 1–25 doi: S0005-7967(05)00214-7 [pii].

Hayes, S. C., Strosahl, K., & Wilson, K. G. (2012). *Acceptance and commitment therapy: The process and practice of mindful change* (2nd ed.). New York: Guilford Press.

Hayes-Skelton, S. A., Roemer, L., & Orsillo, S. M. (2013). A randomized clinical trial comparing an acceptance-based behavior therapy to applied relaxation for generalized anxiety disorder. *Journal of Consulting and Clinical Psychology, 81*(5), 761–773. https://doi.org/10.1037/a0032871.

Hoffmann, D., Rask, C. U., Hedman-Lagerlof, E., Ljotsson, B., & Frostholm, L. (2018). Development and feasibility testing of internet-delivered acceptance and commitment therapy for severe health anxiety: Pilot study. *JMIR Mental Health, 5*(2), e28. https://doi.org/10.2196/mental.9198.

Kashdan, T. B., & Rottenberg, J. (2010). Psychological flexibility as a fundamental aspect of health. *Clinical Psychology Review, 30*(7), 865–878. https://doi.org/10.1016/j.cpr.2010.03.001.

Ost, L. G. (2014). The efficacy of acceptance and commitment therapy: an updated systematic review and meta-analysis. *Behaviour Research and Therapy, 61*, 105–121. https://doi.org/10.1016/j.brat.2014.07.018.

Pielech, M., Vowles, K. E., & Wicksell, R. (2017). Acceptance and commitment therapy for pediatric chronic pain: Theory and application. *Children (Basel, Switzerland). 4*(2)https://doi.org/10.3390/children4020010 E10 [pii].

Plumb, J. C., Stewart, I., Dahl, J., & Lundgren, T. (2009). In search of meaning: Values in modern clinical behavior analysis. *The Behavior Analyst, 32*(1), 85–103.

Roemer, L., Orsillo, S. M., & Salters-Pedneault, K. (2008). Efficacy of an acceptance-based behavior therapy for generalized anxiety disorder: Evaluation in a randomized controlled trial. *Journal of Consulting and Clinical Psychology, 76*(6), 1083–1089. https://doi.org/10.1037/a0012720.

Stoddard, J. A., & Afari, N. (2014). *The big book of ACT metaphors: A practitioner's guide to experiential exercises and metaphors in acceptance and commitment therapy*. Oakland, CA: New Harbinger Publications.

Swain, J., Hancock, K., Hainsworth, C., & Bowman, J. (2013). Acceptance and commitment therapy in the treatment of anxiety: a systematic review. *Clinical Psychology Review, 33*(8), 965–978. https://doi.org/10.1016/j.cpr.2013.07.002.

Thomson, A. B., & Page, L. A. (2007). Psychotherapies for hypochondriasis. *The Cochrane Database of Systematic Reviews, 4*(4), CD006520. https://doi.org/10.1002/14651858.CD006520.pub2.

Twohig, M. P., Hayes, S. C., Plumb, J. C., Pruitt, L. D., Collins, A. B., Hazlett-Stevens, H., & Woidneck, M. R. (2010). A randomized clinical trial of acceptance and commitment therapy versus progressive relaxation training for obsessive-compulsive disorder. *Journal of Consulting and Clinical Psychology, 78*(5), 705–716. https://doi.org/10.1037/a0020508.

Wicksell, R. K., Olsson, G. L., & Hayes, S. C. (2011). Mediators of change in acceptance and commitment therapy for pediatric chronic pain. *Pain, 152*(12), 2792–2801. https://doi.org/10.1016/j.pain.2011.09.003.

CHAPTER EIGHT

Using the Internet to Provide Treatment for Health Anxiety

Erik Hedman-Lagerlöf and Erland Axelsson
Department of Clinical Neuroscience, Karolinska Institutet, Stockholm, Sweden

For the last 20 years, the field of Internet-based psychological treatments has moved forward in a rapid pace (Andersson & Carlbring, 2017). For several health problems, there is now a firm evidence base for Internet-based treatment. The delivery format has been studied in more than 100 randomized controlled trials (Hedman, Ljótsson, & Lindefors, 2012) and is also recommended by influential health-care agencies such as the British National Institute for Health and Care Excellence (NICE) (National Institute for Health and Clinical Excellence, 2011). We here intend to provide a brief introduction to Internet-based psychological treatment and the advantages of this treatment format. This is then followed by a more specific description of how Internet-based therapies can be used to help individuals with health anxiety and which effects one are to expect from such an intervention.

A Focus on Cognitive Behaviour Therapy

There is substantial variation between Internet-based treatments, both with regard to technical complexity and the type of therapist support. A common denominator of most Internet-based treatments is, however, that they are based on cognitive behavioral methods. It is clear to see why cognitive behavioral therapy (CBT) suits well for the Internet format. CBT is a relatively structured treatment, where the main focus is to change concrete behaviors and patterns of thought. Key elements of CBT are psychoeducation (e.g., learning about one's disorder) and practical homework exercises (e.g., gradually approaching a feared situation; see Chapter 5), which goes hand in hand with the Internet format. Many conventional CBT protocols are easily converted to a sequence of didactic material and behavioral instructions that can be presented on a website and that allow the patient to assume great autonomy in working through his or her problem. Another reason for CBT being so dominant in research on Internet-

The Clinician's Guide to Treating Health Anxiety
https://doi.org/10.1016/B978-0-12-811806-1.00008-1

based treatment is that there is a long tradition of working with self-help treatments (also known as bibliotherapy) in the cognitive behavioral field, which made the step to self-help online relatively short. It should be noted that not only CBT but also other forms of psychological treatments such as psychodynamic and interpersonal therapy have shown promising results when delivered via the Internet (e.g., Johansson et al., 2012). However, because CBT is by far the most researched psychological treatment for health anxiety, this chapter deals mainly with Internet-based treatment from a CBT perspective.

What is Internet-Based Treatment?

Internet-based treatment is commonly understood to rely on the same treatment components and behavioral changes as its face-to-face equivalent. In other words, Internet-based treatment is best viewed as a novel mode of treatment delivery, and not as a new theoretical model for therapy. This means that if, for example, excessive reassurance seeking is thought to be a maintaining factor of health anxiety, then just like in face-to-face treatment, an Internet-based treatment should preferably entail components to reduce reassurance seeking.

Internet-based treatment is typically text-based, with approximately 100–150 A4 pages of text compiled in the form of modules, comparable with book chapters and loosely mirroring face-to-face sessions. The modules are presented on a secure website, are usually completed in consecutive order, and each incorporate specific educational material and homework assignments. Similar to face-to-face CBT, the initial phase of Internet-based CBT is characterized by modules that provide psychoeducation about the clinical problem and how one can understand the problem from a cognitive behavioral perspective. Patients learn to adapt the theoretical model to their own idiosyncratic problems and then begin to systematically change their behaviors hypothesized to maintain difficulties over time. The final phase of treatment is focused on preventing relapse and creating a plan for continued improvement after treatment has ended.

In most Internet-based treatments, the patient is guided by a therapist who is the same throughout the treatment and whom the patient knows by name. Guidance is most often provided through asynchronous text messages, that is, a format that is more reminiscent of e-mail than a real-time chat. The role of the therapist is mainly to provide feedback on the patient's homework exercises, but the patient can also send messages to the therapist at any time and typically expect a reply within 48 h. Because all worksheets and questionnaires completed by the patient are stored on the platform, it is easy for both the therapist and patient to access all collected data that are needed to tailor the treatment to the patient's needs (without the risk of losing paper forms).

A thorough clinical assessment before treatment is just as important, if not more important, in Internet-based treatment. This is because the module content, which is mostly composed of self-help texts and sometimes video clips and audio files, is relatively fixed, indented for a specific patient group, and typically cannot be amended over the course of treatment. This means that if a person is misdiagnosed, for example, a person with panic disorder is wrongly diagnosed with health anxiety, it is difficult for the therapist to adapt the treatment accordingly.

Despite the highly structured and text-based format, it is our experience that patients often feel that they are just as well taken care of in this type of treatment as in conventional face-to-face psychiatric care. We believe that this is a crucial explanation for the large effects demonstrated by Internet-based treatment. However, there is also evidence to suggest that the relationship with the therapist is less important for the overall treatment effect in Internet-based than in face-to-face treatment (Andersson et al., 2012).

Advantages of Internet-Based Treatment

There are important advantages of using Internet-based treatment for health anxiety. One that is crucial from both an individual and a societal perspective is that this form of therapy can yield a substantial increase in treatment availability. There are a number of reasons for this. First and foremost, Internet-based treatment requires much less therapist time compared with face-to-face therapy, often about 10 min weekly per patient (Andersson & Lindefors, 2016). This means that a therapist can have up to 80 patients in ongoing treatment, which is about four times as many patients as would be possible in conventional individual therapy. Another way in which Internet-based treatment increases accessibility is that it is independent of geographic distance. This is perhaps not so important in larger cities, but pivotal for persons living in rural areas where the nearest psychiatric outpatient clinic might be so far away that psychological treatment is impossible for practical reasons. In one of our recently conducted trials, some patients lived more than 900 km away from our clinic (Lalouni et al., 2017); we regard it as highly likely that most of these patients would have not started treatment had they been required to come to the clinic on a weekly basis for 10 weeks. Another important advantage with Internet-based treatment is that no real-time scheduled appointments are needed. This makes the treatment format flexible in the sense that both patient and therapist can work with the treatment when it suits them best. The patient does not need to take time off from work to do the treatment, which not only is practical but also means that he or she does not have to face potential stigma that might be associated with discussing one's mental health problem with one's boss or colleagues. From the therapist's point of view, one central advantage of the structure of Internet-based treatment is that one is not tied to scheduled appointments, which makes it possible to work from home. Also, no time has to be spent on booking appointments, and there is no time loss due to the patient canceling or not showing up. Given the lack of trained therapists, the high prevalence of health anxiety, and that a large proportion does not receive evidence-based treatment, we regard the features of Internet-based treatment described here as important because they all contribute to making this type of treatment highly available.

Another advantage of the structured treatment format is that it is relatively easy to ensure that, once the treatment has begun, patients are given access to the best available interventions and strategies for their respective condition. This is because, due to the role of the therapist as support rather than educator, as long as the treatment content is compliant with evidence-based practice, the risk that the patient does not receive the intended intervention is relatively small. The benefits of this should not be underestimated, because so-called therapist factors are a well-documented problem in conventional face-to-face CBT. That is, it is relatively common for therapists to diverge from intended treatment protocols and refrain from using best practice treatment components such as exposure (Waller & Turner, 2016). This, of course, may have detrimental effects for patients who, one would assume, simply want the best tools available for doing something about their problem.

Other advantages of Internet-based treatment that are not so often mentioned but nonetheless important from a clinical perspective are the support systems of the treatment platform. One such key system is integrated self-report assessment of psychiatric symptoms. We typically administer symptom measures weekly throughout the treatment period (see Chapter 5 for validated instruments). These assessments are mandatory in the sense that the patient has to complete them in order to access the treatment platform. The patient's ratings are easily accessible for the therapist (e.g., through graphs), which makes it a simple task for the therapist to quickly detect if the patient is not improving as expected. The treatment platform can also be used to monitor and promote important treatment activities. For example, the platform can be programmed so that the therapist is alerted if a patient lags behind with homework assignments or if he or she has experienced a sudden deterioration of symptoms. Automated reminders to the patient (e.g., via SMS) to complete the weekly self-report assessments are an efficient way to obtain complete data and to promote the patient to log in to the online platform.

Internet-Based Treatment for Health Anxiety

To our knowledge, three research groups (in Sweden, Australia, and Denmark) have contributed to the development of Internet-based psychological treatment for health anxiety. The most well-researched treatment so far is exposure-based cognitive behavioral therapy (CBT), which has been shown to be efficacious in three randomized controlled trials (e.g., Hedman et al., 2011). This is a 12-week treatment that comprises 12 modules, which the patient goes through at a pace of approximately one module per week. Table 1 describes the content of the modules and main homework exercises of the treatment. As can be read from Table 1, the majority of the work revolves around identifying triggers for health anxiety (i.e., situations, symptoms, and thoughts) and systematically confronting these stimuli through exposure. As a means to make the exposure more effective, that is, to help the patient to confront his or her fears without using subtle safety behaviors, the patient in the initial phase of the treatment practices mindfulness training. Content-wise, this treatment is very similar to what is described in Chapter 5 (i.e., exposure and response prevention). Again, the concept of Internet-based treatment is to deliver effective psychological treatment in a new format, and with few exceptions, the delivery format does not imply different hypotheses about the mechanisms responsible for change.

From the patient's perspective, going through Internet-based CBT for health anxiety means putting in a substantial amount of work, several days per week. For an idea of what a typical patient is required to do during a week in this treatment, Table 2 provides a fictitious diary regarding treatment for a patient in Internet-based CBT (note that writing a diary is not a part of the treatment).

As shown in Table 2, Internet-based CBT is so much more than the provision of information, and the treatment is by no means easier than face-to-

Table 1 The Content of Internet-Based Cognitive Behavioral Therapy for Health Anxiety

Module	Main Theme	Main Homework Assignments
1	Introduction to health anxiety, CBT, mindfulness, and self-monitoring	Health anxiety behavior diary, mindfulness training
2	Introduction to the CBT model	Completion of idiosyncratic health anxiety model, health anxiety behavior diary, mindfulness training
3	Interoceptive exposure (i.e., exposure to physical sensations)	Interoceptive exposure, health anxiety behavior diary, mindfulness training
4	Response prevention	Exposure and response prevention, mindfulness training
5	Exposure in vivo (i.e., exposure to real-life triggers for health anxiety)	Exposure and response prevention, mindfulness training
6	Imagery exposure (i.e., exposure to thoughts and mental images)	Exposure and response prevention
7	Imagery exposure and exposure to thoughts about death	Exposure and response prevention
8	Common problems in exposure	Exposure and response prevention
9	Continued exposure and response prevention	Exposure and response prevention
10	Continued exposure and response prevention	Exposure and response prevention
11	Summary of the treatment, the role of values for continued change	Exposure and response prevention, summary of the treatment and most helpful interventions, core values exercise
12	Maintaining gains and relapse prevention	Exposure and response prevention, plan for continued improvement and to prevent and handle relapse, plan for future use of health care

Note: This is a slightly revised version of a previously published table (Hedman, Ljótsson, & Lindefors, 2016).

face CBT in terms of time and energy that the patient has to invest. Sometimes, we hear things like "since I don't have so much time at the moment, I think Internet-based treatment would suit me." We believe that this represents a common misconception of this type of treatment, that is, the treatment is something that mainly takes place online. It is clear to us that Internet-based CBT requires just as strong a commitment to therapy as face-to-face CBT.

Table 2 Typical Treatment Week ("Diary") in Internet-Based CBT for Health Anxiety

Weekday	**Activity**
Monday	Started reading the module text. It's a lot to digest this week, more than 25 pages. Recorded my health anxiety behaviors in the platform
Tuesday	Continued reading. I think I understand most of it, but it's a bit difficult to know if not going to the doctor so often is a good thing or an avoidance behavior. I contacted my therapist to ask about this. Practiced mindfulness training for about 10 min
Wednesday	I received a response from my therapist Maria today. She wrote that if I refrain from going to a doctor because I'm afraid what I'll hear, then it's probably a form of avoidance that is important to break. I'll have to think about this. Kept on recording behaviors that I think might contribute to my health anxiety and practiced mindfulness. The mindfulness exercise made me a bit anxious, I wrote to Maria about this, and she replied that it is perfectly normal
Thursday	My daughter's birthday, not much work done with the treatment except that I tried to squeeze in a little bit of mindfulness practice
Friday	Started with interoceptive exposure today. I found it really hard to do the hyperventilating exercise the first time; I almost got a panic attack. In line with the instructions in the module text, I repeated this exercise several times, and toward the end, it wasn't as frightening although I wasn't perfectly relaxed. Continued recording of my health anxiety behaviors and realized that the reason I think it's so important to have a charged phone is because it feels safe should I have a stroke. Also practiced the mindfulness exercise
Saturday	Did the rest of the interoceptive exposure exercises. None of the remaining 14 exercises came close to hyperventilating in terms of how much anxiety they provoked. I sent in this week's homework report, which mainly concerned how the work with interoceptive exposure has been and what I've learn about that so far. I also had to answer some pretty difficult questions about why exposure is important and what one has to consider when doing it. I think I got most of the answers right
Saturday	My therapist sent me feedback on my homework report. She thinks that I'm doing a good job with the treatment, which was nice to hear. She wrote that because I'm now done with this module, she has granted me access to the next one. I'm too tired to dive into that now but will start reading tomorrow

Treatment Effects, Cost-Effectiveness, and Predictors of Outcome

Our research group has conducted three randomized controlled trials of exposure-based CBT delivered via the Internet (Hedman et al., 2011; Hedman, Axelsson, Andersson, Lekander, & Ljótsson, 2016; Hedman et al., 2014). In the first clinical trial ($N=82$), the treatment was tested against a basic attention control condition where participants instead communicated freely with each other via a text-based online forum (Hedman et al., 2011). The results indicated that Internet-based CBT was highly efficacious, with a controlled effect size of $d=1.6$ at posttreatment on the primary outcome of health anxiety (the Health Anxiety Inventory). At posttreatment, 67.5% of the participants in Internet CBT no longer met diagnostic criteria for health anxiety (hypochondriasis), compared with 4.9% in the control group. Effects were maintained at 1-year follow-up, suggesting that 12 weeks of Internet-based CBT can be long-term effective (Hedman, Andersson, et al., 2013). In a subsequent trial ($N=158$), exposure-based Internet CBT was superior to an active psychological treatment in the form of behavioral stress management in reducing health anxiety. There was no difference in treatment adherence between the two conditions, and the treatments were rated as equally credible, which suggests that there is a specific effect of Internet-based CBT above and beyond that that can be expected from receiving a structured treatment with therapist support (Hedman et al., 2014). In a third trial ($N=132$), where health anxiety was operationalized as DSM-5 somatic symptom disorder (SSD) or illness anxiety disorder (IAD), the results again indicated that therapist-guided Internet-based CBT can be effective in reducing health anxiety (controlled effect size at posttreatment: $d=1.3$) (Hedman, Axelsson, et al., 2016). To our knowledge, this was the first published clinical trial of any type of treatment for the new DSM-5 disorders SSD and IAD, so one important lesson learned from that trial was that the same treatment, which had previously been shown to be effective for hypochondriasis, also worked for these new disorders without any modifications. In the most recently published randomized trial in this field, Newby et al. (2018) investigated the effect of Internet-based CBT over 12 weeks compared with a control condition that received psychoeducation. Participants were required to have SSD or IAD, and the results showed a large and significant improvement, that is, reduction of health anxiety, in Internet-based CBT compared with the control group (controlled effect size $d=1.4$).

In summary, four randomized controlled trials have shown that therapist-guided Internet-based CBT can be effective in the treatment of health anxiety. In two of these trials, by two independent research groups, it could be argued that the treatment was shown to be superior to an active control condition (Hedman et al., 2014; Newby et al., 2018). A pilot study by Hoffmann, Rask, Hedman-Lagerlöf, Ljótsson, and Frostholm (2018) has also indicated that Internet-based acceptance and commitment therapy (see Chapter 7) is a feasible and acceptable treatment for health anxiety, associated with marked reductions in core symptoms. This represents an interesting novel strand of research that tests a slightly different treatment content compared with exposure-based CBT. Of course, randomized trials are needed to establish its efficacy.

As Internet-based treatment requires limited therapist resources, this type of therapy has the potential of being cost-effective. That is, the effects of Internet-based treatment are likely to be large in relation to its costs. To date, there are three published health economic analyses of Internet-based CBT for health anxiety, which all indicate that the net cost of an additional case of remission is low (Axelsson, Andersson, Ljótsson, & Hedman-Lagerlöf, 2018; Hedman, Andersson, et al., 2013; Hedman, Andersson, Ljótsson, Axelsson, & Lekander, 2016). Two studies showed that in Internet-based CBT compared with no treatment (i.e., a waiting-list or attention control condition), one additional case of remission was associated with a net societal cost of less than £500 (Axelsson et al., 2018; Hedman, Andersson, et al., 2013). In other words, Internet-based CBT appears to lead to better mental health while inferring no or minimal costs compared with not providing the treatment.

A question that is often posed is "for whom does Internet-based CBT work?" There are to our knowledge two published studies on predictors of Internet-based CBT for health anxiety (Hedman, Andersson, Lekander, & Ljótsson, 2015; Hedman, Lindefors, et al., 2013). The only stable predictors across those studies were baseline health anxiety and treatment adherence. That is, more health anxiety at baseline was predictive of both a larger reduction in health anxiety, and more anxiety after treatment. Adherence in terms of completing more modules was related to both larger improvements in health anxiety as well as lower end-state health anxiety. Perhaps, the most important finding from these predictor studies is that most clinical and demographic variables (e.g., age, gender, and educational level) seem to be unrelated to outcome. This means that there appears to exist no typical subgroup of health anxiety patients for whom this treatment does not work. Of course, this should be interpreted from the perspective of the participant selection in clinical trials, that is, there is a restriction of a range of predictors as participants with a high risk of dropping out of treatment (e.g., those with substance abuse or who cannot read) are typically excluded. Our clinical impression is that in most cases where face-to-face CBT would work, then, Internet-based CBT probably also works.

How Important is the Therapist?

Some studies have found that having contact with a therapist is associated with larger effects in Internet-based CBT in general (e.g., Palmqvist, Carlbring, & Andersson, 2007). However, there are still few studies that have investigated this question with a design where all aspects other than therapist access were kept constant across treatment conditions. We are aware of only one such study in the treatment of health anxiety (Hedman, Axelsson, et al., 2016). In that study, participants were randomized to one of four conditions: (a) Internet-based CBT with therapist guidance, (b) Internet-based CBT without therapist guidance, (c) bibliotherapy (i.e., the same treatment content but provided through a self-help booklet) without therapist guidance, or (d) a waiting-list control. The results showed that all active treatments were superior to the control condition in reducing health anxiety with large between-group effect sizes ($ds \geq 0.8$) and sustained effects up to 1 year after treatment (Axelsson et al., 2018). The study did not have sufficient power to estimate differences in effect between the active treatments, but the results nonetheless suggest Internet-based CBT can be effective also without therapist contact and when administered as a self-help book without guidance from a therapist. We view this as encouraging as it means that it might be possible to achieve meaningful therapeutic effects also in clinical contexts where it is not possible to provide therapist contact. This in turn could further promote high treatment availability.

Future Directions

Although there has been a stable increase in knowledge about Internet-based CBT for health anxiety in recent years, there are still several important outstanding questions. One important venue for future research is to investigate the effects of this type of treatment compared with face-to-face CBT. Would it be the case that Internet-based CBT is noninferior to its face-to-face equivalent, it could be argued that this new form of CBT should be a part of the standard treatment repertoire. Another important future direction is to conduct effectiveness studies, that is, to explore how well the treatment works when delivered in routine care by regular clinicians.

Summary and Conclusions

Internet-based CBT is a structured treatment that uses self-help texts, video clips, and audio files provided through an online platform to promote the same behavioral changes as in face-to-face CBT. In less than 10 years, four randomized controlled trials have been published showing that Internet-based CBT can be an effective treatment for patients with health anxiety. Several aspects of the treatment, not least that it requires limited therapist resources compared with conventional CBT, make it a promising option for increasing access to effective psychological treatment. Health economic studies indicate that this can be a highly cost-effective treatment that yields large improvements at no or low costs compared with no treatment. Given the high prevalence of health anxiety and the substantial suffering associated with the disorder, Internet-based CBT will probably be an important tool for improving mental health on a large scale in this patient group.

References

Andersson, G., & Carlbring, P. (2017). Internet-assisted cognitive behavioral therapy. *The Psychiatric Clinics of North America*, *40*(4), 689–700. https://doi.org/10.1016/j.psc.2017.08.004.

Andersson, G., & Lindefors, N. (2016). History and current status of ICBT. In N. Lindefors & G. Andersson (Eds.), *Guided Internet-based treatments in psychiatry*. Switzerland: Springer International.

Andersson, G., Paxling, B., Wiwe, M., Vernmark, K., Felix, C. B., Lundborg, L., … Carlbring, P. (2012). Therapeutic alliance in guided internet-delivered cognitive behavioural treatment of depression, generalized anxiety disorder and social anxiety disorder. *Behaviour Research and Therapy*, *50*(9), 544–550. https://doi.org/10.1016/j.brat.2012.05.003.

Axelsson, E., Andersson, E., Ljótsson, B., & Hedman-Lagerlöf, E. (2018). Cost-effectiveness and long-term follow-up of three forms of minimal-contact cognitive behaviour therapy for severe health anxiety: results from a randomised controlled trial. *Behaviour Research and Therapy*, *107*, 95–105. https://doi.org/10.1016/j.brat.2018.06.002.

Hedman, E., Andersson, E., Lekander, M., & Ljótsson, B. (2015). Predictors in Internet-delivered cognitive behavior therapy and behavioral stress management for severe health anxiety. *Behaviour Research and Therapy*, *64*, 49–55. https://doi.org/10.1016/j.brat.2014.11.009.

Hedman, E., Andersson, E., Lindefors, N., Andersson, G., Rück, C., & Ljótsson, B. (2013). Cost-effectiveness and long-term effectiveness of internet-based cognitive behaviour therapy for severe health anxiety. *Psychological Medicine*, *43*(2), 363–374. https://doi.org/10.1017/s0033291712001079.

Hedman, E., Andersson, E., Ljótsson, B., Axelsson, E., & Lekander, M. (2016). Cost effectiveness of internet-based cognitive behaviour therapy and behavioural stress management for severe health anxiety. *BMJ Open*, *6*(4), e009327. https://doi.org/10.1136/bmjopen-2015-009327.

the local psychiatric unit, where he was taken, by my consultant, in his car at the end of the clinic. But it was some years later, after specializing in GU medicine, that my interest in the subject of health anxiety really took off.

While working in GU medicine, I was also employed by Imperial College, following up patients in a research trial, and also involved as a therapist with a new form of psychological therapy concerned with changing the environment, nidotherapy (Tyrer, 2002). I had always been interested in psychiatry and psychology, and it had formed one of my attachments during my vocational training in general practice.

A woman, Isobel (not her real name), in her early 60s attending the clinic was one of the most difficult hypochondriacal patients I had ever encountered. She was convinced that she was riddled with hepatitis C and the herpes virus. There was no clinical or laboratory evidence of either, on repeated testing. She had endless bizarre symptoms that she bombarded me with, so it was difficult to get a word in sideways or have a meaningful conversation. However, her history was interesting and seemed highly relevant to her distress.

She had a brief, minimal, and nonpenetrative sexual encounter with a man a few years before following the separation from her husband. She wasn't worried at the time, but her fears and symptoms had developed over the last year following her husband's death and the birth of her latest grandchild. In GU medicine, we routinely ask about whether there has been any past history of sexual abuse, and she disclosed that her husband had, unbeknownst to her, sexually abused her daughter, getting the girl pregnant 6 years previously, a pregnancy that continued to term. This was Isobel's first grandchild. It was only after the birth of the child that the daughter disclosed who the father was. The police were informed and arrived very early in the morning, arresting both Isobel and her husband. Isobel was subsequently released without charge, but the husband went to prison, and 2 years after his release, he died of a heart attack. He had no further contact with the family.

Isobel felt that distressing as it was, she had got over this, the grandchild had been accepted into the family, and she loved the little girl very much. Meanwhile, Isobel was turning up at the clinic more and more often, completely convinced of her feared illnesses, so after discussion, I referred her to our in-house psychologist. She kept the appointment but explained to the psychologist concerned that she had a medical problem and did not require psychological help. She reattended the clinic to see me requesting further testing complaining that her symptoms were getting worse.

This time, I persuaded her to see a psychiatrist, but once again, although she kept the appointment, she refused to accept any further help from him and returned to see me in the clinic. The psychiatrist did however write me a very helpful letter. He explained that we were fueling her anxiety by repeatedly seeing her and repeating her tests and that we should politely but firmly desist from doing this. So after explaining this to Isobel, in between yet another barrage of symptoms, I said that we couldn't offer her any more help from the clinic and couldn't make any more appointments. In effect, we banned her from coming, something we had never done to any patient before. Several months passed (she had tried initially to make a couple of appointments, which had been gently declined), but this time, she seemed so distressed that the receptionist took pity on her and asked me to see her, which I did.

The presentation was exactly the same as before, although she was even more desperate and possibly becoming depressed. I explained that I did not think it was helpful to do more tests but that I was keen to help her. I explained that I would see her for an hour-long appointment (in my lunch hour) in a week's time, when I would try and get "to the bottom of the problem." I had absolutely no idea what I was going to do.

In fact, I had a meeting with a psychiatrist in London in the interim, so I contacted him, explained the problem, and asked if he could give me any idea as to how I might approach the problem. He said that, as luck would have it, Paul Salkovskis, a psychologist from Oxford, with a special interest in the subject, was talking in the department on the same day and that he would arrange for us to meet up. To his endless credit, Paul spent the whole of his lunch break listening to my case, getting me to role-play Isobel, explaining the basics of how Isobel (and other health anxious patients) think, and encouraging me to have a go at treating her. I was very skeptical but agreed to give it a go and report back to him.

The first thing he stressed to me was that the reason she went on and on about all her bodily sensations/symptoms was that she felt that if she missed one tiny thing out, it might just be the one thing that clinched the diagnosis, so exasperating as it might be, I should pointedly make a careful note of every single thing she had noticed was wrong, even if I thought it was completely irrelevant. So, that is precisely what I did, it took the whole hour, and I made copious notes. I arranged to see her a week later, again for an hour, wondering what to do next. Eventually, after doing some more reading, I decided, if I could get her to listen, to see how the problem affected her life.

When she attended the next appointment, she entered the room; sat down; and to my amazement, said *nothing* and waited for me to begin. It was clear that she was satisfied that I had taken serious note of all her concerns. Possibly for the first time, she had felt properly listened to. She explained that her fears of passing her illnesses on prevented her from touching any of her grandchildren and lately from seeing them at all. Similarly, she couldn't touch her local shopkeeper when handing over her money and had to put it on the counter; sometimes, she was so fearful of contaminating him that she would be unable to enter his shop at all. She had stopped having lunch with her friends in town, for similar reasons. I addressed this by giving her a comprehensive explanation on how hepatitis C and herpes simplex were transmitted (without insisting, once again, that she didn't have these conditions). She listened very attentively, and we agreed to meet again. She didn't ask me to examine her or perform any more tests.

Over the next few weeks, with a bit of long-distance supervision from Paul and some very clumsy cognitive behavioral therapy (CBT) from me, with comments like "I am not sure what to do about that, Isobel, you will have to wait until next time when I have got some advice," her conviction that she had these diseases began to shift. Maybe, it was she had become *frightened* that she had them instead. Paul particularly encouraged me to do an experiment with her around her fears of contaminating others. He asked me to explain that I was convinced that she couldn't contaminate me and to ask her permission to do an experiment to test this out. He suggested I should touch her mouth with my finger and then touch my mouth and see if I came down with any illness by our next appointment. I talked her into it although she was very wary, and I was also terrified that I might develop some bug by the next appointment and put us back to square one. However, all was well, although at the subsequent appointment she entered the room very tentatively and spent the first few minutes scrutinizing me for signs of imminent collapse.

She was now becoming convinced of her *wellness*, could cuddle her grandchildren, had no problems going into the shop, and had started to mix with some friends again. She had no further tests, except once when she said she thought she had "thrush," which turned out to be the case. I had also written to her GP about the psychological help she was receiving, and Isobel explained that she knew she was getting better because when she had to visit him with an exacerbation of her asthma, having not been to the surgery for 2 months, instead of hiding from her as she walked up the path to the surgery, which she had seen him do before (she used to attend at least two or three times a week), he greeted her warmly, shook her hand, and showed her to a chair.

At what turned out to be her last appointment, she spontaneously started to talk about the day she had been arrested by the police and the subsequent interrogation, before she was released the following day. She had been devastated by the revelations of sexual abuse by her husband and felt totally violated by the whole experience. She talked for the whole hour without any interruption by me. At the end, she summed up by saying "I suppose if something bad happens to you like that, you are bound to hurt." We had never addressed the issue in therapy, and she said that she had come to terms with it, in as much as one ever could, and the family as a whole had moved on. She thanked me and said that she was better and didn't feel she needed to come again. The whole experience for me was completely eye-opening and one of the most exciting experiences in my medical career. I suddenly realized we had a lot of patients like this who we were failing to manage properly in the clinic.

It was also evident that although she had accepted psychological help from me, in my position as a doctor in the clinic, she would not have accepted it from a psychologist or psychiatric services, even though it was clear I was learning the therapy as I went along. It may be that the help seemed more relevant delivered in the clinic; perhaps, she felt she knew and trusted me, and she felt safer there because of my medical knowledge. Unfortunately, I never asked her.

Excited by my success with Isobel, I attended an all-day workshop on CBT for health anxiety (CBT-HA) conducted by Paul Salkovskis, and in collaboration with him and colleagues at Imperial College, we conducted a prevalence study on health anxiety within the department. This included a follow-up, which established that the condition was persistent and that these patients were less likely to have a sexually transmitted disease yet were more expensive as they had more doctor and health advisor appointments (Seivewright et al., 2004). This was followed by an intervention study within the department, which showed a highly significant improvement in the patients with health anxiety who were randomized to CBT-HA and which offset the costs of care (Seivewright et al., 2008). I was the therapist in that study, and in my PhD, I found that the second set of patients improved much more than the first (Seivewright, 2009), so it was clear that my skills improved. This then led to a large multicenter trial (Tyrer et al., 2014) that replicated the findings, and subsequent long-term follow-up showed that the positive results were maintained at 5 years; an 8-year follow-up is currently underway. Interestingly, the study also showed that nurses trained in CBT-HA had better outcomes than trainee psychologists (Tyrer et al., 2015).

CBT for health anxiety (Tyrer & Tyrer, 2018) is highly effective, practical, and extremely useful; I have continued to use it within my clinical settings where the time spent saves a lot of extra unnecessary appointments and expensive tests in the long run. In particular, I ran a clinic for patients with chronic GU problems (excluding HIV), which included those with medically unexplained symptoms (sometimes due to depression) and high health anxiety. These conditions were treated within the department by both drug and psychological intervention. It was personally a very satisfactory way to work with clinical freedom. I felt I was able to offer more appropriate and comprehensive care.

One of the most crucial elements in learning how to identify and manage health anxious patients was to understand the way that they think. So in essence, health anxiety has usually been precipitated by a trigger, perhaps the untimely death of a family member or hearing about someone in the press, a person of their age who has developed a life-threatening illness, and suddenly, they start to feel vulnerable, misinterpreting ordinary bodily sensations and changes, or minor ailments as evidence of the feared disease. Each sufferer has a unique often specific fear of what having this disease would mean for them, possibly dying young without ever fulfilling their dreams, never seeing their children grow up, or dying a horrible painful death. This drives the fear and leads to the conviction that there is something wrong. They fail to respond lastingly to reassurance, and the fears always return.

These patients can cause exasperation to the medical profession, or it can lead to ridicule, with family and friends also becoming fed up with their continued preoccupation with the belief that there is something wrong. But the sufferer "knows" they are ill and feels no one is taking them seriously, so the responsibility of monitoring their health now falls to them. They check their bodies, noticing and becoming highly alarmed by minor variations in bodily appearance or function, and increasingly, they check on the Internet, often for hours a day, looking for reassurance, but inevitably feeling worse as any symptom can be a precursor of more serious disease. As they become more and more anxious, their symptoms of anxiety become interpreted to them as further evidence that their condition is worsening. They feel very alone, misunderstood, and very frightened. It is a miserable condition to have, and there is an increased risk of suicide, premature morbidity, and mortality (Berge et al., 2016).

Once I as a physician got a grasp of this, it became incredibly important to ascertain what patients *believed* about what was wrong and not just presume. It is very easy to ask a patient if he/she is worried, and what about, and what is likely to be helpful. I developed a series of "probe questions" aimed at eliciting the fact that a patient may be worrying excessively without suggesting that their problem was "all in the mind." So if I felt there was a possibility of health anxiety, I would ask "Have you been worrying a lot about this problem?" If the response is "Yes," this would lead to the next questions "Do you feel that there might be something more serious wrong?" and "Do you feel that there might be something that we doctors have failed to find?" If these were also answered in the affirmative, then I would go on to say something like "We are very interested in this department in the extent to which patients worry about their health/condition, as excessive worry can make everything much harder to cope with." I might then hand them the short-health anxiety inventory (HAI) (Salkovskis, Rimes, Warwick, & Clark, 2002) or elicit their fears, and if I didn't have time then, I would arrange another appointment to help with this.

I to some extent had the luxury of doing this, but in our hard-pressed health service, a busy GP or cardiologist would not have this opportunity or, indeed, interest. But they would be interested in these patients, usually with medically unexplained symptoms per se, or if they did have an underlying condition, with medically unexplained complications, not coming back repeatedly requesting more time, tests, and investigations. Ideally, in my opinion if these patients could be referred to a nurse practitioner, trained in psychological approaches such as CBT-HA, within the department, a lot of time, distress, and money could be saved, and a much more professionally satisfying outcome could be achieved. This is not "rocket science," it is common sense. We have a tried and tested therapy that works, and we should be putting it in place. Some centers have begun to do this, but it is not common practice. I once attended a cardiac rehabilitation session with a patient with a treated cardiac condition but unexplained chest pain. When he found the physical exercises distressing, he was asked to stop, and the only psychological input seemed to be lying on a mat at the end listening to a relaxation tape, pleasant in its way, but there was no attempt to elicit specific fears or begin to address them.

The crux of CBT-HA is to get your patient to consider two different hypotheses: firstly, that they have the disease that they fear and the other is that they don't have that disease but are just frightened that they have it. Specific techniques and personally relevant experiments are then used to build up evidence for the "fear of disease" model. The approach is collaborative, and the evidence is directly from the patient's experience. It makes sense in their world.

Health anxiety is a very common problem present throughout all spheres of medicine, which causes immense distress. The cost to the health service in the United Kingdom has not been properly determined, but extrapolating from our first study when £33 was saved for each point reduction in health anxiety score (Seivewright et al., 2008) using the short-health anxiety inventory (Salkovskis et al., 2002) over £165 M would be saved annually in secondary care alone through effective treatment.

Unfortunately, health anxiety is poorly recognized and rarely addressed. This is simply not good enough. The condition can be readily identified by a few simple questions, and there is now a growing research base of evidence described elsewhere in this book for effective inexpensive treatments. Not only that, but unlike many other psychological treatments, the benefits for psychological treatment appear to last (Tyrer et al., 2017). The time is ripe for The National Institute for Clinical Evidence (NICE) in the United Kingdom and equivalent bodies elsewhere to review this evidence and develop guidelines for the management of health anxiety. The nature, identification, and basic management of this condition should be an integral part of medical training. Addressing this condition as a routine component of clinical management not only comprehensively enhances patient care but also is inherently more humane.

References

Berge, L. I., Skogen, J. C., Sulo, G., Igland, J., Wilhelmsen, I., Vollset, S. E., et al. (2016). Health anxiety and risk of ischaemic heart disease: A prospective cohort study linking the Hordaland health study (HUSK) with the cardiovascular diseases in Norway (CVDNOR) project. *BMJ Open, 6*, e012914.

Salkovskis, P. M., Rimes, K. A., Warwick, H. M. C., & Clark, D. M. (2002). The health anxiety inventory: development and validation of scales for the measurement of health anxiety and hypochondriasis. *Psychological Medicine, 32*, 843–853.

Seivewright, H. (2009). Prevalence and management of health anxiety in genitourinary clinics. Ph.D. Thesis, Imperial College, London.

Seivewright, H., Green, J., Salkovskis, P., Barrett, B., Nur, U., & Tyrer, P. (2008). Randomised controlled trial of cognitive behaviour therapy in the treatment of health anxiety in a genitourinary medicine clinic. *British Journal of Psychiatry, 192*, 332–337.

Seivewright, H., Salkovskis, P., Green, J., Mullan, N., Behr, G., Carlin, E., … Tyrer, P. (2004). Prevalence and service implications of health anxiety in genitourinary medicine clinics. *International Journal of STD and AIDS, 15*, 519–522.

Tyrer, P. (2002). Nidotherapy: a new approach to the treatment of personality disorder. *Acta Psychiatrica Scandinavica, 105*, 469–471.

Tyrer, P., Cooper, S., Salkovskis, P., Tyrer, H., Crawford, M., Byford, S., et al. (2014). Clinical and cost-effectiveness of cognitive behaviour therapy for health anxiety in medical patients: a multicentre randomised controlled trial. *Lancet, 383*, 219–225.

Tyrer, P., Salkovskis, P., Tyrer, H., Wang, D., Crawford, M. J., Dupont, S., et al. (2017). Cognitive behaviour therapy for health anxiety in medical patients (CHAMP): randomised controlled trial with outcomes to five years. *Health Technology Assessment, 21*, 50.

Tyrer, P., & Tyrer, H. (2018). Health anxiety: detection and treatment. *Advances in Psychiatric Treatment, 24*, 66–72.

Tyrer, H., Tyrer, P., Lisseman-Stones, Y., McAllister, S., Cooper, S., Salkovskis, P., et al. (2015). Therapist differences in a randomised trial of the outcome of cognitive behaviour therapy for health anxiety in medical patients. *International Journal of Nursing Studies, 52*, 686–694.

CHAPTER TEN

Health Anxiety in Children and Adolescents

Charlotte U. Rask
Research Unit, Department of Child and Adolescent Psychiatry, Aarhus University Hospital, Skejby, Denmark
Research Clinic for Functional Disorders and Psychosomatics, Aarhus University Hospital, Aarhus, Denmark

Health anxiety is still only a very new research area in young populations but also an emerging topic in the pediatric literature. This chapter outlines our current knowledge on the occurrence and clinical presentations of health anxiety in children and adolescents. A developmental approach, integrating potential early childhood and family risk factors, to understand health anxiety is provided. This approach can be useful in relation to both the assessment and the development of new treatment strategies of health anxiety in young persons.

Can Children and Adolescents Suffer from Health Anxiety?

The literature often describes health anxiety as uncommon in children and adolescents and with an onset primarily in adulthood (Schulte & Petermann, 2011a; Schulte & Petermann, 2011b). Very few studies have examined the prevalence of severe health anxiety in the form of hypochondriasis in younger age groups. These report that only few children and adolescents meet the ICD-10 or former DSM-IV diagnostic criteria for the disorder (Bisht, Sankhyan, Kaushal, Sharma, & Grover, 2008; Essau, Conradt, & Petermann, 1999; Lieb, Pfister, Mastaler, & Wittchen, 2000). However, the findings may mainly be explained by the lack of developmentally appropriate diagnostic criteria to be used for children and adolescents rather than the disorder being uncommon in this age group (Fritz, Fritsch, & Hagino, 1997). Thus, a medical record review on 124 adult patients treated for severe health anxiety showed that 18.6% reported debut of their first health anxiety symptoms in childhood (age 2–12 years) and 16.1% in adolescence (age 13–17 years), while 65.3% reported onset in adulthood (Morina, 2015). These results corroborate other retrospective studies on adults diagnosed with hypochondriasis indicating the presence

The Clinician's Guide to Treating Health Anxiety
https://doi.org/10.1016/B978-0-12-811806-1.00010-X

Parental Excessive Concern and Preoccupation With the Child's Symptoms

Occasionally, it is not only the child but also the child's parent who presents with excessive and seemingly unreasonable concern about the child's symptoms. This phenomenon has recently been conceptualized as *health anxiety by proxy* (Lockhart, 2016; Thorgaard et al., 2017). It can lead to unnecessary medical assessments and treatments and risk of iatrogenic harm to the child and thereby compromise the child's physical and mental health. Clinically, it is reported that the parent is also likely to fulfill the diagnosis of health anxiety her/himself (Thorgaard et al., 2017).

Case Example

Rachel is a 35-year-old woman with a 5-year-old son. Rachel is currently pregnant again and attends treatment for severe health anxiety. During the last session, she reveals that she performs daily body checks on her son. She looks for bruises as possible signs of leukemia and for atypical motor movements as possible signs of a severe neurological disorder. Recently, she was convinced that there was something wrong with her son's face. She therefore tried to test his facial sensibility by pressing a pencil hard on the skin, which made him cry. Rachel has had her son medically examined so often that he now recognizes their family doctor in the street. Rachel also worries if there is something wrong with the child she is expecting. She is very distressed about how these worries will affect her children in the long run, but on the other hand, she can't bear the thought if she should overlook a serious illness in them. Her husband feels frustrated. He has tried to convince her that everything is all right, but it doesn't seem to help. They have now agreed that he should be the one who decides whether or not their son should see a doctor.

Given the potential negative impact on the child's health and development, it is important to address health anxiety by proxy. The condition is not to be confused with parental problems within the spectrum of factitious disorder or Münchhausen by proxy where a caregiver falsifies illness in a child by fabricating or inducing symptoms (Bass & Adshead, 2007). These much rarer cases require a quite different approach and management. The underlying main problem in factitious disorder or Münchhausen by proxy is that the parents seek attention from health services themselves by inflicting symptoms on the child (e.g., contamination of a central line to induce bacteremia and fever and asphyxiation to induce cardiac arrest). As with health anxiety by proxy, the result of Münchhausen by proxy will often also be that the child is being exposed to unnecessary medical interventions However, as described, in factitious disorder and Münchhausen by proxy, the problem is not, as in parents with health anxiety by proxy, parental persistent and unmanageable fear that doctors are missing a serious illness in their child but very serious parental psychopathology where the effect on the child in the severe cases can be described as child abuse (hence the increasing use of the broader terminology pediatric condition falsification and/or Medical child abuse). Disentangling the underlying parental psychopathology is therefore important in order to design an effective treatment strategy and to prevent parents with health anxiety by proxy being wrongly tagged as child abusers. Still, in some cases, it can be quite difficult to disengage the main problem, and in both instances, the medical care providers and the health-care system can unintentional become the facilitating medical environment where the child can suffer harm related to damaging medical assessments and treatment. Regardless of caregiver intent, medical child abuse can then occur. The main task of health professionals, when managing families with parental factitious disorder/Münchhausen by proxy or with parental health anxiety by proxy, will therefore be to protect the child from excessive health-care utilization and unnecessary medical interventions.

A Developmental Approach to Understand Health Anxiety

Environmental factors, including early childhood and family factors, are suggested to play a large influential role in prevailing theoretical etiological models for health anxiety such as the cognitive behavioral model (Salkovskis & Warwick, 1986) and the interpersonal model (Noyes Jr. et al., 2002; Stuart & Noyes Jr., 1999). A recent systematic review examined the empirical evidence for potential early psychosocial factors. A trend was found toward the association between clinical presentations of health anxiety in adulthood and three factors: (1) intergenerational transmission of health anxiety and illness beliefs, (2) illness experiences during childhood, and (3) an anxious attachment style (Thorgaard, Frostholm, & Rask, 2018).

Figure 2 suggests a developmental explanatory approach of health anxiety. It is not to be regarded as a comprehensive model but rather an attempt to integrate the above findings with central elements from both the

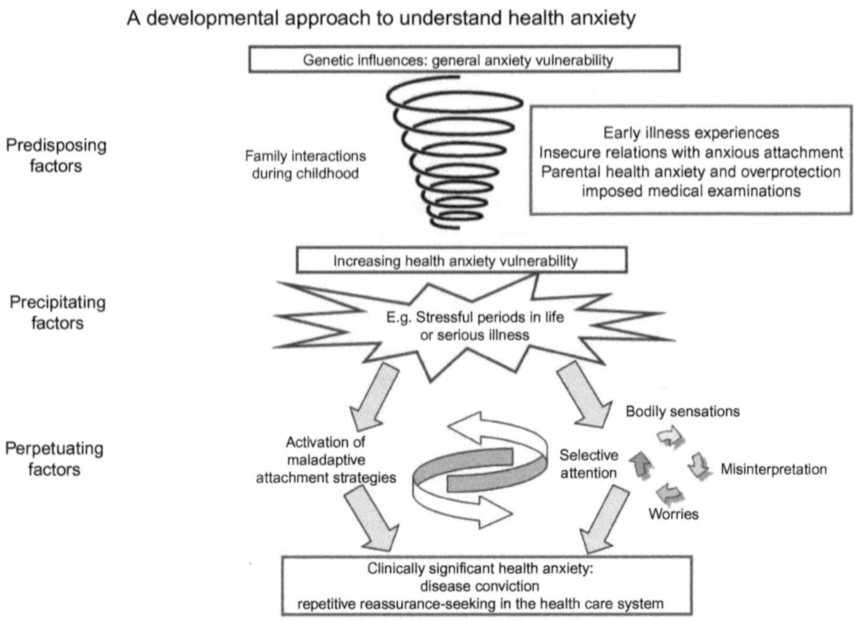

Fig. 2 The model draws on the existing psychological models for health anxiety while emphasizing early childhood and family factors to illustrate potential developmental pathways.

cognitive behavioral and the interpersonal model. It proposes family interactions across early risk domains to illustrate potential developmental pathways of health anxiety. However, it should be emphasized that the empirical evidence for these processes is limited.

Clinically, it is helpful to further subdivide the suggested involved processes into predisposing, precipitating, and perpetuating factors to identify vulnerability (the person's susceptibility to develop the disorder), triggers (factors that are directly involved in the onset of the disorder), and maintaining factors aggravating the pathological processes.

Predisposing factors: It is generally accepted that anxiety runs in families (Drake & Ginsburg, 2012). This is partly explained by a common heritable component, in this model named general anxiety vulnerability. The vulnerability may be shaped into specific disorders in a joint interaction with early childhood and family-related variables (Gouze, Hopkins, Bryant, & Lavigne, 2017). Exposure during childhood to family influences with social learning of maladaptive illness behavior, experiences of illness-related events, and transmission of high parental health anxieties may be involved in the specific developmental trajectory of health anxiety. An increasing vulnerability for health-related concerns over time is then proposed to increase the likelihood of an episode of regular health anxiety later in life.

Precipitating factors: Health anxiety may be triggered by stressful periods and/or the experience of a personal health scare that induces bodily arousal and sensations. Based on the person's negative illness perceptions, established through the family interactions over time, these bodily signals are likely to be conceptualized as threat stimuli that can then trigger the potential perpetuating vicious circles of health anxiety.

Perpetuating factors: As suggested by the cognitive behavioral model, bodily arousal and sensations may initiate a vicious circle of health anxiety with dysfunctional cognitive and behavioral responses such as catastrophic interpretation of the experienced sensations and bodily checking that only increases anxiety and bodily distress (Salkovskis & Warwick, 1986). According to the interpersonal model, the associated distress will at the same time activate the individual's attachment system, which can be seen as a biologically prewired system that has a key role in stress regulation. Insecure or anxious attachment may then manifest as anxious efforts, that is, reassurance seeking, to find support and relief by communicating a need for care through physical symptoms (Noyes Jr. et al., 2003). In the beginning, such behavior may evoke attention, concern, and sympathy from the surroundings but over time lead to avoidance and withdrawal of support and maybe criticism that again impair effective downregulation of distress. As a result, the individual will rely even more on the maladaptive strategies in an attempt to find support from others. Thus, these two vicious circles may interact and mutually reinforce each other through the experience of increasing distress leading to the clinical manifestation of health anxiety.

It is likely that some of the suggested processes in this model may be more important in earlier childhood, for example, the development of anxious attachment, while others may be more salient during adolescence, for example, interactional processes with reinforcement by family (and society) by learned sets of interpersonal or social illness behaviors.

Special Considerations Regarding Assessment

The developmental approach presented above can guide the assessment and an individual case formulation to be used for the further treatment planning. It follows from this approach that an important principle of assessment of young people is the involvement of the family. Part of the assessment should be concerned with the overall family situation and how this

Table 1 Selected Questionnaires for Assessment

Child	Questionnaire	Age Group	No. of Items
Health anxiety	Whiteley-7 index (Fink et al., 1999)	Adolescents	7
	Childhood Illness Attitude Scales (Wright & Asmundson, 2003)	Children and adolescents	35
Parent	Questionnaire		No. of items
Health anxiety by proxy	Parent version of The Illness Worry Subscale (IWS-p) (Garralda & Rangel, 2001)		10
Parental illness behavior toward child	Fetal health anxiety inventory (Reiser & Wright, 2018)		14
	The protect subscale of the Adult Responses to Children's Symptoms (ARCS) (Van Slyke & Walker, 2006)		15

may influence the child's symptom experience and coping strategies. While some parental approaches encourage age-appropriate self-reliance and confidence with regard to coping with illness and physical symptoms, others may feed into problems with worrying or excessive dependence.

The assessment in young children relies primarily on parental information and child/parent interactions, including the potential presence of health anxiety by proxy, whereas more emphasis will be put on self-report in older children and adolescents. The few available standardized questionnaires that may be helpful in the assessment of both child health anxiety and parental health anxiety by proxy are summarized in Table 1. Currently, these scales have been developed for research purposes and are not yet widely used in clinical practice. In addition, various measures of levels of other types of anxiety and depression in the child or adolescent may also be helpful.

Special Considerations in Treatment of Children and Adolescents

At present, there are no specific and specialized programs available for treatment of health anxiety in young persons. The management must therefore draw on existing treatment programs for adults, but at the same time, it should be tailored to suit the developmental abilities of this age group (Greco & Hayes, 2008; Bayer et al., 2011; Frankel et al., 2012). Thus, when adapting adult treatment programs to younger persons, it should be kept in mind that children and adolescents are not simply "little adults." For example, all or nothing, overgeneralizing, and negative filtering may be developmentally normative ways of thinking in young adolescents. Incorporating developmental considerations into treatment design and planning is therefore likely to increase treatment efficacy. However, the translation of developmental principles into practice is neither simple nor direct. In general, the following considerations should be taken into account when treating young people with health anxiety (as well as other mental health problems).

(1) Not only children but also adolescents have less developed memory and attention capacities. This means that psychotherapy sessions should be shorter, and the use of exercises such as mindfulness exposure exercises on bodily sensations should be of short duration, for example, 3–5 min, rather than the longer, often 20–40 min exercises for adults (Greco & Hayes, 2008).

(2) Cognitively, children have limited verbal fluency, abstract reasoning, and logical thinking. Therefore, they cannot be expected to understand and apply the clinical skills being taught in therapy to the same extent as adults. For younger children, it is helpful to use child-friendly material such as cartoons and stickers and more concrete and simplified examples and questions while also providing more support, structure, and feedback. For example, thought bubbles are used to help children identify their thinking. Cognitive distortions typical for health anxiety such as catastrophic thinking about physical sensations and illness can be represented as coming from a "teasing monster" (Frankel et al., 2012). Additionally, a focus on concrete concepts rather than abstract principles may be more effective with less cognitively advanced children, for example, role-play of examples based on actual anxiety provoking situations from the child's life, such as visiting a sick family member or friend, rather than using abstract, hypothetical, future-oriented scenarios. The third-wave behavior therapy, acceptance and commitment therapy (ACT), which has recently been tested as a new treatment for health anxiety in adults (see Chapter 7 on ACT for health anxiety), may be especially suitable for children since it relies heavily on experiential exercises and metaphors similar to teaching methods that young people are familiar with from their educational settings (Greco & Hayes, 2008).

(3) As with any treatment involving young people, attention must be paid to the fact that children and adolescents are part of a larger system involving their family. It will be important to work on the parents' own illness perceptions and illness behaviors and how they understand

and manage their child's physical symptoms and their child's response to these symptoms. Therefore, parents should be involved as a vital part of the treatment process. Based on existing treatment programs for various child anxiety problems, parents should, in addition to assisting with home practice exercises, be given the opportunity to attend an information session before beginning a treatment program with their child and a review session at the end of treatment. Especially in young children, family-based treatments targeting parental health-related anxieties and dysfunctional illness behaviors may be particularly important to reduce the child's health concerns. With increasing age, interpersonal relationship changes, for example, increased importance of peers, formation of cliques, and individuation from parents, should be taken into account in the treatment planning. Thus, in older children and adolescents, direct parental involvement and intervention have been shown to be of less benefit compared with individual or group-based treatment in the treatment of other anxiety disorders in youth (Barrett, Dadds, & Rapee, 1996; Creswell & Cartwright-Hatton, 2007).

New avenues in the treatment of various anxiety disorders in pediatric populations are low-intensity treatment—including the use of bibliotherapy, CDs, mobile applications (mHealth), or Internet-delivered programs. These types of interventions could also be relevant to adapt for health anxiety in young people. With regard to the development of specialized treatment of health anxiety by proxy, this could be inspired by family-based interventions for high-risk families where either one or both parents are diagnosed with an anxiety disorder (Ginsburg, Drake, Tein, Teetsel, & Riddle, 2015). Finally, the role of combined treatment with medication, that is, selective serotonin reuptake inhibitors (SSRIs) and psychotherapy, also needs to be explored in older children and adolescents (Ipser, Stein, Hawkridge, & Hoppe, 2009).

Summary and Conclusion

Despite the increasing evidence of the expression of health anxiety in children and adolescents, the knowledge about its assessment and treatment at young age is still scarce. Emerging research demonstrates that health-related concerns and behaviors can also be common early in life and associated with significant distress and impairment. Clinical approaches based on CBT and third-wave behavior therapy for adults with health anxiety may also be effective in younger persons when appropriate developmental adjustments are made. However, more studies on the developmental course of health anxiety are needed to develop age-appropriate diagnostic criteria and standardized tools for its assessment in younger age groups. Furthermore, work on the development and systematic evaluations of age-adjusted treatment programs, including family-based interventions, remains before specialized treatment for health anxiety in young persons and parental health anxiety by proxy can become widely available.

References

Barrett, P. M., Dadds, M. R., & Rapee, R. M. (1996). Family treatment of childhood anxiety: A controlled trial. *Journal of Consulting and Clinical Psychology*, *64*(2), 333–342.

Bass, C., & Adshead, G. (2007). Fabrication and induction of illness in children: The psychopathology of abuse. *Advances in Psychiatric Treatment*, *13*, 169–177.

Bayer, J. K., Rapee, R. M., Hiscock, H., Ukoumunne, O. C., Mihalopoulos, C., Clifford, S., & Wake, M. (2011). The cool little kids randomised controlled trial: Population-level early prevention for anxiety disorders. *BMC Public Health*, *11*, 11.

Bisht, J., Sankhyan, N., Kaushal, R. K., Sharma, R. C., & Grover, N. (2008). Clinical profile of pediatric somatoform disorders. *Indian Pediatrics*, *45*(2), 111–115.

Creswell, C., & Cartwright-Hatton, S. (2007). Family treatment of child anxiety: Outcomes, limitations and future directions. *Clinical Child and Family Psychology Review*, *10*(3), 232–252.

Drake, K. L., & Ginsburg, G. S. (2012). Family factors in the development, treatment, and prevention of childhood anxiety disorders. *Clinical Child and Family Psychology Review*, *15*(2), 144–162.

Eminson, M., Benjamin, S., Shortall, A., Woods, T., & Faragher, B. (1996). Physical symptoms and illness attitudes in adolescents: An epidemiological study. *Journal of Child Psychology and Psychiatry, and Allied Disciplines*, *37*(5), 519–528.

Essau, C. A., Conradt, J., & Petermann, F. (1999). Prevalence, comorbidity and psychosocial impairment of somatoform disorders in adolescents. *Psychology, Health and Medicine*, *4*(2), 169–180.

Fink, P., Ewald, H., Jensen, J., Sørensen, L., Engberg, M., Holm, M., & Munk-Jørgensen, P. (1999). Screening for somatization and hypochondriasis in primary care and neurological in-patients: a seven-item scale for hypochondriasis and somatization. *J Psychosom Res*, *46* (3), 261–273.

Fink, P., Ornbol, E., Toft, T., Sparle, K. C., Frostholm, L., & Olesen, F. (2004). A new, empirically established hypochondriasis diagnosis. *The American Journal of Psychiatry*, *161*(9), 1680–1691.

Frankel, S. A., Gallerani, C. M., & Garber, J. (2012). Developmental considerations across childhood. In Szigethy E. , Weisz J. R. , & FindlingR. L. (Eds.), *Cognitive-Behavior Therapy for Children and Adolescents*. (1st ed.). Washington, DC, London, England: American Psychiatric Publishing (Chapter 2).

Fritz, G. K., Fritsch, S., & Hagino, O. (1997). Somatoform disorders in children and adolescents: A review of the past 10 years. *Journal of the American Academy of Child and Adolescent Psychiatry*, *36*(10), 1329–1338.

Garralda, M. E., & Rangel, L. (2001). Childhood chronic fatigue syndrome. *The American Journal of Psychiatry*, *158*(7), 1161.

Ginsburg, G. S., Drake, K. L., Tein, J. Y., Teetsel, R., & Riddle, M. A. (2015). Preventing onset of anxiety disorders in offspring of anxious parents: A randomized controlled trial of a family-based intervention. *The American Journal of Psychiatry*, *172*(12), 1207–1214.

Gouze, K. R., Hopkins, J., Bryant, F. B., & Lavigne, J. V. (2017). Parenting and anxiety: Bi-directional relations in young children. *Journal of Abnormal Child Psychology*, *45*(6), 1169–1180.

Greco, L. A., & Hayes, S. C. (2008). *Acceptance & mindfulness treatments for children & adolescents. A practitioner's guide.* Oakland: New Harbinger Publications, Inc.
Ipser, J. C., Stein, D. J., Hawkridge, S., & Hoppe, L. (2009). Pharmacotherapy for anxiety disorders in children and adolescents. *The Cochrane Database of Systematic Reviews, 3.* CD005170.
Lieb, R., Pfister, H., Mastaler, M., & Wittchen, H. U. (2000). Somatoform syndromes and disorders in a representative population sample of adolescents and young adults: Prevalence, comorbidity and impairments. *Acta Psychiatrica Scandinavica, 101*(3), 194–208.
Lockhart, E. (2016). Health anxiety in children and parents. *BMJ (Clinical Research Ed.), 353*, i2891.
Morina B (2015). Debut of health Anxiety, Master Thesis, Faculty of Health, Aarhus University, Denmark.
Noyes, R., Jr., Stuart, S. P., Langbehn, D. R., Happel, R. L., Longley, S. L., Muller, B. A., & Yagla, S. J. (2003). Test of an interpersonal model of hypochondriasis. *Psychosomatic Medicine, 65*(2), 292–300.
Noyes, R., Jr., Stuart, S., Langbehn, D. R., Happel, R. L., Longley, S. L., & Yagla, S. J. (2002). Childhood antecedents of hypochondriasis. *Psychosomatics, 43*(4), 282–289.
Rask, C. U., Elberling, H., Skovgaard, A. M., Thomsen, P. H., & Fink, P. (2012). Parental-reported health anxiety symptoms in 5- to 7-year- old children: The Copenhagen child cohort CCC 2000. *Psychosomatics, 53*(1), 58–67.
Rask, C. U., Munkholm, A., Clemmensen, L., Rimvall, M. K., Ornbol, E., Jeppesen, P., & Skovgaard, A. M. (2016). Health anxiety in preadolescence—associated health problems, healthcare expenditure, and continuity in childhood. *Journal of Abnormal Child Psychology, 44*(4), 823–832.
Reiser, S. J., & Wright, K. D. (2017). *Fetal health anxiety: development and psychometric properties of the fetal health anxiety inventory.* (Personal Communication).
Salkovskis, P. M., & Warwick, H. M. (1986). Morbid preoccupations, health anxiety and reassurance: a cognitive-behavioural approach to hypochondriasis. *Behaviour Research and Therapy, 24*(5), 597–602.
Schulte, I. E., & Petermann, F. (2011a). Familial risk factors for the development of somatoform symptoms and disorders in children and adolescents: a systematic review. *Child Psychiatry and Human Development, 42*(5), 569–583.
Schulte, I. E., & Petermann, F. (2011b). Somatoform disorders: 30 years of debate about criteria! What about children and adolescents? *Journal of Psychosomatic Research, 70*(3), 218–228.
Sirri, L., Grandi, S., & Fava, G. A. (2008). The illness attitude scales. A clinimetric index for assessing hypochondriacal fears and beliefs. *Psychotherapy and Psychosomatics,* 77(6), 337–350.
Stuart, S., & Noyes, R., Jr. (1999). Attachment and interpersonal communication in somatization. *Psychosomatics, 40*(1), 34–43.
Thorgaard, M. V., Frostholm, L., & Rask, C. U. (2018). Childhood and family factors in the development of health anxiety: A systematic review. *Children's Health Care,* 47(2), 198–238.
Thorgaard, M. V., Frostholm, L., Walker, L., Jensen, J. S., Morina, B., Lindegaard, H., Salomonsen, L., & Rask, C. U. (2017). Health anxiety by proxy in women with severe health anxiety: A case control study. *Journal of Anxiety Disorders, 52*, 8–14.
Thorisdottir, A. S., Villadsen, A., LeBouthillier, D. M., Rask, C. U., Wright, K. D., Walker, J. R., Feldgaier, S., & Asmundson, G. J. G. (2017). Measurement invariance across genders on the childhood illness attitude scales (CIAS). *Journal of Psychosomatic Research, 98*, 34–39.
Van Slyke, D. A., & Walker, L. S. (2006). Mothers' responses to children's pain. *The Clinical Journal of Pain, 22*(4), 387–391.
Wright, K. D., & Asmundson, G. J. (2003). Health anxiety in children: Development and psychometric properties of the childhood illness attitude scales. *Cognitive Behaviour Therapy, 32*(4), 194–202.

INDEX

Note: Page numbers followed by *f* indicate figures, *t* indicate tables, and *b* indicate boxes.

F

G

H

I

MIX
Papier | Fördert gute Waldnutzung
FSC® C083411

Kolibri 360 GmbH
Ferdinand-Jühlke-Straße 7
99095 Erfurt, Deutschland
produktsicherheit@kolibri360.de